PAUL U. KELLOGG
AND THE *SURVEY*
Voices for Social Welfare
and Social Justice

PAUL U. KELLOGG
and the
SURVEY

Voices for Social Welfare
and Social Justice

by Clarke A. Chambers

UNIVERSITY OF MINNESOTA PRESS Minneapolis

Library of Congress Catalog Card Number: 77-172931

ISBN 0-8166-0622-6

Preface

WHEN the *Survey* journal had fallen on hard times and was about to fold after more than a half century of recording the story of social service and social welfare, a long-time contributor to the *Survey* wrote to Paul U. Kellogg, its editor, to wish him a pleasant and fruitful retirement and to urge him to take up one last "manifest duty"—to write his life's story and the life story of the *Survey*, for the one could not be told without the other. "For fifty years you have been in constant touch with the best of America," he wrote. "The company of your friends must be unsurpassed—in quality, variety, interest. The story cries for adequate telling. You cannot allow yourself to hesitate or postpone. You will have to Go to It!"

This correspondent undoubtedly did not know how close Paul Kellogg was, then, to the end of his energies. Plagued by sickness and by the numbing fatigue of old age, harassed by the impossible task of trying to find the money to keep the *Survey* going for just one more year, sometimes for just one more issue, he was in no condition to take up the challenge. When he finally collapsed, of a stroke, and was no longer able to keep up the struggle, the *Survey* ceased publication. The last number bore the date of May 1952—fifty years after Kellogg had joined the staff of the old *Charities*, then under the editorship of Edward T. Devine, forty years after he had taken over full responsibilities as editor in chief. During the last six years of his life, Kellogg could not possibly have mustered the energy, the will, or the concentration which the writing of a memoir would have required.

It is probable that even if he had been in good health and robust spirits the autobiography of a journal and of a man would never have been attempted. Paul Kellogg was too modest ever to believe that the course of his own life might be of interest to many others. He knew that what he was doing was of fundamental importance, but the significance lay in what was being done, not in anything intrinsic to himself. Moreover, he was not of introspective temperament—his interests and curiosity were turned outward toward others, toward the world; sometimes privately nostalgic for the universe of his boyhood, he rarely reminisced about the "good old days" or about any of the old days—good, bad, or indifferent. One of the difficulties in writing his biography, indeed, arises from the fact that in conversation and in the myriad letters he wrote he did not often reveal his innermost thoughts or relate past experiences and what subjectively they may have meant to him. He was a born reporter—insatiably curious about the lives of others, about the manner of their existence, their trials, their joys, their failures, and their successes. At the dinner table he could elicit the life story of a casual guest before dessert was served; but not many ever learned about *him*. Not even those who were closest to him can recall that he ever talked much about himself. Whatever the cause, his interest in others came first. Every event he witnessed, every person he met might become a good "story." The stories that did not reach print at once were stored in a reservoir of anecdote, understanding, and sympathy from which he could later draw.

It seems unlikely, then, that Paul Kellogg would ever have set it all down. That would be left to someone else, as curious about him as he was about others. To such a biographer, Kellogg left a great lode of rich ore to be mined and refined—over thirty four-drawer file cabinets of editorial and personal papers; a half century of journal numbers that fill five library shelves. Partly it was a compulsion to save, the old-fashioned squirreling instinct to save anything and everything (including receipts for a ten-cent piece of apricot pie or a nickel cup of coffee). Partly it was the recognition, early in his life, that the *Survey* was important, that the letters and manuscripts of his friends and associates would reveal significant things about momentous events. In the *Survey* office, soon after the First World War, he personally oversaw the establishment of what he called "forget-me-not" files, to hold for posterity the letters and papers of men and women who he knew really counted. Undoubtedly he believed these papers might some day provide the factual evidence for any number of good stories, for he knew the journalist and the historian performed similar functions. (Aboard ship in the fall of 1917 on his way to join the Paris office of the American Red Cross, he studied most intensively of all the reading he lugged along in his steamer trunk Carlton J. H. Hayes's history of modern Europe, the better to understand the war which he was on his way to observe firsthand.)

But history would have to be left to others. The story would have to be told as biography, not spun out as autobiography. Such is the task I undertook some five years ago.

Admittedly there are hazards in attempting a biography of a man whom so many persons still living knew intimately— often with profound affection, and sometimes with antagonism, but always with strong feelings. Two wives and his two children by his first wife still survive; so do many staff and board members, some of whose memories of Paul Kellogg reach back to the years of the First World War. Most of these persons were generous in discussing with me their particular insights into both the journal and its editor; some of them shared personal letters from Paul Kellogg which they had saved over the years and for which no carbon copies existed in either his editorial or his personal papers. The names of the persons whom I interviewed may be found in the bibliographic note. Most of them gave me full liberty to use whatever they said in whatever way I deemed appropriate, but most of them also expressed the preference that I not quote directly or footnote explicitly what they had contributed. I have respected these wishes and the reader will find some anecdotes and observations, without citation, which I drew from these conversations when I was convinced from other independent witnesses or from other evidence that they were valid. I have not put down indiscriminately everything I learned from interviews or from the manuscript and printed record of course; the responsibility of selection is, as it should be, entirely mine.

Paul Kellogg once wrote that the *Survey* was dedicated to "straight reporting and clear-cut presentation of facts and of interpretations close to the facts." He always assumed that evaluation and judgment were integral parts of the process of interpretation. This, too, has been my intent (however imperfectly realized): to tell the story as accurately as I was able, often in the exact or closely paraphrased words of the actors themselves. I have tried to see events as the participants themselves experienced and perceived them without sacrificing the independent perspective that the biographer may enjoy. Anyone who has written a biography will testify how extraordinarily difficult it is to live with his subject so closely for so many months and still discipline himself to that essential objectivity which is also the mark of sound historical writing. I found myself alternately delighted and dismayed, elated and disappointed, exhilarated and bored as day after day, month after month, I immersed myself in studying the records. Other biographers might also bear witness to the kind of tension I felt in myself between a scholar's drive to know all the relevant facts and his desire to fathom all the complex personal relations which make up a man's life, on the one hand, and a reluctance, a reticence, to intrude upon intimate matters of his personal life, on the other.

This is a biography. It is also the story of a journal that stood close to the very heart of the developing profession of social work and the elaboration of social welfare policies over the first half of the twentieth century. To see social service and social policy from the perspective of this "general practice" magazine is to be able to survey the whole development of welfare liberalism in its crucial years. The volume may also be taken as an intensive case study of one progressive who was an active proponent of reform politics from the Bull Moose crusade of 1912, through La Follette's campaign in 1924, democratic socialism with Norman Thomas in 1932, and the New Deal, to Henry Wallace's brand of progressivism in 1948. The book also became a study in the history of journalism, although it had not been my expectation when I embarked upon the project that I would have to involve myself so deeply in the details of publishing a magazine.

But most of all it remains, at heart, the story of a journalist, a reformer, a colleague and associate of professional social workers, whose career as reporter and editor spanned fifty-five exciting years. It is the life story of a sojourner on this earth, a man, Paul Kellogg.

Acknowledgments

AN AUTHOR incurs debts he can never directly or fully repay, not even in kind—friends, colleagues, and students on whom he can try out his ideas with both the spoken and the written word and from whom he receives support, and sharply critical advice. Andrea Hinding, curator of manuscripts at the Social Welfare History Archives Center, University of Minnesota, organized and inventoried the Papers of Survey Associates and of Paul U. Kellogg. Her assistance during the months of research proved invaluable; her critical insights informed my own every step of the way; she gave the draft manuscript a careful reading. With funds provided by the Graduate School of the University of Minnesota I was able to hire research assistants—Clarence Griep and Ruth Porisch. Linda Mack provided cheerful and efficient assistance in the tasks of reading proof and making an index. Richard Patrick Kellogg, who must have inherited or acquired his father's skill as an editor, provided a detailed critique on matters of style, substance, and interpretation that was extraordinarily helpful and saved me from many errors of fact. Others who read and criticized early drafts include George Britt, Mercy Kellogg, Beth de Schweinitz, Karl de Schweinitz, Elsa Greene, Helen Hall, Mary Dublin Keyserling, William Kirk, and Victor Weybright. They will all recognize in this book the contributions they made. My gratitude to them is none the less because I did not always act upon their counsel, and all the judgments had ultimately to be mine.

The book was written during a sabbatical leave from the University of Minnesota. I also received financial support in aid of research from the National Institute of Mental Health and from the Russell Sage Foundation. Without the free time that their grants made possible I could not have completed the project.

My wife, Florence Wood Chambers, listened to me talk out the book over more months than she may wish to be reminded, for the *Survey* project was a jealous mistress. The final draft is far the better for her counsel. She put up with her (often) distraught and (usually) distracted husband during the years of research and writing. When the sabbatical freedom from regular university duties proved insufficient, by itself, for the kind of concentration the task of composition demanded, she encouraged me to go away from campus and from home; in a cabin on the St. Croix River, isolated and entirely alone for ten weeks, I was able to write a rough draft, uninterrupted by academic, neighborhood, community, and family obligations. For the gift of those weeks I am most profoundly grateful.

C. A. C.

August, 1971

Table of Contents

PAUL U. KELLOGG
AND THE *SURVEY*
Voices for Social Welfare
and Social Justice

{I}

The Origins
of Social Work
Journalism

ALL about them, in the latter decades of the nineteenth century, the American people witnessed radical transformations in their ways of life. The country was settled and filled in. Where once there had been prairie and meadow and forest, cities were founded and began to sprawl. Much good farmland remained still to be turned to the plow or opened to grazing, but the shift from countryside and village to town and city gained momentum with every passing year. Young girls and boys headed for the cities to seek, if not fortune (although sometimes it broke that way), new opportunities, new occupations, new modes of existence; while from the far reaches of southern and eastern Europe swarmed millions of folk, most of them of peasant stock, unused to city life but attracted by stories of jobs and land in the New World or squeezed out by the lack of land and opportunity at home.

In the cities they began to pile up, these ambitious, restless young men and women, immigrant and native American alike. They jostled each other for jobs and for places to live. They went underground in the mines to harvest the coal and copper and iron. They poured through factory gates, into mills which belched clouds of black smoke over the landscape. Many of the children went to work in the street trades, in the glass factories, in the canneries, and deep beneath the earth with their fathers and older brothers. Women, too, sought ways to supplement family income, unsteady at best; they labored in the sweated trades, sewed garments in their tenement rooms.

In the squalid, crowded tenements many fell victim to typhoid and to tuberculosis. The poverty that accompanied low wages, long hours, uncertain employment, injury and death on the job weakened the physical resistance of these newcomers to the city. Insecurity was no new experience for the human race, but the insecurity wrought by modern industrialism was different both in degree and in kind. Industrial disease and accidents struck often and without regard to the caution a workman might exercise. A family left stranded when the chief breadwinner became sick or was injured or killed had no resources to draw upon; workmen's compensation, initiated in many Western industrial nations in the nineteenth century, did not come until a generation later in the United States. Even during times of expansion and booming prosperity employment was irregular. From week to week, season to season, year to year, a worker never knew when the caprice of the market or the whim of his employer would throw him out of a job. Workers in their middle years, when family responsibilities ran high, were frequently dismissed from their jobs in favor of younger, stronger, and presumably more malleable workers. In coal, in the needle trades, in the garment industry, production and employment were particularly erratic by the season. Even on the rich Mesabi Iron Range in the wilderness of northern Minnesota, workers frequently faced barred gates as different mines in the great open pit were arbitrarily closed and others opened, without design apparent to the workers and almost always without forewarning. One just never knew.

And that was in good times. In bad times—and they struck every twenty years or so—1873, 1893, 1907—things were even worse. Sudden panics slipped down into long troughs of depression from which recovery came slowly and unevenly. Down cycles of contraction followed wild speculative periods of expansion, as night the day (except that there were no natural, rational explanations for economic boom and bust). Some businesses and companies thrived and grew, went from strength to strength, accumulated capital and plant in good times, bought up less vigorous, less daring firms in bad. In such an economy, with prices and production, wages and employment seemingly beyond the control, to say nothing of the comprehension, of man, the need clearly was for understanding, for coordination and rationalization. What Professor Robert Wiebe has called "the search for order" was on.

Part of the growing complexity of civilization arose from the ever-increasing specialization of social function. Industry, in that breakaway era, demanded great masses of unskilled workmen to do the backbreaking work. But it required men of specialized skills as well to build and operate the sophisticated machinery of modern industry; and it required engineers and managers possessing rare talents for organization. So too in other parts of society. The day of the generalist faded quickly before the mounting complexities of modern existence, and it was in these years that the proliferating professions began to organize: engineers, lawyers, doctors, geologists, teachers, social scientists, economists—and social workers.

The term "social worker" was not yet generally in use, of course; it would be a number of years before a profession of social service would evolve and be recognized alongside other professions. But in the decade following the Civil War persons engaged in charities and correction, in nursing and public health, in care for dependent families, widows, and orphans, for the elderly, for defective and delinquent children, for the crippled and the blind and those who then were known as the "feeble-minded," came together to exchange experiences and ideas in the hope that some small degree of order could be wrought out of the chaos of human need and suffering that life in the modern era entailed. A generation earlier, prison administrators had so begun to gather, and in the major cities of the industrial East business and professional men (lawyers, ministers of the gospel) had launched charity organization societies that in some cities went by the name of associations "for improving the condition of the poor." It came to be widely held that charity to the dependent and defective classes had to be coordinated. Haphazard philanthropic giving was seen as a burden on men of wealth and privilege and an assault upon the character and morale of those who were the beneficiaries of such uncoordinated handouts. The first national conference which brought together all those who were engaged in some branch of "charities and correction" was held in 1873, and delegates gathered annually from that time on to share with one another new techniques for serving the health and welfare needs of deprived persons and classes. They listened to sermons of exhortation and admonition. They went away, presumably uplifted, for another year of serving the unfortunate, and more knowing and efficient in the doing of good deeds.

It was in response to this need to rationalize social services that in Boston and in New York concerned persons caught up in philanthropic and charitable work founded journals to carry news of welfare activities both to the executives and boards of agencies which provided the services and to volunteers and paid employees in the field; while in Chicago, where the settlement house movement had taken hold under the leadership of such notable pioneers as Graham Taylor and Jane Addams, a review for settlement workers was launched out of Chicago Commons.

The Boston journal, *Lend a Hand*—a title suggesting the philanthropic sentiment which lingered into the latter years of the nineteenth century—was established in 1886 under the editorship of Edward Everett Hale and had eleven years of independent existence before it was merged with the official publication of the New York Charity Organization Society (cos), the *Charities Review*, whose first number dated from 1891. While *Lend a Hand* ran to chatty news items, practical advice, and philosophical asides, the more formal *Charities Review* was, in the words of the most prominent welfare editor in that generation, Edward T. Devine, a "dignified, scholarly, educational, and provocative" journal.[1] It had a succession of distinguished editors—John H. Finley (later of the *New York Times*), Paul Leicester Ford (like Hale a man of letters, and an author of popular novels), and Frederick H. Wines (by common judgment one of the great leaders in prison and reformatory work in the decade of the nineties)—and its circulation extended to charities workers in other parts of the country, who found sound analyses and helpful information and advice in its columns. Never a popular periodical outside the profession, it provided continuity for persons engaged in health and welfare work of all kinds between the annual meetings of the National Conference of Charities and Correction (NCCC), whose official *Proceedings* contained the best of the addresses and papers delivered each year.

To meet what it considered to be an unfulfilled demand for a more practical journal of charities practice, the New York COS called on Edward T. Devine to launch, in December 1897, a second official publication under the simple, declarative title of *Charities*. Appearing monthly during the first year of publication, it became thereafter a "weekly review of local and general philanthropy." In March 1901, it absorbed the *Charities Review*, whose more formidable content continued to be reflected in the number that appeared the first Saturday of each month. In 1909 the journal was renamed the *Survey*.

Devine came to a career in social service, like so many of his contemporaries, more by chance than by design, for the profession of social work had not yet been identified. Born in 1866, he had been a teacher in an Iowa school and principal there, for a time, of a small Protestant seminary. Graduate study at the University of Pennsylvania and at the University of Halle in Germany earned him the title of "Doctor" by which his associates always knew him and prepared him for a position as staff lecturer in economics at the American Society for Extension of University Teaching in Philadelphia. His tenure there carried him through the terrible depression which began in 1893. Moved by the suffering he witnessed about him, he gradually turned from teaching toward more applied service for human betterment, and in 1896, at age twenty-nine, he accepted the call to become secretary of the New York COS.

The COS, for its part, could hardly have made a more fortunate choice: Devine proved to be a vigorous, imaginative, aggressive young man, determined to set a course but flexible enough to shift his perceptions of the job as conditions themselves changed. For a decade and a half, until Paul Kellogg took over as editor in chief of the *Survey* in 1912, Devine edited the weekly journal in whatever spare moments he could steal from his more demanding responsibilities as secretary of the largest charity society in the nation at that time. Fortunately he had energy to spare, and *Charities* never suffered from lack of enthusiasm or lack of attention on his part. In addition he somehow found the time to launch the New York Summer School of Philanthropy (an enterprise that in time became the New York School of Philanthropy attached to Columbia University and later yet the Columbia University Graduate School of Social Work), and to initiate movements in New York City for the reform of tenement housing and the eradication of tuberculosis. During many of these years he also taught part-time as professor of social economy at Columbia University. These other careers and commitments were bound to spill over into *Charities,* and as his own interests and concerns broadened and deepened, so too did the journal extend its coverage to comprehend social problems and social services of all kinds, far beyond the limits of "charities" alone.

In the beginning that was not the case, for during its first five or six years, *Charities* reflected the rhetoric and the assumptions of the nineteenth century more than it did modern idiom and ideas. Its first issues rolled out the old rationale for charity organization which had been around for a half century: indiscriminate alms-giving was a drain on limited community resources and a source of moral disintegration for the recipients; to provide support for destitute families required a careful, scientific investigation of all the circumstances which had led to the awful condition of dependency; the trained investigator should enter into the lives of these families "in a neighborly spirit"—he could learn "their sources of weakness and strength" and provide them "always with sympathy, counsel, and service," but "rarely with groceries or coal or rent." The aim was "not to give alms but a friend."[2]

The prevailing view of classes of "deserving" and "undeserving" poor held sway in the early volumes of the journal. In the roustabout society of the nineteenth century there were always those who failed to get ahead, or even to get along for that matter. Some were "feebleminded," or lacking in skill and aptitude; others were victims of bad luck—sickness, accident, and personal catastrophe. If such folk, so the older postulate ran, did for themselves what they could, sought out the assistance of public alms or private charity only as a very last resort, and continued to live upright and moral lives (that is, were prudent, thrifty, sober, and hard working), they were entitled to the support and counsel of their betters. But then there were the "undeserving poor"— the improvident and imprudent, the shiftless, the willfully ignorant, the slatternly, those who were given over to drunkenness, promiscuity, extravagance, wickedness, crime, and vice. However much a later generation might question what was cause and what effect, nineteenth-century bourgeois society knew that the "undeserving poor" deserved but one thing— their poverty. *Charities* was not so unsophisticated as to employ the very terms of "deserving" and "undeserving," but the assumption pattern remained. Charity had to discriminate among different classes of the dependent; casual handouts to those who failed to exert themselves were unscientific and harmful, but to meet the needs of "respectable but long suffering people" was to provide a better chance for those who still maintained their moral fiber. Such service was "both a joy and a mercy."[3]

Sentimental appeals to the power of good to prevail were sprinkled throughout the early issues. The rosy optimism of the favored classes was expressed, for example, in the reprinting of an old poem in the Christmas number of *Charities*, 1898:

> If the world seems cold to you,
>   Kindle fires to warm it!
> If the world's a wilderness,
>   Go build houses in it!
> If the world's a vale of tears,
>   Smile till rainbows span it![4]

Sentiments such as these were more likely to touch the heart of a volunteer friendly visitor to the poor than to comfort a mother of six children recently widowed by a railway accident or a mine explosion.

But the main thrust of *Charities* in these years that bridged the two centuries was practical. It printed annual reports of various social agencies; it carried news notes on agency practices in New York and elsewhere; it periodically provided "cautionary lists" which detailed persons and agencies charitable in declared purpose and name but in reality fraudulent schemes to squeeze money from the unwary, and on the positive side it compiled directories of approved agencies. There were calendars of events, and announcements of special short courses for charity workers and volunteers. Practical in intent, as well, were the recurring warnings against giving funds to persons who just would not work so long as money was handed out to them. These caveats appeared so often and their tone was so anxious and so abusive of one class of mendicants that one wonders, now, at the sources of this fear of being bamboozled by charlatans seeking relief who did not need or deserve it. The substance of a typical article, "Tricks and Resources of Beggars," appeared under many different titles.

Articles concerning social conditions out of which dependency might arise were scattered and few. The evils of tenement housing—crowding, ill health, and immorality—were treated most often. Publicity on early recognition and treatment of tuberculosis consumed many columns of print. There were occasional notices of the need for public parks and playgrounds, and one favorable news note on the prospect of establishing a children's court appeared. More prominent were editorials and articles opposing public aid to private charities, the granting of outdoor relief (that is, the provision of cash assistance to the needy in their homes), and state supervision of private charitable agencies. The 17 June 1899 issue, for example, reported with satisfaction the defeat, for the third year running, of a "destitute mothers' bill, authorizing the payment of public funds in New York City to widows for the support of their children instead of committing them to institutions," this defeat having been secured "by the united efforts of the general charitable agencies of the city."[5]

Nevertheless, *Charities* could declare in the lead editorial of the first number published in the new century that it aimed to be "the organ of the poor and the distressed, pleading for fraternity of spirit, for efficiency of aid, for a more complete understanding of the causes of destitution, for the removal of all which are social in nature and for which the community as a whole is therefore responsible." This statement was balanced by another which rededicated the journal to the promotion of such programs as would "enable the individual to eradicate, as far as may be, his personal defects before they have brought ruin and disaster."[6]

When *Charities* absorbed the *Charities Review* in 1901, the merger resulted in a broadening of the weekly's gauge. The first number of each month, which contained double the twenty pages of the usual issue, began to run longer and more analytical articles, many of which stressed preventive over ameliorative work. The quality of contributions began to improve: now came essays and articles by men and women prominent in their fields — Joseph Lee, Jeffrey R. Brackett, Mary Richmond, Homer Folks, Mary Willcox Brown, and many others. In these pieces the social origins and consequences of need were often noted, but the focus of attention remained concentrated on practice or service whether the subject was methods of charitable cooperation, techniques of visiting the poor, provision for care in county almshouses, institutional care for children, conditions in prisons and jails, provision for the insane, or protective services for neglected children. News items still drew heavily on New York, but increasingly there were reviews of developments elsewhere in the nation and summaries of the proceedings of state conferences and state boards. Late in 1902 *Charities* declared that one of its chief functions had come to be a review of "practical philanthropy, such as will let workers in one line of social effort in one part of the country know what others in other lines of effort in other parts of the country are doing."[7]

Edward Devine had slowly begun to turn the house organ of the New York Charity Organization Society into a journal with more ambitious designs than merely informing and arousing a small clientele of charitable and philanthropic workers in New York and other large cities in the East. The format, the typography, the editorial policies, the range of concerns had shifted but slightly by 1902. The reader in 1902 perused quite the same journal he had read in 1897.

It was to this journal that the Kellogg brothers, Paul and Arthur, from Kalamazoo in the freshwater province of Michigan, came as assistant editors — Paul, the younger, in the summer of 1902, Arthur the year following.

{II}

The Making of
an Editor

To the end of his long life, all the adult years of which he spent in New York City, Paul Kellogg never forgot his origins in what he liked to think of, with some small twinge of nostalgia, as the heartland of America. Sometimes his spoken memory was a rhetorical flourish or an ideological appeal to what he perceived as best from the land of Abraham Lincoln, Jane Addams, and Henry A. Wallace. At other times he would conjure up such names as Eugene V. Debs, Robert M. LaFollette, George Norris, Carl Sandburg—midwesterners all. Although histories headed the disorderly array of books he studied at day's end, there is no evidence to suggest that he was a disciple of Frederick Jackson Turner, or even that he had ever read him, but a sense of the pioneering spirit of a "self-reliant, self-contained people," rooted in the frontier experience and sustained generation after generation, ran deep in his heart. He never doubted that the ideal of sturdy self-reliance combined with the spirit of mutual cooperation, both of which he saw as marks of the frontier community, would prevail as long as the great valley of democracy, and with it the country, stayed loyal to its true heritage.[1]

Thus he spoke on public occasions, thus did he write to close friends and associates, and even to his young son Pat. "You were born in New York—in an apartment house—on a hill of apartment houses," Kellogg began. "But you are a middle-westerner like the rest of us." Now Pat was spending a winter in the better climate of California where he had the chance to

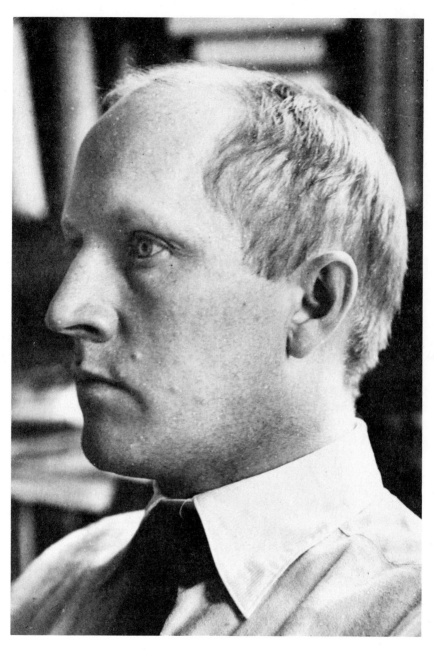

Paul U. Kellogg, the young editor

balance out his eight childhood years in the East: "Which is to look at life with young eyes: and to explore, and pioneer, and carry on the great adventure which was set for us in this new continent—so that always, forever and ever your children —our children—each generation of children—shall keep friends with the youth of the world and share it with all men."[2] The comments read more like an editorial or a peroration of some public speech than a letter to an eight-year-old son, but he regularly so addressed his children and the sentiments were nonetheless genuine.

The Michigan years remained a touchstone for Paul far more than ever they did for his brother Arthur, a year and a half Paul's elder, who followed him to New York and onto the staff of the journal for which they would be jointly responsible until Arthur's death in 1934. Arthur always had about him more brisk workaday practicality and less of the devotion to ideals and sentiments which marked his younger brother; Arthur came to terms more quickly and more easily with the realities of existence in the big city and bothered little with harkening back to boyhood days.

Born in Kalamazoo—Arthur on 18 March 1878, Paul on 30 September 1879—the two worked together inseparably from the day (Paul recalled on his brother's death) that they "set up a coop in our backyard as 'Kellogg brothers—chicken dealers.' "[3] Their paternal grandfather, Israel Kellogg, had migrated in the 1840s from New England to the Michigan frontier, where he set himself up in the lumber industry. From his marriage to Betsy Patrick issued three children: two daughters and one son, Frank Israel, who became the father of Arthur and Paul. Frank Israel Kellogg lived in the shadow of his father whose prosperity in the lumbering industry, in an era when the great stands of forest in Michigan were being slashed down, permitted him a kind of patriarchal authority. The son attended Racine College in Wisconsin in the 1860s and returned to Kalamazoo to take over the family business. By the time old Israel died, in 1880, the lumber industry in Michigan had long suffered decline, and young Frank had neither the vigorous constitution nor the business acumen of his father. The business eventually failed, as did his health, and Frank Kellogg departed for Texas, leaving his wife, Mary Foster Underwood Kellogg, to care for the two young boys. There in Texas he eked out an existence in different jobs, the last one as night clerk in the Hotel Bristol, Houston. Paul's judgment of his father's life (and the adolescent years without a father had not been easy) was typically generous: he had a "fine mind," Paul wrote his own son in 1934, but he was "bruised by the world and the business failures."[4]

Before the failure of the family business in the 1890s, the two brothers played out a typical small-town boyhood. There were Sunday School picnics at a nearby lake, family expeditions to boat and fish, canoeing and swimming on the river, digging for clams, riding their "byks" (as Arthur once recorded in a childish scrawl in a letter to his aunt), attending services at the local Episcopal parish, and going to school, of course. Because there were no playgrounds in Kalamazoo in those years, the boys' parents marked out a small ball diamond on the side yard, and put up there a horizontal bar and a trapeze. Among other scattered documents from these pleasant years there survives a petition, dated 1889, and jointly signed by the brothers: "We the undersigned do hereby petition our father Frank I. Kellogg to grant us *each* an *Air Rifle* instead of evening fireworks. We in return do hereby promise to use them with great precaution, thus causing no danger of an accident. We do here unto set our sign and seal." The Fourth of July petition was apparently granted, for on the reverse side of the document, in a steady mature hand, is the admonition: "They are not to shoot at any kind of song birds, nor point the gun at or towards any person."[5]

Their adolescent years, however, coincided with the hard times of the 1890s. Somehow the family made do. Their mother baked plum puddings which the boys delivered to the Michigan Central Railroad; she baked cookies which they peddled throughout the town. There was the backyard chicken enterprise; and Paul worked part-time as an office boy for the principal of the high school which they attended. Whatever other extracurricular activities they may have found the time to enjoy, it is recorded only that together they wrote and edited the high school paper. They were graduated together in the class of '97, Arthur serving as senior class president and Paul as class historian.

There was no money for either of them to go on to college — a loss which they both felt keenly later in life; for as Paul once complained to his son, it had taken him many painful years of self-directed reading and study to learn what he might have picked up in any four-year college course. Paul took a job in a local bookstore, sweeping out in the morning, closing up at night, making deliveries, opening boxes, washing windows, and waiting on customers. And all that for three dollars a week. "I entirely despised it," he wrote to Pat on the eve of his son's eighteenth birthday. "It was about the only time in my life I did not get joy out of my work." One lesson he had learned, however— he got "an inkling of what it means to be a misfit in your work." Paul moved on to take a position as reporter, and soon as city editor, on the *Kalamazoo Daily Telegraph,* where he was joined on the staff by Arthur. Here the two of them were quickly successful and for the next several years, living at home, they worked and saved their money; Paul, at least, hoped to be able to break away and go east to college where he could take courses that would help him toward that career in journalism he knew would be his lifetime's commitment.[6]

Paul made the break in the summer of 1901, carrying with him to his new home with an uncle, Channing Underwood, in New Jersey a letter from the publisher of the *Daily Telegraph* addressed to whomever it might concern testifying that Paul Kellogg was a "first-class newspaperman . . . efficient, painstaking and obliging."[7] Since his nonclassical course of high school studies did not qualify him to be a regular degree candidate, he enrolled as a special student at Columbia University. Full-time during the academic year 1901-2, and part-time for several years thereafter, he studied sociology with Franklin H. Giddings, history with William A. Dunning, economics with E. R. A. Seligman and John B. Clark, government with Frank J. Goodnow and Felix Adler, American literature with Brander

Matthews—a formidable, distinguished, and stimulating group of scholars under whom to be introduced to the world of serious study.

From several packets of English themes which he saved, one can learn some of the things he had in mind. He sought the "inspiration of the idea," but beyond that he wished ·to learn how to apply facts and ideas to "everyday life," to discover those things which would "explain and guide living men in relation to their present circumstances." He had known he was "in a rut and wanted out of it. . . . I was getting to look at things from the viewpoint of my own particular desk, at that one particular establishment in that one particular town." In another theme he set down a motive which was already a guide and a spur: "Moreover I knew others—working men in particular—in just such ruts. I knew there were evils in this rut system of society but not always why they were evils or why they were. I wanted to know better what was good and what forces are making for good. If I could get out of my rut, I might help them to do so."[8]

To understand the "rut system of society" was his declared intent. In the meantime there were weekly themes to be handed in. Some of them came from books or from newspaper stories— a review of Theodore Roosevelt's *Winning of the West,* an account of George Washington on the Delaware, a summary, secondhand, of a Vanderbilt-Hyde coaching party in New Jersey. Some few were nostalgic — the nutting season back home in Michigan, for example. Others were critical of British and American imperialism. But most of them were human-interest stories such as a tabloid reporter might relate from his daily experiences in the city; their settings suggest that he was taking advantage of his freedom to wander about the city—Brooklyn Bridge, the ferries, Chinatown, Fifth Avenue, the Lower East Side, the Bellevue morgue, the Brooklyn navy yard. He was learning the human stuff of the city as he was learning the fine art of writing an acceptable composition. For a young man who had visited Chicago but once, to take in the World's Fair of 1893, it must have been a heady experience to be thrown into the complex, noisy, bustling society of New York at the turn of the century—strange places and names, exotic tongues and customs, people on the move, people in need as he could never have guessed back in Kalamazoo.

The year's work at Columbia had gone well, but by June his savings were nearly used up. There was enough left, however, to finance a six-week course at the Summer School in Philanthropic Work sponsored by the New York Charity Organization Society. There lectures were given by major welfare leaders: Edward T. Devine, Robert W. de Forest, Jeffrey Brackett, Frederic Almy, Lee K. Frankel, Mary E. Richmond, Zilpha D. Smith, Mrs. Glendower Evans, Homer Folks, Alexander Johnson, Samuel M. Lindsay. (One wonders if ever a more distinguished social work faculty were gathered together.) The thirty-five students, in addition to their formal work in class, made field visits to many different agencies in the city. Devine spotted the eager, curious young man from the hinterland as a person of both ambition and talent and offered him a position as assistant editor of *Charities*; by the term's end Paul Kellogg had written his first signed story—a description of the Summer School program—and accepted what became a half-century job.

Arthur, in the meantime, had continued as city editor at the *Kalamazoo Telegraph* and in June 1902, he married a high school sweetheart, Augusta Louise Coleman. Paul went back to be best man; and Marion Sherwood, the bride's first cousin, whom Paul would marry seven years later, was also a guest at the wedding. The following spring Arthur followed his brother to New York, went through the Summer School in Philanthropic Work, and was employed as another assistant editor at the *Charities* office. The partnership of the Kellogg brothers was a going concern again.[9]

When Paul and Arthur Kellogg joined the *Charities* staff, the publication was already in a period of self-examination and change. Devine, whose set of mind had been formed in the nineties, was sensitive enough to have caught the trend and the meaning of new movements in welfare just then beginning to break away from established norms. It may have seemed brash for a young man of twenty-three, mere months out of small-town mid-America, to offer advice to such a formidable gentleman as Devine, but there always was in Paul Kellogg a gentle and disarming manner that made rather bold proposals seem palatable. Six months after joining the staff, Paul told Devine that *Charities* was too stodgy, too narrow in its appeal to professional workers. The remedy was simple enough—more timely articles that would appeal to a broader lay audience of readers. *Charities* went to twenty-five hundred regular subscribers, he continued, not many more readers than the magazine had had for some years. It had been designed to keep charity workers in touch with each other and to be an "independent and intelligent critic to prevent arrant professionalism among charitable workers." Well and good; those were valuable functions for such a journal to perform. But the unmet need was for a more popular magazine to interest a much larger audience in the social problems with which *Charities* was properly concerned. Perhaps, he suggested, the magazine might be split—one to be a technical journal of practice, the other to serve nonprofessional concerned citizens.[10]

The suggestion that there be two publications, not one, anticipated by some twenty years the division between the *Survey Graphic* (designed to reach a broad audience) and the *Survey Midmonthly* (aimed at serving the practical needs of social workers as they went about their professional business), which the Kelloggs would institute in the 1920s. But for the time the journal remained one. It is impossible to judge the degree to which the Kellogg brothers were responsible for changes in format, style, content, and tone that came to *Charities* over the next several years. Devine could juggle his multiple jobs and responsibilities only by delegating authority in many departments, and it seems probable that although he himself continued to write most of the lead editorials he gave the Kellogg brothers their head on many policy and editorial matters.

Paul recalled, much later in life, the discomfort he felt working for *Charities* "with my midwestern recoil against the very name . . ." It was, in those days, "a life saver to go up to the sixth floor of the Charities building and get a whiff of [Florence Kelley's] insurgent democratic spirit." Florence Kelley, executive secretary of the National Consumers' League, whose office was several floors above the *Charities*'s office in the same building, was already engaged in crusades for the rights of working women, government regulation of conditions of labor, and the prohibition of child labor, and Paul remembered the "edge" that Mrs. Kelley gave to her research, her sensitivity to current problems, her break with "stodgy" ways. "This was research on the firing line," Paul concluded.[11] Paul's recollection was accurate enough, and it is clear that the personal impact of that "impatient crusader," as Florence Kelley's biographer called her, was immediate, direct, and severe.

Whatever the influences were, whosoever had the responsibility, *Charities* began to open itself to new concerns and a new spirit in 1902-3. The publication became more attractive and more readable: the type was changed, variety in layout was introduced, letters to the editor were added as a regular feature of each issue, there were more illustrations and photographs. Many articles continued to emphasize practice, service, and uplift, but articles dealing with child labor and articles detailing and illustrating the evils of slum living claimed more space. In 1904 *Charities* created special departments for news gathering and interpretation in many fields of social service and social action. Some of the departments stressed traditional concerns of practice and service, but even here the emphasis was placed now more on preventive than on ameliorative programs. C. C. Carstens edited the department on "Care and Relief of Families in Their Homes"; Homer Folks addressed himself to the problems of "Dependent and Delinquent Children"; Mary Vida Clark assumed responsibility for describing "Public Care of Dependent Classes"; and Samuel J. Barrows dealt with the "Treatment of the Criminal." Of equal significance were Mary Simkhovitch's department on activities of the "Social Settlements," Florence Kelley's on "Child Labor and Protection of Children," Lawrence Veiller's on "Housing Reform," and Lilian Brandt's on "Prevention of Tuberculosis."

It was in these same pivotal years that *Charities* experimented with special numbers given over to an exploration in depth of dramatic social issues. A special number published 6 February

1904, for example, was devoted to the subject of immigration. Separate articles set forth the relationship of new immigration to labor standards and unionization, to housing congestion in tenement slums, to public health; others investigated the processes of Americanization and assimilation, and the settlement of immigrants outside the great cities. Underlying almost all the articles was an anxiety about the fate of traditional values and customs, religious and ethnic standards, should unrestricted immigration continue at its current pace; but a follow-up issue in May 1904 which dwelt on Italian immigrants included a number of pieces written by Italian-Americans detailing the social and economic conditions in Italian communities in the New World and providing, for the first time in this journal, an analysis of the role of ethnic benevolent and fraternal societies in caring for their own people. The subject must have opened new prospects to old-line native American charity workers who were accustomed to think only in terms of what the Yankee hosts had to offer to the poor immigrants. Although a certain number of familiar stereotypes of the new immigrants popped up in the February number, the May number demonstrated a respect and a sympathy for the integrity of transplanted citizens. The issue on the Italians must have been counted a success, for in December *Charities* did for Slavic communities in America what it had essayed for the Italians in May. This time again it was a first for *Charities*: the editors not only called on Slavic leaders in the United States for contributions but featured observations by leaders prominent in the settlement movement— Mary McDowell, Jane Robbins, Walter Weyl, and Alice Masaryk, for example.

The following year, in the October 1905 number, the pages of *Charities* (expanded to ninety-six for the occasion, the largest issue published to that date) were dedicated to "The Negro in the Cities of the North." Discussion of the conflicting strategies of Tuskegee and Atlanta was consciously avoided, but the number included articles by both Booker T. Washington and W. E. B. Du Bois. An effort was made to present all facets of the subject without the injection of editorial judgments, and certainly the number was a compendium of information on any number of subjects: housing, industrial conditions, employment, rates of crime and dependency, and how the needs of black communities in the urban north could be served by various social institutions—social agencies, the settlements, visiting nurses, the church, the schools, and the courts.

Perhaps the most sensational number for that time was one that included a long and detailed account of a conference of the Society for Sanitary and Moral Prophylaxis, published 24 June 1905. Surprisingly open and direct (surprising, that is, compared to the general run of periodical writing on the subject of venereal disease at the time), the article proposed that society awaken to the "great black plague" of syphilis as it had been aroused to the "great white plague" of tuberculosis. Although the summary included accounts of organized prostitution, its tone was not in the least moralistic or sentimental; the social evil was treated impassively and objectively, as part of the public health movement. At least one reader complained that it was not an issue of the journal "he would like to leave on his library table," but the general response of readers was entirely favorable and even enthusiastic, and there were many requests for reprints. The taboo against the candid public discussion of venereal disease had been broken.[12]

Apart from these special numbers which pioneered new techniques in welfare journalism, every issue began to demonstrate the enlargement of *Charities*'s social view. Articles on medical services pointed to the need for sanitary and housing reforms if public health and personal well-being were to be served. Studies of dependent families singled out uncertain and irregular employment as a probable root cause of family need. The *Charities*'s summary of the 1904 National Conference of Charities and Correction cited with approval those sessions which stressed the need to change the environment in order to bring out the best in all people. "The challenge is not to remold a never-ending series of depraved children," *Charities* reported on one of the main themes of the conference, "but to renovate the community life where it breeds hateful growths in mind or morals." Social work had to classify and study particular individuals and families, true, but it had also to "reach back into the sources of defect and delinquency." The family had to be considered as an organic whole, related to the particular community and the particular environment in which it dwelt. Such were the lessons, as the *Charities* reporters saw them, of the 1904 conference.[13] Social workers themselves were beginning to concentrate more on the *social* aspects of their service; *Charities* reflected those new concerns and new strategies.

By 1904-5 *Charities* clearly had outgrown its name and its home in the Charity Organization Society of New York. The search was on for a new mandate to match the growing sensitivity of social workers and social reformers to the persistence of social problems which lay beyond the control of any single family, group, class, or community. On Edward Devine's initiative and with the active support and guidance of Robert W. de Forest, the society picked up the challenge by creating a National Publications Committee to advise it on how best to transform *Charities* into a truly national journal for all branches of social service and for the broader audience of nonprofessional concerned citizens. Devine and de Forest came up with a list of proposed members, essentially the old-line established names: Jane Addams (of course, always Jane Addams), Daniel C. Gilman, Joseph Lee, John M. Glenn, Robert Treat Paine, and Paul M. Warburg, among others. Paul Kellogg shot off a rejoinder at once. Why not include representatives of new social thinking in America: Jacob Riis, in whose company Paul had toured Nova Scotia one summer; Simon N. Patten, devotee of a new economics and of new social programs; Charles Booth, whose great survey of poverty in London was already a classic; Robert Hunter, young settlement worker in New York, socialist, and author of a recent book with the simple bold title of *Poverty*; Graham Taylor, warden of Chicago Commons and editor of *The Commons*; and Edward A. Filene, Boston merchant with new ideas about the responsibility of the business community for employee welfare? "If you were to call my inclinations youthful, radical and popular, and extremely western," Kellogg explained, "I should describe this first list as oldish, conservative, undemocratic, and extremely eastern." His own hope was for a committee that would be "capable of enthusiasm as well as dignity," for the inclusion of some " 'infectious' " men.[14]

The final composition of the committee ran closer to the original list than to Kellogg's, although Jacob Riis and Simon Patten, at least, were asked to serve; but Kellogg's essential points did not go unnoticed. The charge to the committee asked for policy lines that would lead toward "the more complete development of a progressive journal for social workers; the publication of popular issues, live news, and readable articles that will make practical philanthropy a part of the every-day interest of the general reader; the education of public opinion through connection with newspapers and other agencies of publicity."[15] The letter of appointment concluded: "In our changing American cities a more flexible, continued medium of information is imperative to make available the underlying facts of social conditions which affect deeply the right living and well being of the community."[16]

The merger in the fall of 1905 of *Charities* and Graham Taylor's *The Commons* (which had become since its founding in April 1896 the national organ of the settlement movement) constituted the first practical step toward the realization of these goals. When, the following spring, the renamed *Charities and the Commons* absorbed *Jewish Charity*, the official paper of the United Hebrew Charities of New York, edited then by Lee K. Frankel, a new phase in welfare journalism was begun. Under the new dispensation Edward Devine remained as editor in chief of the combined publications; Taylor and Frankel assumed posts as associate editors; Robert W. de Forest remained as chairman of the Publications Committee and Paul Kellogg as its secretary; Kellogg also became managing editor of *Charities and the Commons.*

Graham Taylor, writing in the last number of *The Commons,* announced to his readers what the merger meant. *Charities,* he wrote, had been concerned essentially with "charitable and reformatory effort, both public and private" and with "creative social work"; *The Commons* had stood for "constructive insistence upon economic justice and fair industrial adjustments, the administrative efficiency of municipal government and the social extension of public education." *The Commons* had never been stronger than it was in 1905, but the time had come to join together in one, national, coordinated enterprise. [17]

Devine and the Kellogg brothers must have known what effect the infusion of the settlement point of view would have on the joint publication. Paul Kellogg himself, in these years, before he moved into a nearby apartment of his own in Greenwich Village, was a sometime resident at Greenwich House, where he lived in daily contact with settlement programs and was infected by the settlement spirit. The settlement impulse had been more neighborly than charitable; very early it had taken its stand on the premise that men were not their brothers' keepers, but their brothers' brothers. More democratic than patrician, more fraternalistic than paternalistic, settlement leaders quickly espoused all social causes in which their neighborhoods were involved—civic betterment, the enforcement of zoning and sanitary codes, slum clearance, public health, industrial justice, minimum wage and maximum hour legislation, and the prohibition of child labor. They had established day nurseries for the children of working mothers, programs in arts and crafts, music and drama; they had assisted in the organization of labor unions, especially among working women, and had walked the picket lines during strikes while gathering food and clothing for family strike relief. They responded to the felt needs of their neighbors.

The Commons had reflected and helped to inspire and to guide this thrust for social betterment. John Palmer Gavit, first editor of *The Commons,* gave the word in a year's end editorial, 1898: "We have neither prejudice against the rich nor veneration for the poor, as such . . . the aggressions of wealth are not to be overcome by some mystical friendliness between classes, or by largeness of heart upon the part of the rich." Philanthropy was inherently disqualified from dealing constructively with injustice and inequality of condition and opportunity. Social justice rested upon the recognition and the acceptance of the existence of human rights to which all men were entitled. [18]

As for poverty and the poor, writers in *The Commons* knew, as did settlement workers themselves, "that the suffering of the poor is not, as a rule, due to individual fault, but to conditions of inheritance and environment." To the poor, "hygienic living" was impossible; there was no chance for thrift. Poverty seemed "to be a linked chain of causes—poverty begetting intemperance, shiftlessness and incompetence, all of which, in turn, beget poverty . . . and behind all these causes the primary evil of irresponsible and defective society." No single line of reform would suffice to overcome the complex problems of persisting poverty; salients of many sorts would have to be initiated: improved housing, the organization of labor, the eight-hour day, public playgrounds and parks, better schools, smaller families for the poor, trade schools, public baths, an income tax, etc.[19]

In the ten years of its existence as an independent journal *The Commons* carried news in depth on all the pressing social issues of the day, including war and imperialism (it was opposed to the Spanish-American War and to the acquisition of overseas territory). It dealt with the causes and consequences of juvenile delinquency, explained and endorsed the creation of special courts for juvenile offenders. (Paul Kellogg's first piece in *The Commons,* January 1905, was an anecdotal account of the reforms instituted in Denver along these lines by Judge Ben Lindsey.) It carried numerous studies of immigrant conditions and contributions. It plumped for direct democratic processes. It explored ways by which public schools could be made social centers for neighborhood life. It stood for free speech and discussion. Whereas at first (like *Charities*) it had drawn contributions primarily from workers in the field, by the turn of the century its list of authors included Allen T. Burns, Robert Hunter, John R. Commons, Richard T. Ely, William English Walling, Henry Bruère, and Jeffrey R. Brackett.

When it merged with *Charities* not only did it bring this broad social vision, this commitment to social action to solve social problems, this rambunctious spirit of openness to ideas and programs of all sorts—it brought along, as well, a national circulation of over three thousand subscribers.

The *Springfield Republican* welcomed the merger in an editorial that identified the potential strength the combined journals might have: "The Union . . . is a matter of large importance in the social betterment movement which, loud as the din of politicians sounds, is the important movement of the day—it is the practical radicalism of the causes which these journals have championed which affords the most hopeful outlook· in the advance of the Republic."[20] The journal, in the years it was published under the combined title, 1905-9, did much to realize this promise.

It was in the first year of merger that Edward Devine served as president of the National Conference of Charities and Correction, a recognition that Paul Kellogg would be accorded a third of a century later. Devine's presidential address, which was printed in full in *Charities and the Commons,* set forth the principles by which he was now animated. The first task of NCCC delegates had always been service to those in need; if agencies had come to prefer prevention to relief, relief was always a legitimate concern. But social work had now to move beyond these specific tasks and address itself to the larger problems of society. Modern philanthropy, he said, embodies "a determination to seek out and to strike effectively at those organized forces of evil, at those particular causes of dependence and intolerable living conditions which are beyond the control of the individuals whom they injure and whom they too often destroy." Personal weaknesses exist without regard to class; but it is the poor alone who suffer the injustices of society. He was not unaware of the forces that would always resist reform —"inertia, indifference, ignorance, prejudice"—but in pecuniary self-interest, perhaps, lay the chief source of reactionism. "Child labor would come to an end in a twelve-month if there were not money to be made in the exploitation of child labor." These things being so, the first prerequisite both for effective service and for successful reform was research into the "environmental causes of distress" as well as into the sources of personal weaknesses and failures. "We are all culpably, incredibly ignorant of the very things which it would be most to our advantage and most to our credit to know." With the knowledge and the understanding that knowledge brings, the serving professions could then devise radical means to strike "against the organized forces of corruption, injustice, and predatory greed."[21]

Devine's address may be taken to represent the essential principles upon which *Charities and the Commons* took its stand in these years. It was, as a new masthead proclaimed in June 1906, "A Weekly Journal of Philanthropy and Social Advance." Service and reform, charities and settlements, practice and social action—these were the balanced ingredients that made up each number, with increasingly every year an infusion of social research into every editorial, article, news item, and book review. "There is no surer safeguard against wrong interpretations than to get at right facts," Kellogg wrote at this time; and so the journal dedicated itself to setting forth the "right facts."[22] The tone of the magazine became ever more pragmatic. Hard-hitting (it did not refrain from drawing what were to the editors logical conclusions), it was rarely sentimental, rarely shrill, rarely sensational; it did not fall into slipshod empiricism that would be content simply to gather the data and let the facts speak for themselves. Hypotheses about the nature of social institutions, it is true, provided systems of analysis by which the facts were collected, inferences and conclusions drawn, but there persisted a kind of implicit assumption that to gather and to report accurately and fully the evidence was somehow to make manifest courses of appropriate action. The editors felt that when the people and their leaders were properly informed, they would draw the right conclusions from the "right facts" and would be spurred to inaugurate effective programs of social service and social reconstruction. Sound research and analysis were to inform and guide both practice and reform.

Charities and the Commons made explicit the essentially educative function the journal was intended to perform. Looking back upon the year just past in December 1907, Devine took assurance from circulation figures that showed ten thousand regular readers for every number, but the real success of the journal, he concluded, would have to be measured "by the degree in which it serves as an educational institution for furthering the understanding of social conditions and the adoption of appropriate remedies."[23] To play this role properly, the social analyst, the journal reporter, must strive to transcend particular interest, class, condition. The journal held no brief for any special interest, he declared in 1908, not for trade unions or financiers or organized capital. Rather, "we seek to observe each impartially and sympathetically and with due recollection that neither separately, nor both together, constitute the whole of society. Our special task," he continued, "is to discover and to report as accurately as we can what financier and trade unionist, philanthropist and social worker, scientist and merchant, and all others, are doing for the common good."[24]

Freedom of inquiry, it followed, was essential to the exercise of editorial responsibility. The journal could be beholden to no class, no group, no special interest. Like a university faculty, it had to be free of external interference and imposed restrictions. But freedom was not "alone the absence of restraint," it was "a positive opportunity for action under favorable conditions."[25]

In all these things, *Charities and the Commons* reflected the typical "progressive" faith of that reform generation. It believed in the efficacy of facts; it believed in the ultimate benevolence of an informed public; it asserted that government could be a great agency for the elevation of the human race; it believed that when the people really knew what the conditions were that stood in the way of social justice, they would take appropriate steps to root out evil; it insisted on open, "scientific" inquiry; it had faith in an elite of well-trained social analysts and practitioners, standing above class, above special interest, impartial and objective, serving only the general good. It preached a commanding faith in the possibility of regenerated mankind if false, corrupt, encrusted institutions were only reformed, as surely they could be reformed if the people took thought, were well informed, and aroused to action, for, in the words of Devine, ". . . we believe in the inherent nobility and the latent tendency towards the good in the human soul. The failure is accidental, partial, temporary. The desire for right living and rational conduct is universal, natural, and in the end dominant."[26]

All of this is to say that *Charities and the Commons*—its editors, its correspondents, its contributors, and without doubt its readers as well—believed in progress, progress which would be achieved, step by step, by radical analysis and evolutionary means. The way was often difficult—social institutions were hard and inflexible, organized self-interest was frequently recalcitrant—but if only "external conditions were made fairly tolerable," Devine replied to one contributor, Richard C. Cabot, who had suggested that "social amelioration" was not the proper province of the social worker, "if children were not put at work prematurely but given the opportunity to play and to grow, if overwork were to cease . . . if sanitary homes were insured, if congestion of population were controlled . . . if savings were safe, the schools provided an education—then character would take care of itself." Everything was not wrong, basically most things were right; "they are better than they ever were before," he concluded, and therefore "it is possible to make them better yet."[27]

Progress, common sense, efficiency, cooperation, enthusiasm, objectivity, facts, democracy, human goodness, social evil, justice not charity, equality of opportunity, the common welfare, education, reconstruction, regeneration, self-determination, spontaneity, freedom of inquiry and personal choice, social advance—these were the words and concepts that recurred and prevailed. They were perceptions of human nature and social process, moreover, on which the new middle class of professional men and women in education, law, medicine, and social work were beginning to build justification for their careers as social bureaucrats (to use the terms that Professor Wiebe has employed in his analysis of history in that generation, *The Search for Order*). Finally, it seemed unlikely to Devine and his associates that any single group by its own initiative and effort could usher in the new day, nor was the reconstruction of society to be achieved at once: "There are other groups," Devine cautioned, "and there is a to-morrow."[28]

But *Charities and the Commons* would do its modest part. It printed stories on the human consequences of industrial accidents, occupational disease, and mine disasters and called for workmen's compensation, preventive medicine, and government regulation of conditions in factory and mine. It documented the personal and social costs of irregular employment at substandard wages for excessively long hours, and proposed regularization of production, minimum wages, and the elimination of the twelve-hour day. It portrayed the ugliness and incoherence of the modern industrial city and explored ways that congestion might be relieved, communities beautified by parks and playgrounds and civic centers, and neighborhoods made more sanitary and healthy. It noted the irrelevance of what so often passed for education in the public schools, and suggested the need for trade schools and for curricula that would be more directly pertinent to the experience of the city-dwelling child. Although it had not, by 1909, become a vigorous proponent of social insurance (that would come later), it had at least broached the subject and in an "Outline of a Program of Social Reform," April 1907, Professor Henry R. Seager of Columbia University proposed that the answer to insecurity in all phases of life and labor was the institution of systems of social insurance against the hazards of "sickness, accident, unemployment, premature death and old age."[29]

None of these broad social concerns was allowed to obscure the journal's responsibility to keep workers in the field apprised of new theories and techniques for more efficient and more humane service to persons and families in need. No area was left uncovered. Penology, recreation, nursing, dependent and delinquent children, family relief, education, camping, charity organization, neighborhood work, care of handicapped and defective persons, treatment and prevention of tuberculosis, institutions for orphans and the aged and the insane—these were subjects explored in detail in number after number. It was a journal, by its own declaration, of "social advance" *and* of "philanthropy."

Events were moving fast, and however eager the journal was to identify new issues, document new social movements, and espouse new causes, it was not always equal to the task. As early as 1907, more sharply by 1908-9, board members and staff began to evidence an uneasiness with the limitations inherent in a journal that still carried the word "charities" in its title. At this juncture came a call from a number of concerned citizens of Pittsburgh for someone to make a broad social analysis of conditions of life and labor in that industrial city. The National Publications Committee of the New York Charities Organization Society took up the challenge: Paul Kellogg was dispatched to Pittsburgh to direct the study. From these efforts came the Pittsburgh Survey, the results of which were published over several years in six volumes; and from his experience there, Kellogg returned to New York determined to shape the *Charities and the Commons* in new ways, to give it a new thrust of concern and action. In 1909 the journal was renamed the *Survey,* and under one variation and another of that basic title would be published from that time until it faltered and died forty-three years later.

{III}

The Pittsburgh
Survey and the
Survey Journal

THE exact origin of the impulse for the Pittsburgh Survey is lost in legend and clouded by the contradictory recollections of participants many years after the fact. The story most often told concerns a chief probation officer of the Allegheny Juvenile Court, Mrs. Alice B. Montgomery, who had read with excitement the special number of *Charities and the Commons* in March 1906, "Neglected Neighborhoods; in the Alleys, Shacks and Tenements of the National Capital," and was determined that some such report on decayed neighborhoods and neglected lives be done for the city of steel. The special number had indeed aroused a great deal of interest around the country, and Mrs. Montgomery's letter addressed to Paul Kellogg as managing editor of *Charities and the Commons* is the only document, contemporary to the events, that was saved in the Kellogg personal papers.

"Would it be possible for you to appoint a special investigator to make a study and a report of social conditions in Pittsburgh and vicinity?" she inquired. "We feel that the people of Allegheny County are not as yet wide awake as to the needs of the poor, and it is almost impossible with our limited corps of workers, to make the systematic investigation and presentation that is needed. We should be very glad for any help that you might give us, or for any suggestions you could offer."[1]

Paul U. Kellogg and the *Survey*

What response was made to this letter is not known, but the request was apparently referred by Edward T. Devine to the Publications Committee of the New York cos where it received the vigorous support of a committee member, Frank Tucker, and an initial appropriation of $1000 was made to explore the feasibility of such a project. At some point William H. Matthews, head worker at Kingsley House in Pittsburgh, threw his influence behind the study. Robert A. Woods, then director of South End House in Boston and one of the leading settlement workers in the country, who happened to be a native of Pittsburgh, helped make initial contacts with community leaders and served as a member of the advisory committee throughout the project. In Pittsburgh Mayor George W. Guthrie, H. D. W. English, president of the Chamber of Commerce, and Joseph W. Buffington, judge of the United States Circuit Court, agreed to serve as referents. Florence Kelley and John R. Commons joined Woods as members of the advisory committee.

In addition to the original grant of $1000 from the New York cos, the Pittsburgh Civic Association put in $350 (a token sum which may be taken as a predicting sign of the amount of concern the citizens of Pittsburgh would later demonstrate when the study was completed); but the bulk of the financing came through the good offices of the Russell Sage Foundation, which had just been established and chose this project as its first extensive investment in social research. Its first grant of $7000 was predicated on the assumption that Kellogg and a small staff would be able to complete their field studies in three months. The three months became a year and a half, and the Russell Sage Foundation appropriated $27,000 in all before publication, and provided another $20,000 as a publication subvention (only a small part of which was later recovered from sales of the six volumes).[2]

Paul Kellogg, secure in the knowledge that Arthur would remain in New York to watch the shop, agreed to take on the assignment after he had made certain that persons in Pittsburgh on whose cooperation he would have to depend were indeed serious in their commitments to the project and intended to push for reforms "once an independent investigation is made by us."[3]

The Pittsburgh Survey and the *Survey* Journal

In September 1907, aged twenty-eight but already seasoned by ten years of writing and editing, Kellogg moved to Pittsburgh and began to gather a staff which would garner facts and data into what one of the staff came to call "piled up actualities."[4] Perhaps because of the contacts and influence Florence Kelley enjoyed, perhaps because John R. Commons had learned to appreciate the scholarly contributions that women had to make, perhaps because Robert A. Woods and William H. Matthews were accustomed to accepting women in the settlements as equal partners in every enterprise, perhaps because Kellogg himself intuitively trusted women (and intelligent and competent women were always attracted to him), and perhaps because educated and trained women were more readily available on short notice than were their male counterparts, tied down to career and family as so many of them were—for whatever reasons, Kellogg's staff included a substantial number of remarkably talented young women, experienced in doing field work, and skilled at making both quick and thorough studies.

Crystal Eastman, graduate of Vassar and holder of a law degree, sister of the noted author and critic Max Eastman, and for the rest of her life an intimate friend of Paul Kellogg's, investigated work accidents and the law. She discovered that industrial accidents, while traceable to worker negligence in some cases, derived more often from the failure of employers to provide reasonable safety devices, or were assignable to the very system of industrial discipline itself. The burden of accidents, moreover, and this was the telling point, fell upon the worker and his family. Elizabeth Beardsley Butler, secretary of the Consumers' League of New Jersey, who joined the staff on the direct recommendation of Florence Kelley, compiled the facts on employment among women workers in canning, confectionery, cracker, glass, metal, garment, broom, and paper-box industries, in the needle trades, in laundries, and in mercantile establishments. Margaret E. Byington studied family life in ninety households of industrial workers, finding not only low standards when measured by criteria of space, sanitation, facilities, and nutrition, but a sense of powerlessness that pervaded everything the families thought and did—the families found themselves cut off from the community by the very length of the workday (twelve hours on the job left little time or energy for anything but bare survival), and by class and nationality (the workers were essentially of new immigrant stock); decisions affecting their lives were always made by others who were socially far distant. Assisting in many different capacities were Beulah Kennard, secretary of the Pittsburgh Playground Association; Helen A. Tucker, on leave of absence from the United States Department of Labor and Commerce; D. Lucille Field Woodward, on loan from the Federal Immigration Commission; S. Adele Shaw and Ann Reed, both of whom were later members of the *Survey* journal staff.

John A. Fitch laid out the social and economic data of labor in the steel industry, in which the one overriding fact of life was the twelve-hour day. He found an atmosphere of intimidation and fear. The workers were afraid to discuss their lives and their grievances with anyone; every element of self-determination was stunted by the pall of authority imposed from above which hung over their lives like the smoke that clouded the skies.

Kellogg gave to Lewis Hine, then an unknown teacher and amateur photographer, the assignment of taking documentary photographs of workers, factories, and homes. He commissioned Joseph Stella to do a series of sketches of immigrant workers and their families. The studies, as they appeared first in serial form in numbers of *Charities and the Commons,* and then in the six separate hardbound volumes, included a great deal of pictorial material: photographs and sketches, maps, charts, graphs, tables, and diagrams.

The designation "pioneering" is used altogether too casually to describe a project innovative in any way, however minor. The Pittsburgh Survey was a truly pioneering adventure, the first major attempt to survey in depth the entire life of a single community by team research. An index of the subjects covered by these volumes would run to many pages, but whatever the topic—wages, hours, conditions of labor, housing, schooling, health, taxation, fire and police protection, recreation, land values—the ultimate aim was, in the words of Kellogg, "to reduce conditions in terms of household experience and human life."[5] Statistical data were woven about by individual case studies; analysis began and ended with descriptions of individual persons as they went about their lives.

Kellogg's role was more than simply that of director and editor. He had to coordinate the work of literally hundreds of persons, not only his chief staff aids who wrote the several volumes, but all those statisticians, social workers, engineers, lawyers, physicians, economists, labor investigators, and city planners who made significant contributions at every point of the Survey. He had to keep his lines open to community leaders, for without their support the work could not continue. He had to keep community agencies, businesses, churches, civic leaders informed of his work at every phase and stage. He had, of course, to manage the budget. He had, finally, to edit thousands of pages of studies and reports, for the results of the investigations found publication not only in *Charities and the Commons* and in six fat books, but in a number of other periodicals: among them, *Collier's Weekly, American Magazine, Review of Reviews, World's Work*, and the *Independent*. The Pittsburgh Survey proved to be creative research and journalism at its very best.

The findings documented in great detail what social investigators, academic scholars, and muckraking journalists were beginning to uncover; but not until the Pittsburgh Survey was completed, and then not again for many years, was there such a compendium of the facts of human existence in modern industrial communities. That hours were long and wages low would not have come as a surprise to the workers, nor did it to many social workers and other professional people whose job it was to know such facts, but the degree and the extent of labor exploitation came as a shock to many readers. In Pittsburgh wage rates, even at the higher end of the scale, were found to be "inadequate to the maintenance of a normal American standard of living." Wages might be higher in Pittsburgh than in those provinces of southern and eastern Europe from which immigrant workers were drawn, but these newcomers enjoyed a "net pecuniary advantage because of abnormally low expenditures for food and shelter and inadequate provision for the contingencies of sickness, accident, and death." The fact of wide-spread poverty was demoralizing, but even more destructive of family life were the excessively long hours of labor and the disease and the accidents that came as a consequence. The community itself was clearly prosperous, industry was booming, but never before, wrote Edward Devine in a summary of the volumes, had "a community applied what it had so meagerly to the rational purposes of human life." The surplus that industry created should come back to the community, he concluded, not in libraries and museums but in wages, in safety, and "by raising the standards of domestic life."[6]

Civic services of all sorts, the Pittsburgh Survey made abundantly clear, were provided without regard to human need. The school system, for example, was financed out of the general property tax, but administered by wards. Rich neighborhoods and middle-class neighborhoods got good schools, poor wards got bad schools; yet the need for really good schools was more pressing in exactly those crowded immigrant neighborhoods where there was the narrowest tax base. So also was the case with hospitals and medical services: where the need was the greatest, the services were most niggardly. Control of typhoid was not alone a public health problem; it was a test of good government. Industrial exploitation robbed workers of a decent standard of living, and of dignity and self-determination; it also deprived the city of healthy and participating citizens.

To Paul Kellogg the Pittsburgh Survey was an effort to find a "human measure" by which to analyze and judge contemporary civilization. The style, he said, was that of Jacob Riis and Lincoln Steffens—to set forth a vast amount of information graphically, "not in goody-goody preachment of what it ought to be; not in sensational discoloration; not merely in a formidable array of rigid facts." The Survey was not designed merely as a criticism of existing institutions or as a social inventory, but as a new point of departure for social action. Somehow the citizens of Pittsburgh must come to realize the burden of "indirect taxation—levied in the last analysis upon every inhabitant of the city—of bad water, bad houses, bad air, bad hours." He was not optimistic; even with this "fearless statement of a range of current needs" there was still a long way to go. "Even our most enthusiastic social movements have encroached but a little way upon the fastnesses of selfishness and inertia, ignorance and privilege."[7]

It is difficult to assess the impact the Pittsburgh Survey made upon events, although the number of references to it in the generation of sociological and economic scholarship that followed testifies to the surpassing influence it had on the course of social research. There was at least one immediate effect upon housing. Part of the description of housing in industrial neighborhoods included an exposé of the atrocious conditions prevailing on Painters' Row, housing some one hundred families on a hillside not far from one of the major plants of United States Steel. Charles M. Cabot, a small stockholder of U.S. Steel, demanded an accounting from Judge Gary, director of that corporation. When he received a whitewash report implying that the investigators for the Pittsburgh Survey were lying, Cabot asked Kellogg for his proof. The truth was not difficult to establish, and on the basis of the detailed field notes, Cabot was able to get the worst of the houses destroyed and the rest fixed up. Cabot subsequently furnished the *Survey* journal with substantial grants for the establishment of an Industrial Department, headed for many years by John Fitch, whose articles published over the next decade and a half are sometimes credited with providing ammunition in the prolonged war to eliminate the twelve-hour day from the steel industry.[8]

The Pittsburgh Survey undoubtedly had a bearing on the move for workmen's compensation. Crystal Eastman went on to be a staff member of the industrial commission that wrote what came to be a model bill in New York State, and the findings of the Survey were frequently cited in other states in support of this reform as well as others. Kellogg himself never pretended that the Pittsburgh Survey was alone responsible for the institution of safety campaigns throughout industry at that time or claimed that it was singly responsible for the successful campaign for workmen's compensation, but he wrote to an economist friend in 1919: "as the first inductive investigation of the causes of work accidents and the incidence of their economic burden, it unquestionably accelerated the moves in both these directions." Looking back from the perspective that a decade provided, Kellogg could take little comfort: "In the Pittsburgh Survey we had to plow deep and break loose the hard pan; and the damning we got for it was part of the day's work. When I think that for ten years people have continued to work the twelve hour day, I think perhaps we ought to have ploughed deeper and been damned harder."[9]

One conclusion above all others is undeniable. The Pittsburgh Survey constituted a major turning point in the career of Paul Kellogg and in the shaping of the journal which, in 1909, took the name *Survey* from the Pittsburgh experience. After Pittsburgh, the old *Charities and the Commons* had to be recast—in name, in concept, in style, in quality—not from scratch to be sure, for many precedents in welfare journalism were firmly grounded by 1909; the foundation had been soundly laid by Devine and by the Kellogg brothers. But 1909 marked the beginning of a new departure.

Some months before he left to take up the Pittsburgh project, Kellogg had been asked by Devine to sketch out a plan by which *Charities and the Commons* could achieve greater independence from the cos, which still provided the financial support covering the journal's annual operating deficit. Devine hoped that the magazine might be made to appeal to a larger audience, but until new sources of income were tapped it seemed impossible either to upgrade its quality or to expand its influence. Kellogg did not have to be urged. In a series of memoranda written in the spring of 1907, he laid out the problems and proposed some tentative answers. *Charities and the Commons* had sought to be "brief and compelling for the general reader" and at the same time "to be consecutively informing for the different groups of social workers." The journal had a limited circulation—seven thousand paid subscribers, a readership of ten thousand—but he judged these were the community leaders who got things done, the people who got "other people, agencies, governmental bodies, to act; lawyers, ministers, editors, officials, heads of institutions and leaders in philanthropic movements." Other than the cos, Kellogg saw the newly established Russell Sage Foundation as the best source of funds; given the fact that Robert W. de Forest was chairman of both organizations, it seemed likely that some cooperative arrangement might win broad support. The danger lay in the journal's losing its critical independence by being the official organ of any body. Cooperation and support were one thing, control was another. If the Russell Sage Foundation could be persuaded to invest $20,000 a year for four years, the journal would be able so to improve its offerings and thus attract new readers and new support that its existence as an independent magazine would be assured. Perhaps the National Publications Committee of the New York cos could be separately incorporated, and that committee, in turn, could be made more truly representative of the readers whose attachment to the journal was not unlike the commitment that people made to other philanthropic organizations. As for ways the subsidy could be spent, Kellogg had definite ideas. The journal would have to add field reporters who could cover emergencies and emerging news stories. Department heads should be made regular members of the staff and paid for their services. Some of the funds would have to be poured into promotion and circulation and into salaries for regional staff members who would serve both as reporters of developments in the welfare story outside of New York and Chicago and as agents through which a national audience could be promoted.[10]

Devine passed along Kellogg's analyses together with a request for $20,000 a year for five years to the Russell Sage Foundation in April 1907, but it was just at this point that the Pittsburgh project was getting underway, so the foundation made a smaller initial subsidy without prejudice of action another year. In fact, this response marked the beginning of a financial relationship which would continue for many years.[11]

Kellogg was not one to pass up an opportunity when it came his way. Finished with the direction of the field studies in Pittsburgh by the summer of 1908 (although he still had a great deal of editing to do back in the home office), he found himself aboard ship on a summer's vacation trip in the company of Robert de Forest. Apparently the two of them used the occasion to discuss at length the future of *Charities and the Commons*, for from Heidelberg, Germany, Kellogg wrote a long letter to de Forest in London, summarizing the sense of their conversations. They had differed on some points, he recalled: "You spoke of the danger to the country from the mistaken enthusiast and I from the man who is spiritually blasé." But "the function of a journal is primarily neither sedative nor irritating; but suggestive and quickening." Although an editorial page with full independence and responsibility for the editor accorded was a necessary part of the journal, presentation of the facts, straight reporting, should take precedence over opinion. Harkening back to the presentation made by Devine in April 1907, Kellogg underlined what was to him an essential point to guide whatever future relations the journal might have with the COS and the Russell Sage Foundation—nothing should be done to jeopardize in any way the independence the journal had enjoyed under the counsel of the National Publications Committee. "I do not conceive of the magazine as so much paper and ink, or as a commercial venture; but rather as a company of men and women, held together toward common ends." Separate incorporation, Kellogg concluded, was essential.[12]

As for its name, "Charities" would have to go. The word was delimiting; it irritated a number of potential readers whom the journal would have to enlist if it were to expand its circulation and enlarge its mandate. (On an earlier occasion, Kellogg had not been quite so cautious on the matter of the change of name. "Charities," he had dashed off in a memorandum dated 1906, appeals primarily to "spinsters and society ladies"; whereas the journal, were it to succeed, must appeal to all those who come to welfare from "a sense of wrong, of justice, of religion, of democracy, of charity.")[13] Discussion of the change in name had been a committee concern for several years. The Chicago contingent, which was closer of course to the "Commons" than to the "Charities" tradition, were agreed that the present name was unacceptable, but when it came to a substitute the best they could suggest was "The Social Sense," or "Social Ideals," or "The New View," or "The Common Good." Others had put forward "The Community," "The Neighbor," "The Charter," "The Forecast," and "The Social Survey"—all suggestive of the kinds of functions committee members thought the journal should perform. In his July 1908 letter to de Forest, Kellogg had proposed that the magazine draw from the Pittsburgh enterprise and rename itself simply "The Survey," and it was this advice the committee accepted at its meeting in December.[14]

From its first number in 1897 down to the change of name, effective in 1909, the journal had gradually evolved into an enterprise very much broader than its original board and staff had imagined. Merger with *The Commons* and absorption of *Jewish Charity* had substantially changed its design. New sources of funding, beginning with the Russell Sage support in 1907, opened up new possibilities for expansion. The whole Pittsburgh experience had shaken not only Paul Kellogg but all those connected with it in any way. Then came the change in name, signifying the beginning of a new era. There remained but one further step to effect the transformation—separate incorporation.

Beyond the annual subsidy from the New York COS and the special grants from the Russell Sage Foundation the journal had received contributions from private donors. Among the early and generous patrons were Robert W. de Forest, Julian W. Mack, George Foster Peabody, Paul and Felix Warburg, Nathan Straus, and Mrs. Raymond Robins, and in 1906 Devine launched a campaign to secure at least one hundred "co-operating subscribers" who would agree to pay at least ten dollars a year. By 1912 the number of large contributors had increased and over six hundred subscribers were paying the basic ten-dollar contribution.

In 1912 all patrons who subscribed ten dollars or more became the original voting members of Survey Associates under the new charter of incorporation. As members they were entitled to attend annual meetings and to vote for election of members of the Board of Directors. As in many such organizations, the effective "election" came at the point of nomination to a single slate put together by a committee of the board itself, and in all the years of its existence there is no evidence that the members ever challenged the list of nominees presented to them. The Articles of Incorporation, 31 October 1912, named the first twelve directors; thereafter four board members were elected each year for terms of three years each.[15] Robert W. de Forest was elected president of the board of Survey Associates, a position he held until his death in 1931. The press of his other careers encouraged Edward Devine to resign as editor in chief at this point of reorganization, although he continued as a major contributor and as a member of the board; Paul Kellogg was named in his place, and Arthur became managing editor. Having been "sheltered in the house of friends," as Kellogg put it, the *Survey* was now launched on its independent course.

It was typical of Kellogg's perception of the adventure that he should choose as the symbol for the *Survey* a drawing of a ship taken from an old map prepared by de la Cosa, pilot of Christopher Columbus; and it was this jaunty caravel, sails full in the wind, that remained at the masthead. "We are essentially a magazine of the New World and share in its spirit," Kellogg explained; "social exploration" was its mission. Appearing together with Columbus's caravel were four other insignia: a surveyor's target, to stand for accuracy; a dial, to suggest the timeliness for which journalism had to strive; the seal of the New York COS; and a cogwheel, the "central axis of motive power in industrial life."[16]

It would be in keeping with Paul Kellogg's style to spin out the metaphor as he so often did—the staff might be considered the crew, Arthur would have to be designated both chief engineer and purser, Paul himself both navigator and captain, and the members of Survey Associates perhaps the passengers on the voyages of discovery . . . but let the metaphor go before its weight sinks the ship. Of crucial importance to an understanding of the enterprise was the Kellogg brothers' perception of the Associates; other journals had editors and staffs and subscribers but no other enjoyed a base of regular members who not only subscribed but contributed time and money. From the Associates board members were selected; from the Associates over the years came fruitful suggestions and leads and the submission of major articles. As the Kelloggs conceived of them, the Associates constituted a core group of independent professional persons who were the expert specialists that society would have to accept and whose talents the nation would have to employ if rational control were to be asserted over the drift of life. They formed an elite corps whose services, if democratically directed, could establish order over the latent anarchy of modern life. Before they could be made into a true community of public servants they would need to learn from each other the essential information and design of each other's separate professions. It was to the processes of mutual education that the *Survey* was chiefly dedicated. Educators, lawyers and jurists, doctors and nurses, engineers, ministers, public administrators, social scientists, business managers, technologists, social workers—if these professionals could learn to communicate with each other they might come to share a social vision and acquire a common body of social knowledge and processes by which the nation could be moved down the path of welfare and progress. Through the *Survey* such a community of elite groups might be forged.

{IV}

An Era of
Reform and the
Coming of War

THE years beginning with the Pittsburgh Survey experience were hard-working and creative years for Paul and Arthur. Married in 1909 to Marion Pearce Sherwood, who had come east from Kalamazoo in 1907 to do secretarial work in the *Charities* office, Paul seemed little distracted by his new condition of marriage and later fatherhood. Richard Patrick arrived in February 1911 — Richard for Marion's grandfather by whom she had been reared; Patrick was a surname on Paul's side of the family, but family folklore has it that Paul favored the name because it claimed an Irish ancestry to which he was romantically attached. Mercy Pearce, named for Marion's Quaker grandmother, was born in April 1918, soon after Paul's return from an overseas assignment with the Red Cross. Arthur and Augusta (or "Gussie" as she was more often called) remained childless. Paul was a devoted if often absentminded father, and Uncle Arthur was always a source of delight to the children. The work of the Kelloggs was demanding, and they threw themselves into the enterprise with unstinted vigor, although Arthur's enthusiasm, while no less than his brother's, was laced with a certain wry sense of life's ironies which was entirely alien to Paul's style. The *Survey* proved to be a jealous mistress for them both. They came to the office early and stayed late; they lugged bulging briefcases home at night; weekends were as often devoted to business as to family; neither of them got away often for family vacations in these years, and Paul was away from home with some frequency promoting the *Survey* and seeking out stories in the field.

They were heady years, moreover, for the two reformers both in their thirties, still young enough to be swept by the enthusiasms which marked the cresting years of the progressive era, but mature and experienced enough to move with some authority in the realms of social advance. Later in life, when progress did not seem as assured as it had when the Kelloggs stood in the presence of a goodly company at Armageddon and battled for the Lord, Paul recalled in a nostalgic letter to his dear friend Lillian Wald that life had felt "young and hopeful to us" in the years before the war. [1]

So it did. The Pittsburgh experience had tested Paul's latent capacities and he emerged confident of his own ability to do what he set his will to accomplish, and that assurance matched the confidence of an age which was coming to believe that all things were possible if men applied their social intelligence to solving the problems which beset society. There was no lack of challenge, the world's work was to be done, the world's work *could* be done.

It was natural that Kellogg should have worked through the National Conference of Charities and Correction toward the goals of social reform. The NCCC had established, in its 1909 convention at Buffalo, a Committee on Occupational Standards. Sherman Kingsley, a prime mover at the meeting that year, arranged for Paul Kellogg, fresh from the Pittsburgh Survey, to be its first chairman. It was his task—before Florence Kelley took over the chairmanship in 1911, and Owen Lovejoy in 1912 —to stake out the field, to identify those problems which were most pressing, and to propose lines of inquiry and study which seemed most promising. Working closely with Florence Kelley, Julia Lathrop, John B. Andrews, Crystal Eastman, and Father John A. Ryan, Kellogg arranged for papers and reports to be discussed at the 1911 NCCC meeting on such subjects as the limitation of hours of labor, workmen's compensation, industrial hygiene, and the level of industrial wages. After three years of

committee activity, the delegates to the national conference in
1912, acting in their individual capacities and not in any official
way, endorsed the platform brought to them for their consideration by the Committee on Standards of Living and Labor (as it
had come to be called), of which committee Kellogg was still
an influential member.

It was this platform that John A. Kingsbury, acting for the
social workers on the committee, carried to Theodore Roosevelt who saw to the inclusion of large segments of it in the Progressive party platform that year. If social welfare leaders ever
had a candidate and a program behind which they could unite,
it was TR and the Bull Moose party in 1912. Edward Devine
argued in the pages of the *Survey* that fall that the real responsibility of the profession was not to engage in a partisan campaign,
but to remain outside of party politics where it could promote
causes for the common good without regard to the shifting successes and failures of particular candidates and parties. Loyalty
should be to issues, not to persons, he insisted.[2] Others were
not so cautious. Jane Addams, Owen Lovejoy, John Kingsbury,
Henry Moskowitz, the Kellogg brothers, and a host of others
endorsed the Bull Moose candidate and campaigned actively for
him.

At the time, Kellogg had expected that active participation
in the drafting of the platform and in the campaign would lead
to a "new alignment" in public life, regardless of how the campaign came out. Noting in the pages of the *Survey* that the NCCC
platform had been taken up in Roosevelt's great "Confession
of Faith," he declared: "It is a truism of political history that
minority parties ultimately write the platforms for all parties. In
time, the causes which they have the temerity to espouse, are
taken up by the established organizations when direct appeal to
the latter may have proven fruitless." Not all would agree with
that estimate, he admitted, but he saw the opportunity greatly
to accelerate the process of reform by such acts.[3] When challenged later by the observation that Roosevelt's candidacy had
done little but assure Wilson's election, Kellogg demurred:
". . . as a matter of fact, the social and economic planks of the
Bull Moose platform gave a shove to more state legislation in

those fields than had been enacted in the preceding thirty!"[4] As for national action, "more social legislation . . . was passed in the two following years than in ten years preceding," he wrote at the same time to another correspondent. "The planks or standards had been seeded down in public interest."[5]

Out of the deliberations of the NCCC Committee on Standards of Living and Labor had come an urgent demand for the creation of a federal government commission on industrial relations. A symposium printed in the *Survey* in 1911 had given focus to the proposal and a special committee composed of welfare leaders and their associates in reform movements was established—Edward Devine, chairman, Lillian Wald, Florence Kelley, Allen Burns, Rabbi Stephen Wise, Adolph Lewisohn, and Paul Kellogg, who wrote the various formal statements of need and edited a short series of popular pamphlets. Congress established such a commission in 1912, but because Taft's nominations of commissioners to represent the "public" included no prominent social worker or economist and no woman at all, the committee was forced into the uncomfortable position of fighting against confirmation of all of Taft's nominees. Congress delayed action until the new president, Woodrow Wilson, could name a new slate, but his nominees, although they seemed at first more acceptable to the committee of social workers and reformers, of which Kellogg continued an important member, proved not to fulfill the expectations the original proponents of the commission had entertained and Wilson's chairman, Frank P. Walsh, turned out to be more flamboyant and less constructive than they had envisioned. There followed several years of sniping and guerrilla warfare between the commission and members of the committee with claims and counterclaims and the exacerbation of hard feelings on all sides. The affair was ugly and drawn out over several years, and it led to no constructive results whatsoever. The commission held a number of public hearings concerned with the relations of management and labor in a number of key industries, but its findings satisfied none of the parties.

The committee's proposals and positions reflected accurately middle-class progressives' fears of industrial violence, and the hope that citizens could rise above economic self-interest, that institutions of government could be led to represent the "public's" interest and to seek the common good, that class differences could be overridden and arbitrated. Not one of these progressive expectations was realized in the United States Commission on Industrial Relations, as Kellogg and Devine and their friends perceived it; by these criteria it would have to be judged an utter failure. The wonder remains that the disappointments of committee members, while expressed in personal attacks on the commission, did not lead to more bitterness, or to a reassessment of the premises upon which hopes had been founded. For Kellogg at least, the failure of the commission, as he and the others had conceived its functions, may have had some such consequence, for although he never gave up his belief that the instrumentality of government might be used for the promotion of the *general* welfare, his espousal in subsequent years of unionization, and his conviction that labor would have to organize to win by its *own* actions (both economic and political) those rights which society frustrated or denied, may have arisen in some part out of what was to him the unhappy experience of the commission in these years just before the war.[6]

In light of these concerns and of the increasing activity of social welfare leaders in the political and industrial arena, it was logical that the *Survey* should turn more and more to the exploration of broad social issues. It did not neglect its function as a journal of social service practice, but the balance was certainly tipped in favor of social action as opposed to traditional professional matters. John Fitch's Industrial Department was the only special section of the magazine directed by a full-time staff member. The Health Department claimed the attentions of another staff member half-time, and all the other social work departments were put together by unpaid volunteer contributors, working with the clerical assistance of *Survey* personnel of course. Kellogg reflected the enthusiasm of welfare people generally for social action; beyond that he himself was not unaware of the competition of the *Masses* and, after 1914, of the *New Republic,* whose mandate and potential readership overlapped with the *Survey*'s, even though the *Survey* publicly disclaimed any intent ever of becoming a journal of opinion.

An Era of Reform and the Coming of War

In his annual report to members of Survey Associates in 1914 Kellogg estimated that the space devoted to news of social movements had quadrupled in the preceding decade, and to the Reverend Samuel Z. Batten, one of the most aggressive and radical of the social gospelers, he confessed: "We have published industrial matters to a point where some of our friends feel we are destroying the balance of The Survey; and yet the pressure for publication in that field from many directions has not itself been fully met."[7]

The subjects for social exploration were as many and varied as the agenda of all the social movements combined. The editor assigned top priority to industrial topics—hours, wages, conditions of employment, industrial accidents and mine disasters, occupational disease, the exploitation of the labor of women and children and immigrants, and the progress of labor legislation on all these items (this last a regular section edited by John B. Andrews, secretary of the American Association for Labor Legislation). Other related topics claimed almost as much space: the health and moral hazards of tenement house living; discrimination against immigrants and Negroes not only in employment but in all areas of their lives; the need for schools, hospitals, parks, and playgrounds and, beyond these, for comprehensive city planning; conditions of prison life, juvenile courts, improvement in procedures for probation and parole; the growth of alcoholism, and the organized business of prostitution (which the *Survey* tended to regard more as an economic than as a moral problem); prospects for social insurance against the hazards of unemployment, sickness and accident, and old age; the extension of the suffrage to women. Even the topic of birth control received occasional (if cautious) reference.

The journal did not ignore social work practice but it carried far less such news from the time it first began publication under the title of the *Survey* down through the years of war and reconstruction; just as social work itself was beginning to move from ameliorative to constructive measures so did the *Survey* both reflect and lead that trend. Edward Devine, in a guest editorial early in 1916, set forth the new spirit of a "profession in the making." Welfare demanded "thoroughly trained experts in the broader aspects of social work," but these specialists, if they were to be part of the spirit of the contemporary age, would be moved by a "vision of a new social order in which poverty, crime and disease, if not wholly abolished, will certainly be vastly diminished." Hospitals were to be considered no longer merely as refuges for the sick but as community health centers.[8] And in another piece, which appeared as the nation accelerated its preparedness program, Devine demanded that welfare measures—infant and child protection, health insurance, humane care of the mentally defective, and town planning alike—be considered not as a cost that the nation might or might not choose to assume but as an investment, whose returns would be measured "in terms of life, vigor, efficiency, power of creation, and capacity for enjoyment."[9]

Such was the spirit in those years—guidance for skilled social service, a crusade for industrial justice, a move beyond preventive programs to constructive community measures. It was fitting that the *Survey* should have responded to a plea from Simon N. Patten that a committee of "brotherhood and social aspiration" be called together to compile a book of hymns which welfare workers, of whatever religious persuasion, might sing together. The *Survey* did in fact commission such an ecumenical effort, and although it reported that the jurors disagreed all down the line on tune and harmony and text, they finally selected a hundred hymns of aspiration and faith, liberty and justice, peace, labor and conflict, brotherhood, and patriotism. These hymns, the *Survey* boasted, sang notes of "cheer, courage and inspiration"; there were none of "atonement, sin and sacrifice." We have persisted in "holding to the sunny way," the *Survey* concluded. "There is so much of gloom without singing it!"[10]

It was no wonder that John M. Glenn complained to Kellogg in 1916 that the journal seemed "to be more and more getting out of the field of social work. . . . It is becoming more a journal of opinion, less a journal which deals with facts." He went on to suggest that the editor had worried too much about the success of the *New Republic*, had been too much influenced by the *Call* and the *Masses*; these magazines, Glenn insisted, were not in any sense rivals of the *Survey*, which had quite another audience. Especially did he object to space given over to articles on "feminism, on twilight sleep, on birth control," and articles devoted to what he interpreted as attacks upon national preparedness.[11]

Such files as survive from the prewar years indicate that Glenn's objections, whatever weight they may have carried because of the authority which he himself exercised owing to his connections with the Russell Sage Foundation which continued to pour subsidies into the *Survey,* were a minority expression. Welfare, not service, was the rage in these years; the *Survey* served the needs of its constituency and led them to new insights. The *Survey*'s primary work, Kellogg explained in 1915, "is as an investigator and interpreter of the objective conditions of life and labor and as a chronicler of undertakings to improve them. The points of view of those who contribute is almost as diverse as their places of residence."[12]

The *Survey* was not a journal of opinion as were the *New Republic* and the *Nation.* Paul Kellogg's energies went not into shaping policies in regard to public issues which he might then pour out in editorial columns; in fact in these years the *Survey* featured only occasional editorial essays and guest columnists, not Kellogg, usually wrote them. It was rather in the solicitation and selection and editing of articles that Kellogg influenced the direction the magazine took. The points of view, the interpretations, the proclamations, the exhortations were buried in the articles themselves and in the cartoons and sketches and illustrations which accompanied the printed text.

The Kellogg brothers continued, however, to play an active part in the public promotion of those causes which the *Survey* itself analyzed and interpreted. In late March 1913, for example, Paul and Arthur with forty-five others endorsed a plea to President Wilson that he include social legislation along with revenue and currency and tariff bills when Congress assembled in special session. The ad hoc group, chaired by Devine, asked serious consideration for workmen's compensation legislation to cover federal government employees and workers in interstate commerce, for an eight-hour day for women in the District of Columbia, for the creation of a coordinated health service, for mental testing of immigrants, for improved conditions for American seamen, for the abolition of contract convict labor.[13] Paul Kellogg also worked with Joseph Chamberlain and Jane Addams to encourage the Progressive party to take up the cause of national health insurance.[14]

When it came to the presidential campaign in 1916, Kellogg, like so many of his friends, was disappointed in all the parties. The Progressives had been held together only by Roosevelt's personality, he feared, and when the party turned from reform to preparedness for war, nothing remained for a reformer to support. The Progressives had not originated reforms—politics could not be innovative in that sense—but "like all creative minorities, it has set issues before the public . . . and its existence has been a pressure . . . for action."[15] But it seemed to Kellogg that the Progressives in 1916 had joined with the Republicans in a platform that was "a preachment of militant, self-reliant, self-righteous nationalism." The Democrats under Wilson had set an enviable domestic record by rifling the Bull Moose platform of 1912, but Wilson tended, especially in foreign affairs, to react to events rather than creating opportunities for asserting policies on his own initiative. As for the war and the shape of the postwar world no party and no candidate seemed prepared to take those steps which would be essential if a "new order" were to be built "out of the wreck of war." Rather than being paralyzed by the fear of differences within the nation, especially of the tensions that existed between various national groups, Kellogg proposed that political leaders set in motion constructive debates which might draw upon the special understanding that immigrant peoples had of European affairs, discussions which might begin to point the way toward a constructive resolution of European problems.[16]

The *Survey* endorsed no candidate and Kellogg himself did not in the pages of the journal announce his preference, but he did join with many other "Social Workers for Wilson" in a public statement of support in the closing weeks of the campaign. Wilson had proved himself to be a man of "broad social vision," concerned with advancing the "social welfare of the whole people." He had won constructive legislative enactments:

the Federal Reserve, rural credits, workmen's compensation, a national child labor act, the Seaman's Act, the Clayton Act; he had pursued in diplomacy a course of "reason and negotiation"; he had appointed sound performers to office: Louis Brandeis (whose confirmation as justice of the Supreme Court had been explicitly endorsed in the *Survey*), Newton D. Baker, Frederic C. Howe, and Julia Lathrop.[17] When Jane Addams wrote to confess that she had been "quite unprepared for the distinctive period in American politics developed under the brilliant Party leadership of President Wilson," and to urge that the statement be made more forthright in Wilson's support, Arthur Kellogg (one of the chief movers of the committee and one of the authors of the statement) replied that the committee "would have hesitated to have added much that was specific about President Wilson, for we found a considerable amount of luke-warmness; and to have said anything about the Progressive party would have complicated matters, for we found a rather astonishing number had been Democrats for some time and voted for Wilson in 1912."[18]

Arthur Kellogg did not specify exactly which persons on the committee had been in Wilson's corner in 1912, but he was trained to accurate reporting and he was never swept away by political emotions so it must be assumed that his observations were essentially correct. Arthur and Paul had both campaigned for Roosevelt in 1912 and endorsed Wilson four years later; so did Jane Addams; so did Frederic Almy who claimed that he always voted "for social work rather than for a party label," and when Wilson proclaimed all the principles of the Bull Moosers, whose policies were "victorious though the party is dead," he naturally shifted to Wilson as the social work candidate.[19] Most of the eminent settlement movement leaders had made the same shift, and Professor Arthur Link's thesis that Wilson's domestic reform program brought over enough former Progressives to make possible his reelection by however narrow a margin is corroborated by this evidence.

By 1916, however, for the Kelloggs and the *Survey* as for the nation, American policy in regard to the European war clearly took precedence over other concerns. To the small band to which the Kelloggs attached themselves very soon after the outbreak of war in the summer of 1914, the issue was never simply whether to stay out or go in, whether to hold aloof or intervene; rather they sought to explore lines of national conduct which might open channels to mediation of the conflict, to ways in which American influence and authority could be brought to bear on a just settlement without the necessity of the United States becoming an active belligerent.

From his travels on the continent of Europe in the summer of 1908 Paul Kellogg had come away favorably impressed with German efficiency and with the system of industrial welfare and comprehensive social insurance which the Empire had instituted. Skeptical of all authoritarian procedures, he wished that these ends might have been achieved by more democratic means, but at least Germany had acted positively whereas in the United States nothing had been accomplished along these lines at all. Psychologically it was difficult for Kellogg to ascribe the sins of autocracy entirely to the side of the Central Powers; the industrial autocracy which still made men afraid in Pittsburgh was too fresh in his mind. Moreover, he knew from his reading of history that war was inhumane, and brutalizing, and that the proclamation of high ideals often obscured the imperialistic designs by which governments were truly guided (the Mexican and the Spanish-American wars came readily to his mind). The condition of peace, on the other hand, represented those virtues cherished by every good progressive—social stability, the supremacy of reason over emotion, and a people united in brotherly affection one to another. [20]

When, in September 1914, Lillian Wald invited a small group of friends to meet with her at the House on Henry Street, Paul Kellogg was among those who talked far into the night about the implications of war which would in time become the overriding condition of their lives. Identifying themselves at first as the Peace Committee and conceiving of themselves, in Kellogg's words, as a "small, active junta," the group held informal conversations that came to involve Jane Addams (when she was in New York), Oswald Garrison Villard, Louis P.

Lochner, John Palmer Gavit, Crystal Eastman, Frederic C. Howe, George Kirchwey, Washington Gladden, and Frederick D. Lynch among others. Although during the first year or so of its gatherings the group proposed no formal resolutions, its members tended to oppose preparedness programs which distracted the American attention from seeking a negotiated peace and which diverted funds from health and welfare to the manufacture of engines of death. In time as the meetings became more formalized, the group assumed the name of the American Union against Militarism.[21]

As for the *Survey,* the editors and staff tried scrupulously to keep the columns open to a free exchange of divergent views when the war seemed a relevant concern to the chief functions of the journal. Paul Kellogg's first editorial response to the war, in the fall of 1914, expressed his anxiety that the war— "with its inevitable disaster to the humane instincts"—might set back the cause of reform. The agenda for reform at home was far from realized, he said, and he pledged that the *Survey* would be alert "to check anti-social encroachments which may be attempted under the cover of the general pre-occupation." The fate of basic welfare measures—health, industry, prisons, asylums, unemployment, poverty—was now in question; if other papers and journals let themselves be distracted by events in Europe, the *Survey* would continue to report and interpret the welfare scene.[22] For the next several years the *Survey* held to that course. It carried articles on problems of relief that the war had brought in its train; it reported on the economic dislocations that occurred when the preparedness campaign gathered speed; it pressed and pressed hard for the enactment of welfare measures in state and national politics; it surveyed the impact defense had on the provision of welfare services; it set forth the need for ever greater coordination in the raising and spending of funds by councils and federations of private community agencies (anticipating the drive for the creation of community chests which would arise during the war years). But until the winter of 1917 it did not specifically comment on the diplomacy of peace and war as such.

By February of 1917, however, Kellogg had persuaded

himself—or rather, had been persuaded by the sweep of events those winter weeks when the trend toward intervention accelerated—that he would have to use the columns of the *Survey* to set forth his personal views on the war crisis. He felt that to refrain from speaking out on the most pressing issues of the day in deference to the usual mandate of the journal would be a failure of editorial responsibility. To Jane Addams he reported a meeting of the American Union against Militarism which was "the most gripping experience I have ever been through." Rabbi Stephen Wise had proposed that American intervention was now the only way that Prussianism could be stayed. But others—Amos Pinchot, L. Hollingsworth Wood of the Quakers, and Emily Greene Balch—had countered that it was war itself that would bring Prussianism to the United States and that America's entrance on the side of the Allies would prepare the ground for a counteralliance that would threaten democracy for a century. Kellogg's own contribution that night had been to suggest to Rabbi Wise that he "arouse the German-born Americans to a lifelong enlistment in the cause of overthrowing Prussianism—through moral and intellectual fire rather than through force."[23]

Over the Lincoln's birthday holiday—working "soberly, slowly and hopefully," as he reported his state of mind to Jane Addams—he drafted a piece which he intended to have printed not as an editorial, but as an article over his personal signature, for although he could no longer keep quiet he could not commit the *Survey* officially to his own position.[24] He circulated galley proof of the article among the staff and to select friends but not to members of the board because, as he later explained, his action did not seem to involve any departure from standard procedures in such matters; it was as natural and appropriate to turn to the staff and not to the board as for a faculty member of a university to turn for advice to his colleagues and not to the trustees.[25]

His personal statement appeared as "The Fighting Issues," in the 17 February 1917 number of the *Survey*. "Military operations and international politics are not, as such, the subject matter for the *Survey*," he began. "Neither are meteorology and hydraulics. But when a flood comes down a great valley, sweeping over everything in its course, the rushing waters take on human content; and the relief work, the organization of social action, the prevention of future disasters through forestation and flood control, become our concern. So with war." The extension of submarine warfare and the consequent break with Germany forced the nation now to weigh ends and means and to judge the social consequences of whatever course it chose. To destroy the fact and the spirit of Prussianism was a legitimate goal; but the war itself had Prussianized England, and the overthrow of Prussian militarism in Germany was a task appropriately left to the German people, Kellogg argued. But most significantly, if the United States intervened would it not become just another of the military powers and thus lose the authority it otherwise carried for a just peace? He could not bring himself to believe "that a settlement resting on conquest and exhaustion and maintained by force can last." He praised Wilson for the patience he had demonstrated over so many difficult months, and he hoped that the president might still find a path by which "peace without victory" could be brought about. A peaceful and neutral United States would continue to be a "great moral example" to the world, Kellogg concluded, but a belligerent nation would be swept by hatred and lost would be "the world's only great reservoir of good will and resource for the generous purposes of reconstruction." He joined Jane Addams in the hope that the American people might mobilize themselves in the " 'opposite direction from war.' "[26]

No other single editorial decision in the whole history of the journal ever aroused such controversy. Letters of praise and denunciation, divided about evenly, poured in; many agreed, many disagreed but respected Kellogg's right to express his own views, some wrote to ask that their subscriptions be canceled. More importantly, a number of the board members who favored the interventionist course that Wilson now seemed to be taking expressed sharp displeasure not alone with the substance of Kellogg's article but with the procedure by which he had sought staff but not board advice on a matter of such importance. The difficulties became compounded when the board learned that the

editor, on his own initiative, had solicited other articles which
would discuss the war issue from other perspectives. Dr. John
Grier Hibben, president of Princeton University, had been asked
by Kellogg to put in article form a speech he had delivered in
which he had urged American intervention in order to preserve
the liberties and humanities of Western civilization from destruction; and when he declined, Kellogg had requested his Boston
friend and patron Richard C. Cabot to shape an article along
such lines, for it was a position, Kellogg observed, that many
prominent social workers held.[27]

In several meetings held late in February and throughout
March, the board debated what action, if any, should be taken in
regard to the editor's assertion of editorial independence, and
what now should be done in regard to the printing of the Cabot
draft favoring intervention and a manuscript article written by
John F. Moors opposing American belligerency. Since a number
of members of the board including its vice-chairman, John
M. Glenn, who presided in the absence of Robert de Forest,
agreed that the question of war went beyond the scope of the
Survey, a "truce" was declared by the terms of which Kellogg
would refrain from printing any more articles on the war until
de Forest returned to the city and the whole question of editorial
responsibility and independence could be resolved. Glenn, writing for the board, absolved Kellogg of any charge of error; if the
editor had erred it was on the side of "fairness and generosity."[28]
There had been threats of resignation on the part of at least
three board members, and some consideration of asking for
Kellogg's resignation as editor, but Kellogg accepted the board's
action gracefully. When Cabot shot off a telegram to Kellogg
complaining that the truce was unfair—"Consider the stopping
of my article an outrage. What fairness in declaring truce just
after a series of pacifist articles and just before a patriotic one"
—Kellogg replied that he himself was still committed to keeping
the *Survey* "open as a channel where social workers and thinkers
of your point of view and mine can meet and express themselves
on even footing." And then, anticipating the pressures for con-
formity that war would surely bring, Kellogg added: "Ahead of
us, if ever, we need such a free press."[29]

Six months later Paul Kellogg included in a letter to Arthur, written from Red Cross headquarters in Paris, a statement of appreciation to the board: "The editor desires to express his appreciation of the sincerity, the fire of conviction and the spirit of accommodation based on long association, which marked this period of deliberation and decision at a time when men's nerves were on edge and so many fellowships snapped under the strain."[30]

By the time de Forest returned from California in mid-April, the nation had gone to war and no one, apparently, had the desire or the will to prolong further a controversy which events had rendered obsolete. There were other more pressing matters to attend to now. By default, however, Kellogg had won his point, at least so *he* felt, and by acting as though he had in the years that followed he did in fact successfully maintain that principle most dear to him of editorial independence and editorial responsibility. The board would subsequently discuss editorial policy and work critically and constructively to make the *Survey* a better journal, one in accord with their perception of its proper functions, but never again did they entertain seriously the thought either of overriding the editor or of seeking his resignation on the point of editorial prerogative.

As for the substantive issue of war and peace, Kellogg acquiesced in the national decision, taking some comfort in Wilson's having "lifted the plane of our entrance into the war from that of neutral rights to an all-impressing fight for democracy."[31]

The issue was joined. The nation was at war.

{V}

War and

Reconstruction

PAUL KELLOGG counted among his closest friends persons who were absolute pacifists, associates who could find no justification at all for the human suffering that war invariably entailed. His own instincts almost persuaded him that they were right. Just two weeks before Congress declared war he wrote to a cousin about a half-uncle, Paul, after whom he had been named, who had died of a fever contracted during the Mexican War: "It was only after many such young men had given up their lives, and long after the war was over, that the country came to realize it was not a simple war of patriotism and right, but was in part at least the result of the agitation of slave-holders of the South who wanted more cotton lands for slavery." His understanding of that experience, he concluded, made him "want to stop and think and try to see through the clouds of words when there is war clamor on, so that we will be sure that ours is a just cause and war is the only way to advance it."[1] A half year later, after he had witnessed the "excruciating" horrors of war firsthand, he wrote home to his wife: ". . . of the millions who have gone down—of the men at each others throats—only the few had enmity toward one another. . . . the scheme of things which made this war possible must be junked before Pat grows up."[2]

Down through March of 1917 he had stood with his closest friends—Lillian Wald and Jane Addams—on this momentous decision, but once the nation was at war, abhor violence though he did, he accommodated himself to the fact of American belligerence and bent his energies toward making certain that the war would be waged with a due respect for the rights of dissenters on the home front who persisted in their opposition to the war, and toward encouraging a peace whose terms would justify if they could never redeem the sacrifice of blood. When, under the intense pressures of war, members of the American Union against Militarism began to split apart— some to hold the pacifist position, some into the defense of civil liberties (a group that formed itself into the American Civil Liberties Union), and some into an informal committee of citizens seeking the formulation of peace terms while the war was still being waged— Kellogg sided with the latter group (which by 1921 had formed itself into the Foreign Policy Association), without ever breaking friendship with old associates who followed other paths. In fact he was often called upon in these years to mediate differences between contesting factions within the circle of welfare work. At the NCCC conference in June 1917, for example, Kellogg put himself forward as a buffer between conflicting members of a panel addressing themselves to the consequences of American belligerency, endeavoring, as he reported the hectic debate to Jane Addams, "to make clear why conference delegates and citizens generally should be interested in a fresh statement of terms of peace and not leave those tremendous issues of foreign policy to the extremists."[3]

It was at that convention that Paul Kellogg helped Roger Baldwin draft an open letter to Woodrow Wilson, a statement endorsed by over five hundred conference delegates which pledged support for such steps as would "elicit a fresh statement of peace terms by the allies, repudiating autocracy, disclaiming conquests and punitive indemnities and focusing the liberal forces of all mankind for a democratic organization of the world."[4] On other occasions Kellogg lent his support to a petition from the American Association for Labor Legislation to Newton D. Baker, secretary of war, urging that industrial standards not be relaxed under the exigencies of war, and pleading that the United States hold to the example of Canada and Australia and not resort to military conscription.[5]

It was in accord with these guidelines that the *Survey* went to war. Pressed by a shortage of newsprint, rising costs of production, and a decline in revenue, the journal found it difficult to respond to the new challenge of war without cutting back on some of its traditional services. Kellogg urged the staff to strive for shorter articles and crisper style, to hold space each number for war-related news, and always to lead readers to recognize the social aspects of war and "to look ahead to times after the war."[6] The *Survey* hired Bruno Lasker, at that time a staff member of the Mayor's Committee on Unemployment of New York City, to head a new Foreign Service Department which carried items on war relief, on American service agencies working overseas, on the activities of immigrant groups in the United States, and on events which were giving shape to postwar reconstruction. Lasker, who proved to be a valuable member of the *Survey* staff for the next several years, a contributor to its pages and a private critic for many years thereafter, had emigrated some years before the war from Germany to England where he had been engaged with B. Seebohm Rowntree in his studies of unemployment, social insurance, housing, and city planning. Lasker's presence on the staff strengthened Kellogg's determination to turn part of the *Survey*'s attention to developments abroad and to the task of reconstruction in the postwar world.[7]

In war, even more than in peace, Kellogg declared in his annual report to members of Survey Associates at the end of 1917, the *Survey* sought to show the ways in which social work could be kept from becoming a mere "mender and patcher" and become instead an "affirmative force" for social progress. The journal had assigned top priority throughout the year to keep "industrial, civic and social welfare in America from being impoverished by sluicing all money and energy into war activities." It had played up the ways in which public health, child and infant welfare, and all the other agency services supported the end of national strength and morale. The editorial page had been scrapped in favor of columns setting forth different points of view on a variety of issues, making that section of the journal more a forum than a pulpit.[8]

New times and new events created new issues. To these the

Survey responded. It published articles on food conservation, on how to make family income stretch in the face of inflation, on the care and rehabilitation of men crippled in battle, on the new meaning of Americanization programs especially among those who were officially classified as "enemy aliens," on the enforcement of prohibition as a war-related expedient, on the migration of Negroes from the rural South to northern defense industries. It carried reports on social conditions in and around army bases and defense centers, on war risk insurance, on American relief efforts in such far-flung places as France, Belgium, and Italy, Russia, Armenia, and Palestine. It followed closely the participation of labor as an equal partner with management in the defense effort, and publicized government actions to maintain industrial standards for all workers and to extend special protections to women working in industry. In one special supplement, printed just before the war's end, the *Survey* took note of the new impact of the findings of modern psychology for all divisions of social work—casework, public welfare, children's aid, parole, hospital social service, reformatories and training schools; the inference to be drawn was clear: social work education should begin to consider training its practitioners not for service in particular institutional settings but for a common understanding of basic issues and attitudes.

Just to keep the *Survey* appearing on weekly schedule required minor miracles, to say nothing of shaping new lines of inquiry to match new developments in welfare. Paul Kellogg served the Red Cross in Europe from September 1917 until early winter 1918, and although he wrote occasional reports on his activities back to the *Survey,* the main burden of editing was left to Arthur. Two other staff members took jobs overseas, three left to do war work in the United States, both the circulation and the advertising managers resigned to take other positions. It was to a skeleton staff that Arthur Kellogg pleaded: let there be no excuses for failure to meet publishing deadlines "because of the idiosyncrasies of suburban trains and habits, the arranging of outside programs, the meeting of committees on the state of the union or the persistence of personal callers"; "let us concentrate all our editorial conferences, suggestions, questions and

Paul U. Kellogg and the *Survey*

snooky little visits between 10 and 11 o'clock in the morning";
"let us cut down the pelting memos . . . and speak out what we
have to say"; "to all outsiders let us be 'out' all afternoon, and
stick to uninterrupted writing."[9] By the end of the war Paul
Kellogg despaired of getting out the journal under wartime conditions; the office "is wobbling along like a stage camel," he
confided to his brother, "loosely hung, badly in need of system,
sorely in need of clear-cut placement of responsibility."[10]

That the *Survey* in these years had the appearance of bits and
pieces thrown haphazardly together, that typographical errors
proliferated, that the writing often seemed hurried and even
slapdash, that the pages were gray and drab should be no surprise. Given the handicaps under which the journal labored, it
is a wonder that it appeared at all.

Paul Kellogg had originally intended to visit the European
war zone as a field reporter for the *Survey,* but before those
plans could be implemented he was recruited by Homer Folks
to join the Paris staff of the American Red Cross. He arrived in
September 1917, made firsthand surveys of Red Cross work in
Belgium, France, and Italy throughout the fall and early winter,
and, on the basis of his observations in the field, compiled a
report for use of the head office in Paris summarizing his findings and projecting lines of Red Cross activity and policy in the
months to come. What began as a six-week assignment was
strung out five months and more. Frustrated by censorship and
by the bureaucratic confusions that inevitably accompanied such
assignments in wartime, fatigued in body and "wilted" in spirits,
he was homesick as any soldier and "greedy to the core for
letters." It came to be primarily his personal loyalty to Folks
and to Edward Devine (who accompanied Kellogg on the Italian
leg of his journeys) that kept him on the job.[11]

His task finally completed, Kellogg stopped off in England on
his way home to judge for himself the social climate in the other
great democracy of the alliance. His first engagement there took
him to the meetings of the Labour party in Nottingham where he
felt at once, and for the first time in months, at home among
people of his "own kind."[12] His "own kind" he meant not as a
national identification but purely and fully in an ideological

sense; here were men speaking of a postwar world in which social institutions everywhere would be re-formed. He spent an evening alone in the company of Robert Smillie, president of the great British Federation of Miners, and the force of the Scotsman's personality and character Kellogg would never forget. Here was a pacifist and a socialist who had not called out his miners as long as the war was on because he had known that a German victory would smash democracy everywhere; rather he chose to keep his men on the job while fighting for a peace that would secure the good life for all common men. Kellogg recalled how lonely he had felt in Belgium and France and Italy, but at Nottingham he "saw this great belt of Britishers, and the thousands they spoke for, striking out for things I believed in."[13] With the deliberations of the British labor movement still ringing in his ears, he dispatched an enthusiastic note to Jane Addams detailing his "encouragement and faith in the coherent power of the workers."[14]

To Kellogg the British labor movement held forth the hope of a world in which the communal sense would be harnessed not for war but for positive measures of brotherhood. This form of social democracy aimed at coordinating all the productive forces of modern industrial society without bureaucratic regimentation. It appealed to him, moreover, as a folk movement, complex and varied, sensitive to individual rights and needs, nondogmatic in program. It promised procedures by which the workers themselves, working through shop councils, could play a daily role in shaping the policies of their own factories and industries, not only in matters of wages and hours and conditions but in spheres of decision making hitherto confined to the managerial classes. It promised controls both democratic and decentralized. In national politics it stood for free public education, national health programs, comprehensive social insurance, municipal planning, civil liberties, and complete adult suffrage that would enfranchise women.

On the international scene the British labor movement, as Kellogg interpreted it, sought the utter destruction of the old balance of power and war system; it stood for self-determination of nations, of peoples, of classes; it would work toward international cooperation, the common people of the world united for a new order. As Kellogg judged the world climate in the spring and summer of 1918, as the Allied forces prepared to launch their last great military efforts which would bring victory on the field of battle by fall, the British labor movement represented "the only force in western Europe competent and desirous of throwing its strength alongside President Wilson's in securing a democratic outcome in the settlement of the war."[15]

These were the goals and these the modes toward which Kellogg and the *Survey* had been tending since August 1914. The editor's first report to Survey Associates following the outbreak of the European conflict had been to that point—the *Survey* must prepare at once for that era of opportunity for "sound social reconstruction here as well as abroad which we profoundly hope will follow in the wake of war. For, whatever its brutal cost in life and blood and spirit, war has thrown a lance on the shield of complacency, of letting things be as they are."[16]

The statement became the preamble to editorial policies to which the *Survey* would adhere for the next four years. Hardly a number was printed that did not contain some news, some projection of plans for the postwar world and suggestions for what might be done while the war was being waged to secure those desired ends, for Kellogg knew that the future was always being formed in the present. It was for that reason that Kellogg had opposed America's entry into the war: to become a belligerent would be to place in jeopardy the impartial authority of the nation for a just peace. In 1915 the *Survey* published a series of articles around the central theme of "War and Reconstruction," in which Jane Addams, George H. Mead, Edward A. Filene, Emily Greene Balch, Simon N. Patten, Frederic C. Howe, and others pointed the way toward a vital internationalism (to be neutral was not to be indifferent, wrote Jane Addams) which would move toward a better world order. Unless the neutral nations took the lead in planning for peace, now, Europe would be left at war's end prostrate and embittered — an armed camp.[17]

From 1914 through 1919 probably no word of substantive importance occurred more often in the pages of the *Survey* than "reconstruction." Indeed, when Kellogg commissioned Bruno

Lasker to set up a special department on reconstruction in September 1918, he went so far as to suggest that the *Survey* should "stake our claim to the term," as though it were something unique to the journal's vision of a succession of finer tomorrows.[18] Whether on the home front or on the international scene, the *Survey*'s central impulse pointed toward the day of victory and peace when the resources that had been mobilized for war could be turned to the creation of a new civilization. Thus when victory came, the *Survey* exulted at the "release of mankind from nightmare"; now all men were free "to face toward the future which is to be whatever the nations choose to make it"; perhaps there would come revolutions, financial crises, reactionary movements, social degeneration, but not if men willed these things not to happen. "We shall be likely to get what we expect and predict."[19]

The rhetoric was intense, but the *Survey* did not stop with fine and rejoicing words. In the issue which greeted the Armistice, Edward T. Devine laid down at length the hope and the strategy to which he and his associates were dedicated. What had the nation learned from war? To train injured soldiers in new skills—why not apply this lesson to the rehabilitation of all handicapped workers? To apply progressive inheritance and income taxes to the war effort—the "large lesson" could be turned to the "common advantage" in an era of peace. War expenditures had proved that the nation had the resources to provide a decent standard of living for every family in the nation; there was no longer any acceptable excuse for poverty. The nation had come to accept the reality of collective bargaining in industrial relations; that lesson, too, could be turned to social progress. In war, the American woman had become a "citizen and a worker"; from then on wives would share "when they like in the responsibility for earning an income." American Negroes had made enormous gains; now they sought not "indulgence" but "self-determination." The red lights were dimmed and must not be lit again. War had alerted the American people to problems of health; the nation need now but create a coordinated national health program. Industry had accepted the logic of rational planning for economic stability and worker welfare.

The brotherhood forged in the common sacrifice of war could be enlarged in peace. "America has come into the current of the world's history," Devine concluded, "and nothing in the old world is henceforth foreign to our interest."[20]

As a first practical step toward the realization of these ends, the *Survey* called a Conference on Demobilization to which over one hundred invited delegates, leaders in all fields of social service, came for two days in late November to discuss the agenda for the postwar world. Felix Adler, president of the National Child Labor Committee, who presided over the conference, set the expected tone when he appealed to welfare workers to mobilize a moral force equal to that which had won the war. The keynote should not be "demobilization," cried one delegate, but "mobilization for the tasks of peace of the social spirit which has been generated so abundantly by the demands of war."[21] When the special committee appointed by the conference reported the following spring, it began with the assertion that social workers, by the very nature of their professional activities, knew the "bad effects of overwork, overcrowding, inadequate income, irregular employment, inefficiency, thriftlessness, unorganized industry and industrial unrest." Social work, it was clear, had a special responsibility to lead in the formulation of a national program of reconstruction.

The program of specifics that followed read like an updating of the social justice planks of the old Progressive party, which welfare leaders had helped to compose in 1912. It called for permanent compensation and insurance for war veterans; federal aid to elementary, secondary, and higher education; the restoration of civil liberties (which wartime censorship and controls had whittled away); a system of probation in federal courts; a separate cabinet department of public health; an acceleration of federal-state extension work in rural areas; a comprehensive program to conserve natural resources; in industrial life the preservation of the wartime federal employment service, the extension of the Woman in Industry Service, the maintenance of the Divisions of Negro Economics and of Arbitration and Conciliation in the Department of Labor; and the creation of a cabinet department to coordinate public works in times of unemployment.[22]

Throughout 1919 the *Survey* devoted large sections of the first number of each month to news on reconstruction concerns. It also featured extensive summaries of the reconstruction conventions and conferences sponsored by all the well-established progressive reform groups—the National Child Labor Committee, the National Consumers' League, the American Association for Labor Legislation, the Women's Trade Union League, and others.

Progress at home constituted but one salient toward reconstruction; the other aimed at a world in which peace, self-determination, and democracy would be secure.

Paul Kellogg considered Kalamazoo a proud heritage, but he was quickly open to new modes, new ideas, new styles. In New York he moved quickly and with remarkable ease (remarkable, that is, for such a disarmingly unpretentious young man) on different levels of New York society, all of which were "internationalist" in one way and another. The immigrant people he came to know in settlement house neighborhoods spoke to him of their homelands—far-distant places in Russia, Italy, Armenia, Poland, places that Kellogg began to know through the stories they told. At dinner at the Henry Street settlement, with Lillian Wald at the head of the table ladling out the evening's soup, the young journalist met social workers, politicians, artists, labor leaders from all parts of Europe. The leaders of the old German Jewish community in New York he came to know and to depend upon for counsel (and for money, for the most generous supporters of the *Survey* over a half century were members of these families)—Julian Mack, Lillian Wald, the Warburgs, the Laskers, the Lewisohns, the Lehmans, the Morgenthaus, Julius Rosenwald in Chicago, and Samuel B. Fels in Philadelphia. They all looked toward Europe, had family in Europe, traveled in Europe. Robert de Forest, of French Huguenot ancestry, moved with authority and ease in international circles. The young man from the inland province of Michigan questioned, he listened, he learned.

Being a progressive (and a Progressive) Kellogg naturally

became a Wilsonian. He opposed America's entrance into the war it is true; but the Wilson of "peace without victory," the Wilson who proclaimed a "war to end wars," a "war to make the world safe for democracy," the Wilson of the Fourteen Points — these were expressions of a man and an ideal to which Kellogg was wholly devoted.

After 6 April 1917 Kellogg operated the *Survey* in accord with the tacit understanding he had with the board "not to re-open the question of justification of the war, once the country was committed to it."[23] He would not thresh old straw but look ahead, and what better way to look ahead than to keep the columns of the *Survey* open to manuscripts which would define the shape of the world to come from many different points of view? To the board, in May 1917, Kellogg made an essentially Wilsonian statement of his hope that the *Survey* could explore the terms of a postwar settlement "which will pave the way for enduring peace, for the liberation of oppressed peoples, and for a fabric of security and justice which will not only free the world for democracy, but free it for a renaissance of social well-being."[24]

When Paul Kellogg returned from Britain in March of 1918 it was with a sense of exhilaration, which had been aroused in his heart by the bold acts of the British labor movement, but this was soon tempered by a sense of dejection and even panic provoked by the apathy and indifference in regard to the terms of the peace settlement he found in America. In England he had seen men stand and cheer the mention of Wilson's name; but in America no organization existed to stir up support for the president's diplomacy, Gompers and American labor were on the wrong side, the Socialist party was stubbornly clinging to its antiwar position and thus vitiating whatever influence it might have had in shaping the postwar settlement. Only the League to Enforce Peace seemed alert to pressing issues, but its energies were absorbed in working out the machinery for international control.[25]

On Kellogg's invitation a group of his friends gathered at the Columbia University Club the evening of 23 April 1918 to hear his report. Arthur Kellogg was there (he could always be counted on). Among the others were S. K. Ratcliffe, a British correspondent; Norman Angell, whose book *The Great Illusion,* published before the war, had helped form Kellogg's views on world politics; Winston Churchill and Ernest Poole, American novelists and members of many reform groups; Henry Mussey, Charles Beard, and J. W. Slosson, historians and political scientists of progressive temperament; and Herbert Croly, editor of the *New Republic.* Kellogg poured out his anxieties: in America there was no organized support for Wilson's democratic principles; the liberal forces were inarticulate while the forces of reaction, nationalism, and imperialism were everywhere strong; the House commission might constitute the best informed delegation when the time to talk peace terms arrived, but it would not be able to draw on an informed body of citizens. Kellogg had no blueprint for a new citizens' organization but he hoped if one were formed it would not become a limb of the Wilson administration; he knew that it would have to be nonpartisan and draw on younger men in both parties and that it should avoid becoming "a pacifist group under a new name." Like the British labor movement, he urged, it should support two goals—a vigorous prosecution of the war and the creation of "a democratic order of world relations."[26]

Before the gathering broke up late that evening, the guests had reached a consensus that they should meet again, that a small committee on organization should explore what next steps were required, and that a small delegation should be selected to establish contacts with leading liberal journals—the *Dial,* the *Nation,* the *New Republic,* the *Survey,* the *Independent,* the *Public.* Before adjourning they agreed to call themselves the "Committee on Nothing at All," a name they jokingly agreed to until formal organization that fall of the League of Free Nations Association (LFNA).

For the next several months they met informally, from time to time, to hear papers and speeches on relevant topics. Arthur Gleason dropped in to talk about the British labor movement; Thomas Masaryk discussed the role of small nations in any postwar league; Joseph Chamberlain analyzed international trade routes; John Reed described conditions in Russia; others discussed race and nationality, international boundaries and waterways, the structure of the proposed League of Nations, and access to raw materials.[27]

During the winter of 1918-19, while Wilson was in Paris negotiating with the victorious powers on the terms of the settlement, the LFNA sought every means to publicize its support of what it held to be the true Wilsonian principles—collective security, self-determination of nations, and equality of economic opportunity for all nations. Many members of the LFNA were shocked when the specific terms of the proposed treaty were released; whatever his motives might have been, it appeared that Wilson had compromised at many essential points with the forces of reactionary nationalism. But what could be done? To attack what were to them the weaknesses in the draft treaty was to strengthen the hands of Wilson's enemies in the Senate; to keep silent was implicitly to condone those clauses which they knew to be retrogressive. To pass advisory resolutions was a natural way to confront the dilemma which troubled all good Wilsonians. So pass resolutions they did: calling for ratification of the League of Nations but asking also for liberalization of the Covenant to strengthen the representative quality of the Assembly, to provide for easier amendment, to protect national minorities within the nations, and to encourage the admission of Germany and Russia just as soon as they qualified by establishing stable and democratic governments. In all these deliberations and resolutions, Paul Kellogg played an active and influential role. By March of 1919, however, the LFNA began to fear that to press too hard for liberalization of the Covenant was to risk dividing liberal support for the League of Nations and to jeopardize its chances for ratification in the Senate. Whatever private reservations the members of the LFNA might have, they must close ranks and back the president.

It was not all that easy, of course. Events moved too fast, and Senator Lodge's complex maneuvers of delay rendered it impossible for the well-intentioned members of the LFNA to pursue a consistent and coherent line. For their own understanding and satisfaction, one presumes, members of the board spelled out their own reservations; in July, following a referendum of their members, they urged ratification of the treaty without the Lodge reservations but with clarifying resolutions; in November the LFNA dispatched its president to confer with Colonel House and to urge that Wilson be persuaded to accept some of the reservations, to seek modification of one, and to reject outright the other five; and in April 1920 the committee was still discussing the possibility of asking President Wilson to resubmit the treaty with his own acceptance of the reservations.[28]

It cannot be said that in the country at that time any other organized group concerned with the fate of the treaty and the Covenant of the League of Nations did any better than the League of Free Nations Association, but that was, undoubtedly, small comfort to Kellogg and his friends. Each time the board came to a new resolution, it was quickly rendered obsolete by events in Washington, or by events in Paris, Moscow, London, Rome, and Tokyo.

Paul Kellogg, for one, was not easily discouraged. In May 1919 he helped to draft a resolution, endorsed by some five hundred delegates to the National Conference of Social Work, calling both for support of the League and for such changes and clarifications as would meet the test of Wilson's Fourteen Points.[29] In July, in a signed article in the *Survey*, Kellogg set forth his own personal views of what might be done, but its thick prose and tortured analysis were clues to the confusion events had created in the camp of the Wilsonians. Kellogg's concluding recommendation that the treaty be ratified without reservations but with appended interpretations and clarifications was no more feasible and no more pertinent in the context of political realities at that moment than were the shifting resolutions of the LFNA which he had helped, from time to time, to draft.[30] "Reconstruction" was going sour, and nothing Kellogg and his friends could say or do made any real difference.

From Paris, a friend and associate of Kellogg's wrote in March of 1919 to describe the disillusion of French liberals and French labor with Wilson. The compromises that Wilson made with the forces of national self-interest would likely throw labor in Europe into "the hands of the extreme left bolshevik crowd who have always said that nothing good could come from the bourgeois and that Wilson might be a good man but was impotent."[31] A letter posted the end of April was even more despondent: "this peace conference is enough to ruin any remnants of what one might call a *Survey* constructive mood," he wrote. "One has small faith in liberal bourgeois efforts these days. People around the conference—even those who have worked on it and who began with ardent faith in it—have lost faith in the League of Nations."[32]

As for the hopes aroused in Kellogg's heart by the British labor movement, Arthur Gleason, who had collaborated with Kellogg on an enthusiastic book on the subject, wrote from London in July 1919 that the British people were "tired out," fearful of America's financial superiority, disappointed and disillusioned with Wilson.[33] Later that month he wrote again: "We are in the presence of an incalculable tragedy. The first born are dead. Shall we not try to speak with restraint and dignity?"[34]

Perhaps that was all that was left. The new era had come but it bore no resemblance to what Kellogg and the *Survey* had imagined it would be. Perhaps that *was* all one now could do— to try to speak with "restraint and dignity."

{VI}

Survey Graphic and the *Midmonthly* in the 1920s

PAUL KELLOGG and his associates on the *Survey* suffered a number of disappointments before they were willing to recognize that somewhere on the high road to the promised land humanity had inadvertently taken a wrong turn. The failure of Wilsonianism was the first blow. Industrial warfare, the collapse of unions in the great strikes of 1919, the harassment of aliens and dissenters, inflation, the politics of normalcy, the striking down of child labor and minimum wage legislation by the Supreme Court, the Harding scandals—these followed hard and fast. The twenties, as events unfolded, proved inhospitable to the reform and reconstruction on which the *Survey* had set such store.

No wonder the young men and young women of this generation are disillusioned, Kellogg poured out his heart to an old friend in mid-decade: ". . . they saw the church in all the countries at war apparently forsake Christianity; social leaders go back on what they were teaching of the sanctity of human life; socialism go on the rocks; a war for democracy unravel at Versailles."[1] To Crystal Eastman, who had written inquiring about opportunities for doing publicity work in reform movements if she were to return to America from England, Kellogg sent a warning: the issues had all changed, it would't be easy to pick up her old career, "psychology rather than labor legislation is on the map. . . . You see the war set us back about ten

SURVEY GRAPHIC

JUNE, 1922
TWO SECTIONS
SECTION I

eDUCATION
with a little e
What is America going to do about the
Schooling of Democracy?

WHERE GIRLS GO RIGHT
by VAN LOON   [Appears in Section II]   Paintings by BARTLETT

years, and we are only now passing a compensation law in Missouri, only beginning to prick up our ears to health insurance, or old age pensions."[2] And to Ramsey MacDonald, in whose labor movement Kellogg had invested so much of his heart, Kellogg wrote that while he could be put down "as more encouraged" than most of his associates, he could see only "islands here and there" of hopeful social movements; there was in America "only an archipelago of promise."[3]

78

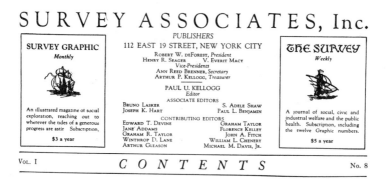

SURVEY ASSOCIATES, Inc.

PUBLISHERS

SURVEY GRAPHIC
Monthly

An illustrated magazine of social
exploration, reaching out to
wherever the tides of a generous
progress are astir Subscription,

$3 a year

112 EAST 19 STREET, NEW YORK CITY

Robert W. deForest, *President*
Henry R. Seager   V. Everit Macy
Vice-Presidents
Ann Reed Brenner, *Secretary*
Arthur P. Kellogg, *Treasurer*

PAUL U. KELLOGG
Editor

ASSOCIATE EDITORS
Bruno Lasker   S. Adele Shaw
Joseph K. Hart   Paul L. Benjamin

CONTRIBUTING EDITORS
Edward T. Devine   Graham Taylor
Jane Addams   Florence Kelley
Graham R. Taylor   John A. Fitch
Winthrop D. Lane   William L. Chenery
Arthur Gleason   Michael M. Davis, Jr.

THE SURVEY
Weekly

A journal of social, civic and
industrial welfare and the public
health. Subscription, including
the twelve Graphic numbers.

$5 a year

Vol. I   *C O N T E N T S*   No. 8

Always on the alert for any signs of a "renaissance of interest in social and economic questions in a period which has seemed to be one of general sag," Kellogg sought to survey new forces "such as the mounting interest in psychology, in international affairs, in the arts; not as competing interests, but as forces which can come to the refreshment of movements for public welfare." So he declared his strategy to a social work friend on the eve of the 1926 annual convention of the American Association of Labor Legislation at which he was to chair a session given over to testing "The Pulse of Public Reform."[4]

Such were the goals of the *Survey* in these years of "sag": to seek, discover, and describe every island of hope; to scout out all the new movements in psychology, art, city planning, social service as they bore on welfare; to hold the faith and wait for a better day. These—with as much dignity, poise, and grace as a discouraged generation could muster.

The Kellogg brothers knew what heroic efforts would be required if the *Survey* were to fulfill its mission, for at war's end they confronted a host of immediate and pressing problems: a skeleton (if loyal) staff, depleted by the wartime service of many associates who, after the Armistice, went on to other careers; financial reserves consumed by inflation; revenue from subscriptions and advertising and gifts shrunk by the distraction of friends and supporters whose attention and energies had been diverted to other causes during the war.

The first task was financial, for unless the capital were secured all else would fail. So, not for the last time, Paul Kellogg

Paul Kellogg in foreground at an annual
banquet of the Survey Associates.

turned his energies and attention from editing to the raising of
money. Not exclusively, of course, since the journal had to meet
its weekly publication deadlines, and Paul carried chief responsibility for designing the issues, soliciting articles, and reviewing
manuscripts; but the week-to-week responsibility devolved essentially upon Arthur who, at various times in the early twenties
when effective staff could not be hired, and often for months
running, covered the desks of managing editor, director of circulation, and business manager.

The difficulties of meeting the annual budget were compounded early in the new decade when the Russell Sage Foundation gave notice it intended gradually to reduce its subsidy,
which was then around $20,000 a year, until in four years its
support would be phased out. The *Survey* board, whose members had been selected largely on the basis of their prominence
in the fields of social welfare, although there were always a
certain number of wealthy philanthropists serving as well, were

as helpful in raising funds, Kellogg once complained, "as a wet rag. It practically all came down on the staff and repeatedly we did not know on Mondays where the money for printing bills and payrolls was coming from."[5] Some large contributors had been scared off by the tone of militancy, especially on matters of industrial relations, that the *Survey* had adopted during the years when "reconstruction" had been its chief focus.[6] Even the Jewish philanthropic communities in New York, Boston, and Philadelphia, on which the *Survey* had normally been able to rely for large donations, had turned instead to financing the relief of Jewish refugees abroad. A prominent coordinator of various Jewish welfare projects, who had usually been able to find several thousand dollars a year for the *Survey* among his patrons, had to turn back the pleas of Kellogg in 1922 for still another try: "I am being so constantly importuned to raise funds for one enterprise or another, that not only have I reached the point of saturation, but have worn out my welcome with a great many friends, who, the moment they see me, ask: 'What are you schnorring for now?'"[7]

Fortunately, Kellogg had been able to persuade Ann Reed Brenner to join the staff in 1917 to assist with the raising of funds. He had known her first when she was a young and very eager assistant in the Pittsburgh Survey. She had subsequently married a man much her senior, the Russian-American sculptor Victor David Brenner (who among other notable pieces had designed the Lincoln penny), and not content merely to be the wife of a distinguished artist she eagerly grasped at the chance to carve out a career on the *Survey*. It was Ann Reed Brenner perhaps as much as any other person—although Agnes Brown Leach, member of the board in these years, would have qualified as a close second—who provided a valuable liaison with wealthy patrons. Kellogg never lost the open and disarming manner which had been his from Kalamazoo days, and he had learned respect for others from his mother; but in the early years he often displayed a candor in personal relations which the rich, accustomed to a certain deference from those who came seeking financial support, sometimes found annoying. Completely wrapped up in his own enthusiasms, Kellogg did not always fully appreciate that the *Survey* was but one among many interests for the journal's patrons.

Mrs. Brenner raised hundreds of thousands of dollars over the many years she worked for the *Survey*. Arthur Kellogg had her measure from the beginning. "Things are going first rate," he wrote to Paul. "I'll say that A. Brenner has the prescription for this game. She talks the talk of these people. . . . She has a lot of real friends here and when she runs out of them she scrapes up a brother-in-law or a cousin or something that went to school with her or knew her best friend in kindergarten— great stuff."[8] For a quarter of a century, Mrs. Brenner was responsible, working in tandem with Paul Kellogg, for securing the financial contributions that made possible the continued solvency of the *Survey*. It was to her contacts in the world of the arts, moreover, that some of the graphic brilliance of the *Survey* in these years can be traced.

Paul Kellogg and Ann Reed Brenner, complementing each other in every way, labored to put the *Survey* on new financial footings. It was an endless task, of course, but by the middle years of the 1920s substantial gains had been registered. They increased, every year, the number of readers who, by paying ten dollars or more a year, qualified as cooperating members of Survey Associates. They persuaded established patrons to give larger annual sums; they added new names to the roster of those who agreed to invest $1000, even $5000, a year in the "Founders' Fund"; they enlarged board membership from its original constitutional limit of twelve in order to bring aboard a greater number of large contributors. By 1922 when the Russell Sage Foundation dropped its subsidy, the Founders' Fund held guarantees of $50,000 a year for the next four years; and beyond these special developmental moneys, the journal could count on an additional $40,000 to $50,000 a year in regular donations. These contributed funds were almost evenly matched by commercial receipts from subscription and advertising revenue so that the *Survey* had a total annual budget of around $180,000 in the 1920s, enough to permit the operation of the journal at a higher level of quality than had ever been possible before.[9]

It had been Paul Kellogg's ambition for a number of years

to establish a journal whose appeal would extend beyond the sphere of social work, philanthropy, and welfare. To serve the professional needs of workers in all the diverse fields of social service—charities, the settlements, health, penology, etc.—was an essential function of the *Survey,* he believed. Since there existed no other journal that covered all the general fields of practice, since in many of the specialized departments of social work there existed no technical or scholarly journals at all, the *Survey* had a mandate to keep its professional readers apprised of all relevant developments bearing on social service. Beyond the restricted circle of the social workers and their friends there were men and women vitally concerned with the whole health of society whose interests were not served by any periodical. The journals of opinion—the *New Republic* and the *Nation*—provided sustenance for part of this social hunger, but they did not offer a balanced diet of information on complex measures and policies in education, health, and welfare. They were, moreover, as Kellogg saw it, enlargements of the editorial page of the daily newspaper; a new journal might become an extension of the news columns of the daily papers, not devoid of interpretation and evaluation to be sure, but providing news analysis in depth and on a regular basis.

Probation workers, doctors, nurses, caseworkers, settlement residents, members of agency boards, visiting teachers needed information on what was happening in their own fields of service; they also needed, in Kellogg's words, "to be carried a peg further" in their understanding of community forces and social problems. And then there was "that wider group of socially-minded laymen," leaders who were the "leaven" of change in their own communities, who needed to be informed of the general significance of social work practice in its many specialized departments and aroused to the constructive opportunities for social change.[10] For both audiences—the professional social workers and concerned citizens—a new journal could seek "to bring social criticism and appraisal to bear on public affairs; to evaluate the human significance of developments in science, engineering, the professions and arts."[11] Such a journal could broaden horizons ("nothing human is foreign to our interest"), shake up established ways ("life overturns all our constructions, soon or late"), provoke citizens everywhere into an awareness of new programs for social reform ("programs which are still too unshaped to win attention unhelped").[12]

Hence, in 1923, the *Survey Graphic* was created as an independent journal of social exploration and interpretation. Published the first of each month, it continued the partner, indeed the brother, of what came now to be published as the *Survey Midmonthly* (or the *Mid* as it was affectionately known to the *Survey* staff). The *Graphic*'s ancestry went back some years to the enlarged first-of-the-month number that the old *Charities* printed after it absorbed the *Charities Review* in 1901, a tradition that the *Survey,* after the reorganizations of 1909 and 1912, maintained on a sometime basis. Beginning in October 1921 this tradition was formalized as the *Graphic* number of the *Survey*: an event of symbolic weight in Kellogg's mind as evidenced by the new cover design he commissioned Hendrik Willem Van Loon to design—a sailing ship, like the old caravel the *Survey* had adopted as its trademark in 1909, but larger and faster and more modern in design. There was in the old caravel, Kellogg wrote, "an inquisitive lift to the prow, a rakishness to the lateen rig, which conveys unmistakably that here is a craft bent on high discovery." Now there was a sister ship: "The winds are skirling in the cross-trees. . . . So we are off to chart the seas, linking to our quest for fact and experience a frank experiment in the technique of social interpretation." In the first-of-the-month *Graphic* number the journal would search out "common ground of mutual understanding"; in it facts were to become a "basis for judgment."[13] The success of the drive for a *Graphic* Founders' Fund of $50,000 a year for four years made it possible, in 1923, to enter upon a new twice-a-month publication schedule, an arrangement that lasted until 1949 when financial exigencies forced the merger of the *Survey Graphic* and the *Survey Midmonthly* into a single monthly journal known simply, once again, as the *Survey.*

"I have hugged the dream of the *Graphic* for ten years past," Kellogg wrote to his former boss, Edward Devine, in 1922.[14] Having so cherished the prospect, Kellogg devoted the lion's share of time, energy, and money to the *Graphic*. The *Graphic* paid its contributors (at modest space rates); the *Midmonthly* received manuscripts from volunteers in the serving professions. Paul Kellogg had his hand in the planning of every *Graphic* number; the shape of the *Midmonthly* was left to a series of associate editors whose job it was to hold the *Mid* to schedule without the funds to pay contributors or to invest in striking layout and supporting pictorial materials. A reader could subscribe to the *Survey Graphic* alone, or jointly to both publications: social workers, it was implied by this arrangement, were expected to be joint subscribers if they wished to receive the professionally oriented *Midmonthly*.

The intent from the beginning was made explicitly clear to board, staff, friends, and readers. The *Survey Graphic,* Kellogg wrote by way of explanation to John Palmer Gavit, "is our long dreamed of plan of developing our illustrated magazine numbers into a periodical which would reach out beyond the narrow circles consecutively interested in social work and movements. The keynote of the thing," he continued, "is interpretation and we are going to employ photographs, etchings, drawings and text of a sort which we hope will get a new hearing for the big human concerns which lie underneath all this technical discussion of social problems."[15] If the *Survey Graphic,* drawing on the Founders' Fund, could become such a high-quality magazine that it could claim a readership large enough to cover its operating costs and perhaps even show a surplus (a financial situation that had never obtained with the *Survey* and its predecessor publications), then it would win true autonomy and would be able to carry the *Midmonthly,* whose appeal had built-in limitations. Such, at least, was the hope—a hope never realized, for regardless of quality and gains in circulation, the two journals always operated with a large annual deficit that had to be met out of donations, foundation grants, and endowments.

To justify the continuing need for outside support, Kellogg put forward the analogy of a private university or library or laboratory. The journal, like them, was an experiment in adult education, not a commercial venture. It required donations to establish "desks" just as a university might set up endowed "chairs." Its methods of research were inductive; it began with firsthand observation and primary sources and proceeded on the basis of the evidence to draw conclusions. These conclusions were not ethereal abstractions, but concrete practicalities—"social research" was to be an "aid to constructive social action." It was a "novel experiment," Kellogg admitted, to make "a periodical rather than a campus the stage of an educational project," but that was the *Survey*'s unique mission as he saw it. Here was an opportunity for men to learn "by their united intelligence" how to "master the material universe and control its forces for the general good."[16]

It followed that scholarship and service, kept "divided and insulated," were as "sand without cement." Research unrelated to social need, research left unapplied, was sterile and thin; service that did not rest on solid and sound study quickly became aimless and ineffective. Scholarship and service working harmoniously together were "shuttles of understanding, weaving through concerns and vocations, the fabric of the common welfare."[17]

It followed also that the pages of the *Survey* were to be kept open to all points of view within the family of welfare. Contributors were expected to hew to no editorial line, but were left free to follow their own bent just so long as the facts were accurately reported and the conclusions followed logically from the evidence. The pages of the *Survey Graphic* and the *Midmonthly* were held open as a public forum, as a pooling place of different experiences and proposals. By his selection of subjects to be covered, and persons to write articles, by editorial nudging once manuscripts were submitted, Kellogg could (and did) shape the general strategy and direction of the journals, but he conscientiously sought out persons of different perspectives to write on controversial topics. As professors and deans were entitled to academic freedom, not so much as a personal right but as a guarantor of truth in the open marketplace of ideas, so, Kellogg argued, were authors and editors privileged, not so much for their own self-enhancement as for the social good.

It followed, finally, that the gathering and testing of evidence were to be pursued with the utmost rigor and caution. Open to many different points of view, gentle and permissive on most things, Kellogg was tough and insistent on several points: no slipshod reporting, no lazy writing, attention to concrete detail. Staff members assigned to an analysis in depth of some new development in welfare service or policy typically began their research by writing to a large number of experts in the field for advice and for leads. In the interwar era of the twenties and thirties, when funds were more readily available than they later came to be, staff writers regularly traveled in the field to pick up firsthand understanding and a direct and immediate "feel" of a subject. Once the evidence had been gathered, and the process sometimes covered many weeks and even months, the draft manuscript was sent to persons who had been interviewed and to other experts. When an article dealt with a controversial subject, care was exercised to include representatives of all sides of the controversy among the critics. Discovery of a direct conflict of evidence sent the author back to recheck the facts; differences in evaluation led to a reexamination of the author's own judgments. The pace was not leisurely, there were deadlines to be met, but *Survey* reporters were not faced with the pressures of filing daily stories before an issue of a paper was put to bed. Kellogg wrote to one of the staff covering the steel strike in 1919, for example: "It is all the more important for us to have a keen and sure footed and unshakeable analysis than it is to try to beat the daily press or the other weeklies."[18]

Articles that seemed to bear some risk of provoking charges of libel (the *Survey* was sued but once, and that once unsuccessfully), Kellogg sent to the *Survey*'s lawyers to be checked out. The editorial files of the *Survey* bulge with letters explaining these procedures to skeptical or suspicious citizens—industrial managers, labor leaders, public officials, and agency executives whose counsel was being sought. Kellogg's secretary must have wearied, over the years, of typing out the same explanation, with only minor changes in the opening paragraph to meet particular circumstances: "Our custom is in any investigation of this sort to send the first draft of the completed findings to the responsible authority or agency under investigation for either criticism or facts which should be weighed by us in making our public presentation. This, of course, puts us under no constraint and at the same time establishes a relationship of good faith with any department or agency under investigation and appraisal."[19] Such letters went out in countless numbers as the *Survey* sought by such procedures to guarantee the factual accuracy of its articles and to build a reservoir of good will and understanding from which it could subsequently draw.

A noted journalist once wrote to Kellogg to commiserate with him on the lot of the editor. "You will probably recall William Allen White's statement," he wrote, "that everyone believes he can do three things—poke a fire, mind a baby, and edit a newspaper."[20] It was not all that simple and they both knew it. Part of Kellogg's brilliance as an editor arose from his experience as a reporter: he understood firsthand the hazards under which the reporter in the field labored to get his story down accurately and right. He never lost the reporter's instinct for the breaking of a good story; he could "see around corners," as one friend put it, and anticipate where next the news would break. He knew that the reader was moved by human interest, not by vague abstractions which lay woolly and thick on the mind.

Time and again manuscripts were returned to authors with admonitions: Point up what these economic questions "mean in the lives of the people concerned"; bring these "larger questions down to earth"; strive for "more intimacy and informality"; create an atmosphere of "getting 'close in' "; let the reader know "how people feel" about this event. Keep your point of view "plastic, experimental," your style "pliant and distinctive." "The more concrete" your article is, "the better"; rely "on the old text that example is better than precept." Pare down the prefatory paragraphs; your article is "all porch." Personalize your article; make the subject "crinkle"; you have a "pretty sober thesis here, if you can riffle at least a third of its surface with humor, it would count tremendously." "For the love of Mike, don't make it a formal article. Tell it in a human, anecdotal way, just as you would in a smoking car." "Many of our contributors are stiff with dignity and heavy with social problems, so don't be afraid to strike an informal and whimsical note." Seek out the "human drama" in these events; move from concrete cases to generalizations; speak directly to parents among our readers who "are baffled, perplexed, and striving." We receive so many manuscripts "charged with precious values but imbedded in habits of technical presentation. . . . journalism has something to teach all of us, in bringing out the drama of experience so that it packs a lesson." Tell the story "simply and unpretentiously," get away from the "formal record," and avoid "the manner in which the economists or the philosophers or the literary people would handle the thing." Your manuscript is "promising—with passages of real charm—but it is still too much like a report"; look for the "f'r instance." Your manuscript has some fine ideas but "you went more social worky than the social workers."[21]

So the advice to staff and authors ran, year after year. To cite these snatches of editorial advice out of thousands of examples is, in some measure, to do an injustice to Kellogg's quality and style as an editor. He was rarely abrupt, except occasionally with the oldest and closest of friends. Letters to contributors customarily began—and ended—with complimentary words; if there were anything salvageable in the first draft of a manuscript, that bit was praised before suggestions for revisions were made. As he became older he sometimes lapsed into folksy habits of expression that detracted from the freshness and bite that had been characteristic throughout his long career, but at their best his comments were incisive without appearing harsh.

The editor's habits were impossible to break: he lived with a blue pencil in his hand, and he never stopped rewriting his own words or the sentences and paragraphs of others. Members of the staff recall that they had sometimes to steal manuscripts off his desk top to get them to the printer by the deadline. At his camp at Lake Memphremagog in the Province of Quebec, where he spent two months, usually August and September, every summer throughout the 1920s and early 1930s, he would lose himself in editing manuscripts and outlining special issues for the coming year. To one of his associate editors he wrote, soon after settling in at his vacation retreat one summer: "A sun swept lake is lapping at the rocks twenty feet from my table, the nights are cool, and now that I've caught my breath after my long trek I'll hope to clear my bag full of stuff, section by section." There followed ten single-spaced pages, typed by his wife from his own scrawling pages of manuscript notes, detailing the administrative work and editorial plans that needed attention.[22] And that was just the beginning of his vacation work. On trips to conventions, or on swings around the country to raise money, he would gather a briefcase full of leads to stories that had to be written and leads to persons who might do the job. Striding to his office from his row house in Greenwich Village at 184 Sullivan Street, his mind fixed more on the day's business than on the flow of traffic, he narrowly missed being run down by single-minded cabbies or truckdrivers hundreds of times. It was no wonder he was the despair of his wife and children.

As for those myriads of authors whose manuscripts Paul Kellogg blue-penciled, their feelings (if one can believe the correspondence) were usually marked by gratitude and delight. John Palmer Gavit, the oldest by tenure of the regular staff, and by all odds the most salty, did not take lightly the editing he got along with everyone else, and on one occasion complained of Kellogg's copy editing: "If to look lustfully is adultery, believe me I am a veteran murderer of copy-readers."[23] But others, despite an author's pride, were grateful for the skilled attention they received. "Dear (though Drastic) Editor," the distinguished Scottish sociologist Sir Patrick Geddes began one letter of appreciation. "You are perfectly right. You have made my yarns *much* more readable for your public. . . . I welcome your changes as a true collaboration."[24] Alain Locke, professor of philosophy at Howard University, and for twenty years a frequent contributor of articles to the *Survey,* wrote in much the same language. "I cannot thank you adequately for the labor of love and friendship you have put on the original mss. . . . But for knowing how much this lies in the tradition of Survey editorship and collaboration, I should hate to sign it. But most Survey articles, to those of us who know, are pretty much the same joint authorship."[25]

For Kellogg one of the hardest parts of his job was to rewrite professional pieces by specialists prominent in their fields who were not accustomed to writing for a general audience. That so many of the big names in welfare wrote awkward prose, thickly larded with jargon, was a challenge to his skills both as diplomat and as stylist. He assigned top priority to rewrite work since the chief purpose of the *Survey* was to make clear to concerned citizens complex developments in fields beyond their area of technical competence. As editor Kellogg was both catalyst and midwife. In his presence, responding to his gentle prodding and cross-examination, persons frequently awakened to the realization that they had a story to tell. It was Kellogg's task— and the responsibility of his editorial associates—to provoke them into putting the stories on paper and to guide the manuscripts through numerous revisions until they saw print in the pages of the *Graphic* or the *Midmonthly*. The process was arduous and often painful. "Do you remember Mrs. Springer's pet phrase to helpless authors?" a staff secretary once inquired. " 'Your manuscript was interesting and well written. All it needed was a little tightening.' . . . She might have added, 'We hope you can still recognize it.' "26

The temptation always lying before editors is to impose their own views on the pages of manuscript that eventually become columns of type. Kellogg shaped the general outline of the journal and determined, in constant conference with others, its thrust of analysis and action. But he exercised restraint and aimed chiefly at helping an author to tell his own story better. As a reporter he had learned the subtle ways by which a correspondent can pile the evidence to support one conclusion or another. In the columns of the *Survey* he encouraged staff and authors to write their stories as dynamically as they could, but always with first regard to the objective accuracy of their accounts. "My father was a lumberman," he wrote to one reporter, "and always said you could pile boards so that all the knots were up, or down, or let them stack as they came."27 By and large the *Survey* let the facts "stack as they came."

These were exciting days to be working on the *Survey*. Paul and Arthur Kellogg were at the height of their powers, young enough to move with gaiety, old enough to be seasoned and at ease. The brothers had worked together so long that they knew each other's minds intuitively. Paul could afford to be softhearted because he knew he would be rescued by Arthur if his sentimentality went too far. When Paul gave permission to a young woman to join the staff as a volunteer in order that she might learn to write, Arthur snapped, "if that is what she wants, let her go to journalism school. . . . B.L. says that he has had experience before with women who 'wanted to write' and under the best of circumstances that species is more trouble than help."[28]

The *Survey* was at home at 112 East 19th Street, a quiet side street whose location, Arthur exulted, discouraged "casual cranks who are prone to call on magazine editors." The offices filled the entire top floor of a loft building and Paul announced that the staff was pleased to "put up with cold water and such like with good cheer," for they enjoyed "windows on four sides and two sky-lights to boot." Regular staff members carried keys to Gramercy Park, a small private yard of green grass and trees that provided a haven particularly in the hot summers.[29]

The staff—some eight to ten regular members in the 1920s — were young and on the make. The pay was low, but young men and women were given responsibility quickly, and they wrote freely for an intelligent audience of readers with no worry at all about the pressure of advertisers. Weekly staff meetings were frequently thrown open to visiting dignitaries; at lunch and teatime the staff held open house for all kinds of guests from all over the country and the world. Arthur's door was always open to clerical and professional staff, and he could settle a grievance or relieve an anxiety with warmth and a crackle of wit. Even if it was a decade of social "sag," things were exciting enough at the *Survey* office, and for those who worked there that was what mattered most.

Reform didn't get much of a hearing in the "period of roaring American post-war prosperity," Paul Kellogg observed in 1932. But the *Survey* kept the faith, as did so many of those other movements which found in the journal their chief comfort and strength; and, at the pivot point around which so much agitation for progress revolved, the editor rejoiced that he had been able to catch "glimpses of some of the old fire of social adventure — which showed not only that there were embers left, but hinted of new kindlings."[30]

{VII}

The *Survey* Journals: Service and Reform

THE professionalization of social work in all its divisions accelerated rapidly during the war years and the decade that followed. It was in 1917, long after the philosophical base of welfare work had shifted in emphasis from amelioration to cure and from cure to prevention, that the National Conference of Charities and Correction changed its name and became the National Conference of Social Work. In the same year a National Social Workers' Exchange was created which, four years later, was transformed into the American Association of Social Workers, a group whose primary objective was to define and secure professional standards for social work. Accompanying these movements was the creation of professional social work schools: whereas in 1915 there were but five, by 1930 there were at least forty.

Dr. Abraham Flexner, at the 1915 NCCC conference, had suggested criteria by which the progress of an occupational group toward professional status might be measured: the existence of formal educational training, both theoretical and applied; the development of a specialized body of knowledge and of special techniques and methods of procedure; the establishment of standards under the supervision of state governments; the creation of professional associations; and the elaboration of codes of ethics and practice.[1] Toward each of these goals social workers strained in the 1920s. The American Association of Social Workers, for example, concerned itself with the task of defining various specialized areas of social work, with recruiting able young men and women into social work careers, with improving salaries and status, with drawing up codes of ethical practices, with inaugurating special schools and short courses for workers already in the field. It attempted to define both the responsibilities and the rights of agency workers, whether private or public, and insisted on the right of social workers to participate in policy formation as well as in policy execution. It sought to establish objective standards for the accreditation of professional schools and the certification of trained personnel.

These were developments that the *Survey* had to report, interpret, and evaluate. It was not a task that Paul Kellogg came to with much relish, for his own personal commitment was always to the public policy and social action thrusts of welfare work, and insofar as social workers came to focus upon new methods and techniques, especially in casework and in the new and exciting field of psychiatry, they tended to focus on the adjustment of the individual to his environment, rather than on the transformation of the social environment within which the individual lived. "The drama of people's insides rather than the pageantry of their group contacts and common needs [was] foremost," Paul Kellogg observed of the 1920s from the vantage point of 1930.[2] Where professionalization demanded specialization, the field of vision was invariably narrowed for all but the most discerning and most broadly concerned workers. Specialization required objective and scientific attitudes toward both the problem area and the client himself. Enthusiasm for reform was not high among the qualities making for success in research, theoretical or applied.

Of all the forces making for professional parochialism during the 1920s, perhaps none was more significant than the new developments in psychology. Psychology and psychiatry opened new frontiers, however, and since the *Survey* functioned most happily when it could report discoveries in previously uncharted lands, its pages were jammed with news of forays into virgin areas of the psyche.[3]

The *Survey* Journals: Service and Reform

To all these professional trends and developments the *Survey,* and after 1923 especially the *Survey Midmonthly,* responded. It was a profoundly difficult task of interpretation the *Survey* set itself, for there were few precedents from which to draw and the problems themselves, at least in the degree of their intensity, were new to that generation. Never had there been such specialization of knowledge in both science and social science, never was there a greater need to know. Not only did social work have to be interpreted to the lay public, but different branches of social service had to be explained to each other, and basic research into human behavior, social structure, economic processes, and the dynamics of politics had to be analyzed for both audiences, the professional social servant and the concerned citizen.

Karl de Schweinitz, by that time already one of the recognized leaders in welfare, set forth the central problem, as he saw it, to Arthur Kellogg in 1918: "Knowledge has been democratized," he began. "Nowadays everybody must know everything, from international relations to the prevention of tuberculosis. At the same time we've never in the history of the world had such an intensification of specialization. The function of the interpreter is to take the discoveries of the specialist and make them part of the knowledge of the general public."[4]

There lay the mandate of the *Survey Midmonthly* during these years, and the Kelloggs knew it. To a much larger extent than before the war, the *Survey* filled its pages with summary analyses of current research in social work and related fields of knowledge. Americans enjoyed a knack for both pure and applied research, Paul Kellogg observed, but that skill had not generally been matched by the ability to make known the processes and findings of research to others in such ways that effective use could be made of newly created understanding. The need, he wrote in 1929, was "to conceive of applied research as an organic process, in which interpretation, by the investigating staff or by co-operating agencies, begins early and calls for considerable share of the budget, of time, money, imagination and energy, so that findings will pollinize both the general public and key forces in a democracy."[5] When agents of research lacked

Arthur P. Kellogg

Paul U. Kellogg

the will or the ability to engage what Kellogg called the "centers of initiative" then the *Survey* had to step in and attempt to do the job.

A balance was difficult to strike: on the one hand highly technical developments had to be put in terms simple enough to be generally understood, on the other hand lay the danger of distorting facts and conclusions when complex studies were reduced to simplified terms. "We are trying to get a wider hearing for materials that are usually salted down in books or wrapped up in the gray matter of experts," Kellogg explained, and one of his chief boasts was that books and monographs that reached but a relative handful of readers engaged the attention of thousands when condensed in the pages of his journal.[6] The journal staff had to survey fifty specialized journals every month, cover a hundred or more annual professional conferences, and skim hundreds of books every year to identify those articles, speeches, and special studies which deserved summary and criticism. But when pressed by some readers and critics to popularize these findings, Kellogg drew the line: "We do not deliver ourselves with finality on a lot of things that are very complex and much in process," he replied to Homer Folks who had written to urge that the *Survey* draw more explicit conclusions for "constructive policy" from the articles it published. "It is irritating to people that like to have things done up in neat and authoritative ribbons," he continued, "but it leaves something to providence and to people to work out on the job." And to Folks's proposal that just as the *New Republic* carried the subtitle "A Journal of Opinion" the *Survey* should add to its masthead "A Journal of Action," Kellogg replied that if a new subtitle were to be invented it would be "A Journal of *Experience*."[7] Kellogg meant, of course, the experience of diverse others, not the experience of himself and the *Survey* staff. "If the *Survey* has any genius or justification," he explained to Philip Cabot, "it is that people of different minds join in making it possible as a gatherer of facts, a pooling place for experience, and a forum of discussion. It is one of the few places where people who come at things from different angles get within arms' reach of each other."[8] The *Survey,* furthermore, was moved by a pragmatic view of the world as open and unfinished.

Until 1923 when the two central functions were divided into two separate (if still related) journals, the *Survey* drifted without clear design or direction. Once its passion for "reconstruction" had played itself out, and by the end of 1919 even the most exuberantly optimistic had been forced to recognize that utopia lay a few years in the future, the *Survey* floundered about, printing fragments of stories from all over. Funds were low, a new staff had not yet been pieced together, it was an effort just to get the magazine printed to say nothing of planning ahead. The pages took on a cluttered appearance. Arthur Kellogg compared the *Survey,* at that juncture, to "a little white hen" trying unsuccessfully to cover "a big clutch of eggs."[9]

John A. Fitch, director of the Industrial Department, together with S. Adele Shaw reported the great steel strike of 1919 in depth and at length, and news of that great struggle and its aftermath filled many columns in subsequent years. This was the continuation of a story which went back to the exposé of the steel industry in the Pittsburgh Survey (Fitch had done the analysis), and the *Survey* handled the beat in the same old way. With a special grant from the Cabot Fund, Fitch and three assistants spent several months in the field in the summer of 1920 checking out the prevalent notion that the steel industry had effectively gone on an eight-hour day, three-shifts-a-day schedule during the war. The evidence of field investigation indicated that although such was the case in some of the more progressive plants, for most workers the long day, the long week, and the long turn were still the rule. They discovered that what had been true in 1907 was true still in 1920: long hours meant physical and mental strain and the demoralization of family life; the lack of self-determination among the workers, rendered more severe by the breaking of the union and the strike in 1919, was destructive of personal morale and of constructive citizenship. As for resolutions, the *Survey* had nothing to offer beyond what it had always proposed—that the public, aroused by a recital of the true facts, would rise up and demand that justice be done. "Neither health work nor work with families, community upbuilding nor training for citizenship can go forward effectively in districts where the twelve-hour day governs," the *Survey* cried in words that echoed its protests of the prewar era. When the steel industry accepted the short workday a couple of years later, the *Survey* claimed some credit for having awakened the public conscience, but the editors were unable to draw a line of influence between the journal's persisting crusade and the decision of the steel owners to do what was, by that latter date, in their own self-interest.[10]

No other single story claimed quite the space given over to conditions in steel. With the dissipation of reconstruction as a lively issue, the *Survey* turned to news stories that were grist for other journals as well: the beginnings of prohibition, the emergence of new states in central Europe, the plight of refugees, inflation, the shortage of housing, immigration, civil liberties, unemployment during the short depression of 1920-21, moves toward disarmament, and the problem of the American Indian. The *Survey* devoted special numbers to the creation of the Irish Free State (26 November 1921), and in cooperation with the Bureau of Industrial Research to the technology and economics of the coal industry (25 March 1922), but neither number created much of a stir.

For the social workers among its readers, the *Survey* continued to summarize professional developments by department: Child Welfare, Family Welfare and Social Organization, Public Health, School and Community, Civics, Crime and Conduct, Foreign Service, and Industry (as the departments were variously identified during these immediate postwar years).

The reorganization of 1923 opened new opportunities that the staff, operating now with a higher budget, were quick to seize, and for the succeeding fifteen years or so, both publications moved ahead to new levels of quality. The *Survey Midmonthly* continued to provide technical information and advice for professional social workers, but it focused less on the summary and analysis of specific forms of service given in specific settings and more on what the profession came to know as "generic" social work, that is, the basic concepts and functions that underlay all practice. The *Mid* explored the sticky problems that arose for all practitioners when faced with the issues of privacy and confidence: what were the client, the agency, and the public entitled to know; what appropriately should the social worker withhold? As social work became more deeply professionalized how should the trained expert relate to boards of lay citizens who knew less and less about techniques and procedures of practice? As social workers achieved official accreditation and certification in what new ways should they work with volunteers? What implications for social work education arose from the breakaway in psychological studies in these years; how could new, and often conflicting, theories and evidence in psychology be incorporated in all divisions of graduate social work curricula? What responsibility did the profession have to keep the community informed of new modes of practice in light of the ever-increasing popularity of community chest drives in raising funds for all health and welfare services? What authority was it appropriate for community chest boards to assert over social work service?

There were no official lines for contributors of articles to follow because the *Mid*'s editors and staff themselves did not pretend to know the answers. So they kept the pages open to different points of view and to representatives of different segments of their reading public—professional social workers and social work educators most prominently, of course, but doctors and lawyers and teachers, too, and lay chairmen of agency boards, and directors of community chests, and citizens without professional social work training who were concerned with the level and quality of social services in their communities.

Of one thing at least the *Midmonthly* was certain—that its readers, professional and lay alike, needed to have kept constantly before them the larger issues which society confronted: poverty, dependency in old age, chronic illness, employment insecurity, race antagonisms. Social policy, as the *Mid* saw it, lay in everyone's domain; but it was the special province of the serving professions to lead the community in the recognition of unmet social needs and in the elaboration of programs that would create an environment in which the self-determination of individuals, families, and natural social groups would be enhanced. The right of each person, each family, each neighborhood, each economic group to determine for itself the paths it would choose: this was the basic philosophical premise from which all else followed. There were no ready-made, packaged remedies at hand; therefore, social workers had to be learners as well as doers and teachers.

Among the fifteen thousand or so subscribers to the *Midmonthly* in the mid- and late-twenties there must have been many readers surprised to read of the persistence of poverty in the midst of generally prevailing prosperity; yet hardly a number went by without some reference to families and communities that stubbornly remained poor. And what did it mean to the poor themselves to live so far below the standards of affluence they could observe all about them? Social workers had a peculiar responsibility to make known the answers to this question, for the poor were inarticulate, and what profession was more in daily contact with social need? Karl de Schweinitz (to cite but one example among many others) set forth what it meant: "It is what poverty does to the spirit that is most terrible of all," he wrote in 1928. "Think what our most prevalent evil, overcrowding, means: never to have a room to oneself. To sleep three in a bed. Never to have so much as a drawer in a bureau where one's own little possessions can be put, and never to have a chance to think apart. Always to anticipate with dread the coming of each new baby. Never to have respite enough from turmoil and confusion to enjoy the members of one's own family."[11]

Other articles in the *Midmonthly* told of the trend in industry and business toward the dismissal of workers in middle age. The modern pace seemed to set a premium on those qualities associated with youth—quickness, agility, strength, and adaptability; workers let go in their forties or fifties, moreover, were not around at retirement time to constitute a moral obligation for their employers. The increase in life expectancy at birth from forty-two years to fifty-eight in just two generations further compounded the problem. Suggestions were made for ways by which workers dismissed in their middle years could be retrained and reemployed; as for the old, society would have to come to accept some public system of old-age pensions. Social work, and society, had slowly come to accept the fact that dependent children were better cared for in their own homes or in foster homes than in institutions; was it not also logical, and more humane by far, to provide pensions for the old so that they could live out their days in their own homes, or in foster homes, rather than in the poor house?[12]

An issue less popular even than concern for the aged, if comparisons are made with the pages of other journals and papers in these years, was the *Midmonthly*'s recognition that provision of health care, not only for the very poor but for hundreds of thousands of families living well above the poverty line, was pathetically meager, especially in light of the technical skill of the medical professions and the remarkable capacity of the nation's economy generally. Early diagnosis and treatment constituted the very best of preventive medicine, but families neglected to visit the doctor, not daring to add the costs to already overburdened family budgets. When chronic illness came, family savings were quickly exhausted. To seek charitable assistance or not to pay one's bills was always a blow to family pride and self-respect. If contributors to the *Midmonthly*'s pages had no solutions to propose, at least the problems were exposed, and before many more years had passed the journal would explore and then endorse any number of proposals including eventually comprehensive, compulsory health insurance.

As for employment insecurity, the *Midmonthly* in number after number devoted pages to evidence that even in times of prosperity a large percentage (8, 10, 12 percent) of the total labor force were idle at any given time. The public should learn, an editorial insisted in 1924, "that in good times and bad, millions of men and women in these prosperous United States are deprived of an opportunity of making a living." The creation of a coordinated system of public employment bureaus would help; so too would the planning of public works for times of seasonal and cyclical slump; employers had a special obligation to seek, through means of modern scientific management, the regularization of employment in their own industries and plants; and society would have to assume the responsibility of protecting workers and their families from "hardship and destitution" by "an adequate system of out-of-work insurance." Such measures were "not counsels of philanthropy, but essential elements in a sound program of economic and industrial organization."[13]

From the beginning of the century the forerunner journals to the *Survey* had explored the special problems Negroes from the rural South faced when they moved to urban and industrial centers in the North. So too, in the twenties, consistent with the acceleration of this migration during and after the war, the *Midmonthly* described the severe insecurities and handicaps the Negro citizen confronted in the North. Negroes were the last to be hired and the first to be fired; they were not enlisted in labor unions; they were crowded into segregated ghettos from which there seemed to be no escape; except for certain small ghetto businesses there were few opportunities for a black middle class to establish itself; they faced discrimination in recreation, in schooling, and in access to public facilities and accommodations. In race relations, as in other areas of social tension, deprivation, and conflict, social workers must inform themselves and help to educate the larger public.

The *Midmonthly* in these years attempted to define the place of social work in a changing society and its relationship both to client and to community; it provided up-to-date summaries of new techniques of service; it worried about the broad implications of professionalization; and it sought, by social interpretation, to alert its readers to the persistence of social problems and to lead them toward ways of prevention and resolution. It was equally assertive in reporting on new understandings of psychology and human behavior, on the one hand, and in surveying social and economic conditions on the other. Both the "retail" (individualized service) and the "wholesale" (social policy) sides of social welfare demanded its attention, and through its pages the attention of its readers.

The *Survey Graphic*'s concerns and functions ran parallel to these, but its emphasis and its style were different, for although its "bailiwick" lay close to the "dull grey province of the dismal science" (as Bruno Lasker described it), it sought by photographs, cartoons, pictorial graphs and charts, etchings and woodcuts,

essays, poems, and personality sketches to publish a journal
"shot with human and beautiful and youthful vistas."[14] The goal
was to engage the attention of a wide audience by use of graphic
and literary arts in partnership with the social sciences, to catch
the eye and the heart as well as the intellect. Dedicated to
exploration and discovery, it derived its guiding principles from
liberal pragmatism: the gathering of social intelligence so that
man could master his environment as he had learned to master
nature and manipulate the forces of the universe for human
progress.

Roscoe Pound and Louis Brandeis were the legal scholar
and jurist most frequently cited; in education, the name of John
Dewey held sway; the *Graphic* appealed to Lewis Mumford and
Sir Patrick Geddes when discussing the promise of city and
regional planning; Robert Marion LaFollette was the *Graphic's*
favorite politician—after his death in 1925 there was none until
Senator Robert Wagner came along; in religion it preferred
John Haynes Holmes, Reinhold Niebuhr, and Father John
Ryan; in historical studies it reflected the "new" historians,
James Harvey Robinson, Harry Elmer Barnes, Charles and
Mary Beard. The British Fabians and the British labor move-
ment were still its models of what democracy applied might
mean for human welfare. It praised those businessmen who
were searching for ways to regularize production and employ-
ment, ways that modern industry might become both more
efficient and more humane through scientific management.
Lewis Hine provided its documentary photographs; Hendrik
Willem Van Loon drew its frontispiece illustrations.

The *Graphic* was chiefly enamored of the process whose
name was borrowed from Justice Brandeis—"social invention."
"The invention of a domestic relations court or a psychiatric
clinic, the institution of a shop-council, or the application of
the insurance principle (which in twenty years has revolutionized
our treatment of trade accidents) to the hazards of sickness and
unemployment"—such inventions, as Paul Kellogg saw it, were
proof and promise of man's inherent capacity for self-determination. For his lead editorial in an early number of the newly independent *Graphic,* Kellogg chose the title "Gangway!" That

word summed up his driving hope for a better world through social engineering. Let man be seized by that vision, let him dedicate himself to science in the affairs of society, let him employ his intelligence for humane ends, then it would be "gangway" for progress.[15]

Kellogg complained of the "sag" that marked life in the twenties, but the *Graphic* itself was never more exciting. In the depression era it had to record dismal stories of human want and social conflict, and attempt to trace complex legislative and executive plans, associated with the New Deal, in terms that an intelligent but lay public could understand. In the forties war and reconstruction consumed its attention. But in the twenties the *Graphic* could afford the time and space to explore the arts, literature, history, and education, the emergence of a "new Negro" in the Harlem renaissance, the revolution of the common man in Mexico, the life style of the Gypsies, experiments in the group theater, and new forms of treatment for the mentally ill. After the great Mississippi flood of 1927, brilliantly reported for the *Survey* by Arthur, it campaigned for comprehensive regional planning for natural watersheds; it crusaded to save the Palisades of the Hudson from commercialization; it warned of the dangers of fascism, Italy being the case sample; and it raised the flag of world peace. The thirties may have seemed more significant to the *Graphic* staff, if the criteria of importance were political reforms, but surely they had more fun in the twenties.

Space that had earlier been claimed by news of religion when Graham Taylor, a minister of the gospel as well as warden of Chicago Commons, was still an active member of the staff was gradually turned over to news of what the Menninger brothers were doing for mental health out on the plains of Kansas, and what new theories of education were doing to make the schools more directly relevant to social need and more exciting for the students. And just in case school and college teachers might miss the ways in which the *Graphic* could be used to bring the world into the classroom, the editors added a new educational department that outlined course syllabi in the social studies.

Less by editorial, and more in article after article on a great variety of subjects, the *Graphic* made its stance known. It stood, for example, for experimentation in all phases of modern life. The Neighborhood Playhouse on the Lower East Side in New York, where Alice and Irene Lewisohn conducted their "artistic and social experiments," was singled out by the *Graphic* because here was theater conceived "as a social force, as an educational institution, and as a vehicle for artistic creation." It put on good plays, and trained young men and women in acting, the dance, set design, and costuming, but its larger justification lay in other contributions: it directed the "play instinct into artistic channels"; it restored the "folk tradition in drama and dance"; it combated "the crass ugliness of a mechanized age"; it "enriched the life of a community"; it created "a new vision and new forms for the theatre of today and tomorrow."[16]

In a special issue, 1 June 1927, devoted entirely to the opportunities in contemporary education, the same cluster of values was evidenced in all the articles and in the thrust that Beulah Amidon, editor of this special number, gave to the issue as a whole. To become effective and good, modern education would have to seek to "integrate school experience with life experience"; it would have to be practical and related to the real present world. Contributors criticized schools that offered classical and "squirrel cage" curricula in which children were made to study what did not interest them and prevented from following their own interests. Bruno Lasker wrote with enthusiasm of the Lichtwarkschule in Hamburg, Germany, where rigid curricula had been abandoned and textbooks largely discarded, where teachers taught from example and experience, and where relevant classroom experiences engaged the students by beginning with present concerns and going on from there. Robert Bruère surveyed the Antioch College experiment where students studied half the year and worked at practical jobs the other half. And Alexander Meikeljohn described the new experimental college opening that fall at the University of Wisconsin where students would help to shape their own programs, where the books that the professors themselves read would be substituted for dusty textbooks, where a community of scholars, some young, some older, would be created out of shared experience, and where, best of all, experimental courses would be opened not alone to a presumed intellectual elite, but to a cross section of all students, for "all normal persons are capable of understanding."[17]

As in the theater and in education, so also in recreation the *Graphic* praised the modern theory that significant human experience lay "in contact with reality—in living now, not in preparation for life at some later period." Through poetry and song and play men were restored, made whole, re-created. Through sound programs of recreation Americans could learn to overcome their devotion to prevailing fallacies—"belief in the machine, belief in means, in all the secondary things." The prewar generation had perceived play as medicine, as a way that youth could be kept fit for work and kept out of mischief, wrote Joseph Lee. "Speed" became the great "prevailing vice" in America and "efficiency came very close to it." But in the modern generation men asked to what ends, and substituted the ennobling of life for efficiency. The modern practice of recreation, moreover, exalted the democratic ethos—play should become "a public function, an essential part of public education and of government provision for the public welfare."[18]

Growth, relevance, democracy, self-determination, mutual cooperation, self-expression: these were the value assumptions from which the *Graphic* and its contributors proceeded. Thus, toward the end of the decade, when the *Graphic* devoted a special number to an analysis of what modern psychology had to offer to an understanding of the processes of human maturation, the separate authors discussed different measures of psychological maturity from different perspectives, but on most points they were agreed: the mature person knew "personal autonomy"; he had the capacity to make himself over to meet changing circumstances; he was not subservient to social institutions but lived, critically, in tune with them; he cared for others; he was self-reliant but strove in cooperation with his fellow man for humane goals.[19]

The *Survey Graphic* believed also in social planning, in the engineering of society—in its necessity and in its possibilities. Never before had man had such sophisticated means at hand to render order out of chaos; but everywhere chaos reigned. People piled up in congested cities; they fled to sprawling suburbs which had no sense at all of community integrity. Urban society encroached on open space, chopped down woodlands, threw up ugly, awkward buildings on sites of natural beauty and destroyed the natural interdependence of city and countryside. In modern cities men lived fragmented and fractional lives; driven by the mania for speed and efficiency they found no comfort and no ease; they were distracted and demoralized. But it need not be so, for modern technology provided the means by which man might remold society closer to the heart's desire. The electronics revolution, in particular, prepared the way for a new era of decentralization. Electric power was clean and fast and could be transmitted long distances at relatively low cost; no longer, therefore, did industrial centers have to pile up factories and people in places where the availability of other sources of power (burning coal to make steam) dictated the location of cities. High-power electric transmission lines rendered decentralization positively economic. It was almost that simple. And the radio and the telephone and the automobile provided an ease of communication and transportation that worked toward the same possibility. Of course men would have to change their established ways: artificial boundaries of cities and counties would have to give way to governments organized in accord with the natural economic and social relationships within a region, for example, if comprehensive social planning were to move ahead. Simple in concept, the actual implementation of social engineering was certain to prove extraordinarily complicated in execution, but to most writers in the *Graphic* the logical necessity for regional planning seemed both irrefutable and irresistible.[20]

Paul Kellogg was a man of many enthusiasms; his buoyancy and optimism were not easily squelched, not even by events which ran strongly counter to his expectations as when his hopes for reconstruction were dashed in the postwar years. No social possibility more engaged his enthusiasm in the twenties than his vision of a world renewed by the kind of social planning that modern technology made feasible. Announcing a special number of the *Graphic* which would be devoted to "giant power," Kellogg pulled out all the stops: "Instead of the misery which came with the piling up of the factory towns under steam, does electric power transmission lift up the hope of overcoming drudgery and capturing new leisure, a hope especially of spreading our production, of decentralization?" he asked. "Does it foreshadow a recovered village life," he rolled on, "no longer isolated and ineffective, but capable of meeting the great center on even terms; in touch with all civilization through radio, telephone and press; but free of the regimentation of the cities?"[21] To one prospective contributor to this special number, he pleaded that the issue was "too emergent, too precious, too buoyant, too promising" not to win his cooperation and support.[22] The extravagance of language may have reflected, in this case, the tension in Kellogg's heart between his nostalgic longing for the neighborliness of his old home town, Kalamazoo, and his equal love for Manhattan, his adopted city. Perhaps he saw in the decentralized industrial village, powered by "clean" electricity, the chance to reestablish on a more cosmopolitan and civilized level the essential elements of a vital community in which men could once again deal with other men as persons rather than as economic or social units. If the sense of community, which Kellogg presumed to have prevailed in the nineteenth century, had been broken by modern technology, perhaps that spirit could be restored now by a higher technology harnessed to humane ends.

Whatever the case, his enthusiasm was shared by the men who contributed articles to the "Giant Power" number. Gifford Pinchot, who wrote one of the key articles, viewed the possibilities in quite the same spirit. Electric power could usher in a new era of economic diffusion and social decentralization. The pall of smoke would be driven from the skies; men could truly go back to the land; here was a "hopeful task in social engineering." Here, in the power field, Pinchot concluded, "perhaps more than from any other quarter we can expect in the near future the most substantial aid in raising the standard of living, in eliminating the physical drudgery of life, and in winning the age-long struggle against poverty."[23] The village ethos was made even more explicit in Joseph K. Hart's essay, "Power and Culture," in the same number. In cities driven by coal and

steam man had "lost contact with nature," and had "lost practically all of the integrity of craftsmanship," Hart observed. "The
industrial city is too inhuman to be the home of the human
spirit." But now man had a chance to begin anew. "Life need no
longer be subordinated to steam: Industry can be decentralized
—the smaller community can be regained, with its old humanities." Decentralization of living, Hart concluded, in turn would
"regenerate our culture by releasing it from the city's hot-houses,
where it attains a superficial brilliance, and restore it to its native rootage in reality."[24] All contributors to the special number,
differ as they did in detail—some stood for public ownership of
electric power, for example, while others opted for private ownership and control under varying degrees of public regulation—
were agreed that on this issue man could *choose.*

Electric power and regional planning—technology and social
engineering—seemed an unbeatable partnership to the *Graphic*
throughout the decade. It was a binding consensus. But even on
a matter of such wide agreement, Kellogg was open to counter-
vailing opinions, and printed a rejoinder from Charles A. Beard.
The movement for regional planning had wide appeal, Beard
confessed, but it had "grown mainly out of speculations concerning a more esthetic and more efficient life, rather than out
of some primordial urge among the masses toward order and
symmetry." Furthermore, these idealistic plans did not command
the allegiance of businessmen and politicians who were the
ones who controlled decisions. Those "who possess the goods"
which the social planner "proposes to re-arrange" see things in
quite another perspective, Beard continued, and self-interest
was not easily made enlightened. Resistance to social planning
came from "special interests" and "private rights" and until
the planners learned how to deal with vested interest they were
just "dreaming dreams and seeing visions."[25]

Beard's tart rejoinder, in retrospect so very sound, caused
no one on the *Survey* staff to reexamine his enthusiasms, not
in the pages of the journal in these years, at any rate. Beard had
raised embarrassing questions about dealing with power realities
and with vested interests so tenacious that they would not easily
yield to the devices the *Survey* had always relied upon—logic

and good will. The *Graphic*'s declared commitment to the goal of social planning was not easily deflected, however, and when, some years later, it seemed that Franklin Roosevelt was about to inaugurate an engineering of society, Kellogg and his associates welcomed the New Deal exactly because it seemed, for a time, to be a realization of their own best hopes.

Balancing this faith in planning was the *Graphic*'s joy in human variety. The planning they had envisioned, after all, prophesied decentralization and the participation of all men and groups in decisions binding on their own lives. It was democratic planning at the grass roots they were enamored of, not the ordering and regimentation of life from above.

It is in this context that the *Graphic*'s romantic interest in exotic peoples and movements can best be understood. Whatever pertained to the "folk" moved Paul Kellogg to delight. As editor he devoted special numbers of the journal to the Irish Free State, to education and land redistribution in the Mexican countryside, and to the Gypsies. The Irish, the Mexican peasants, the Gypsies—all of them "children of the earth," as one author titled an article on the customs and manners of the Gypsies. It was the presumed "natural" or "primitive" quality of the "folk" that undoubtedly appealed to Kellogg, for he was always attracted to those human beings who refused to conform, who refused to give in to the pressures of regimentation in modern life. In his preface to the number on the Gypsies Kellogg poured out his admiration for these "audacious" people who "in the great grinding cities" continued to "live their own untrammelled lives in defiance of twentieth century industrial civilization." The defining quality of being a Gypsy, as Kellogg saw it, was "to live as Gypsies do—care-free, simply, on the go."[26]

From a distance he loved the Irish (and claimed an Irish ancestry which could not be established in genealogical fact). After he discovered the nationalistic drive of the Mexican people for political and cultural self-determination, their programs for land reform and for popular education in the countryside, he guided the *Survey* to analyses of Mexican affairs. Articles and news items on Mexican affairs outnumbered notice of Canadian events manyfold, even though by any objective measure the neighbor to the north was surely as significant to the *Survey*'s natural interests as the neighbor south of the Rio Grande. Kellogg's favorite artists were always those who worked with folk themes, especially when their styles reflected the primitive strength of the common folk; he had little taste for abstract art, and it is not surprising that he was powerfully attracted by the heroic murals of Diego Rivera and José Clemente Orozco and won permission to reproduce their paintings and prints in the pages of the *Graphic*. Then there was the Orient, especially India where Gandhi, clad only in loincloth, plotted the downfall of the British Empire and directed a social movement marked by utter simplicity and folk-wise naiveté. If Kellogg walked the streets of American life shod in practical, ground-gripper shoes, he kept in his closet a pair of light Gypsy boots that he slipped on when the spirit moved.

Some of the same motives may have been operating in Kellogg's mind as he set out to plan a special number on Negro life and culture in the capital city of Black America, Harlem; if so, they were quickly transcended, and the Harlem number of the *Graphic*, published 1 March 1925, became the single most notable achievement of the journal in these years.

Before the war, when Kellogg was a young assistant editor on the staff of the old *Charities and the Commons*, he had helped to put together a special number on the Negro in the industrial and urban north. Sometime in 1924 he conceived of bringing that story up to date by concentrating on a single community, and by shifting the emphasis from "Negro needs, and Negro grievances, to the Negro's contributions."[27] In Harlem, Kellogg wrote in a preview of the special number, "Writers, poets, artists, professional men, social workers, express a social and cultural ferment which is as interesting in its way as the resurgence of Celtic Ireland or the revival of native culture in Mexico."[28]

To edit the special number Kellogg called on Alain Locke, professor of philosophy at Howard University. The choice was a happy one: Locke was young and eager, and because of his youth committed to neither of the old lines of policy and style

associated with the names of W. E. B. Du Bois and Booker T.
Washington; he had many good contacts with cultural leaders
of all sorts in the Negro community, and he quickly learned
to work on easy and friendly terms with Kellogg.[29]

Together they put together a compilation of articles, poems,
drawings, and essays from among the best Negro spokesmen
for that generation: James Weldon Johnson, executive secretary
of the NAACP; Charles S. Johnson, research director for the
National Urban League; W. E. B. Du Bois, then the most effective voice of black militance. There were poems by Countee
Cullen, Claude McKay, and Langston Hughes. Walter F. White
contributed a telling piece on the complexities of the color line;
Arthur Schomburg, who was then gathering the great archives
on the history of the black man in America, wrote an essay on
the Negro past; and Elsie Johnson McDougald added a cutting
analysis of the "double task" of Negro women in their struggle
for both "sex and race emancipation."

In his own lead article, and by the influence he exerted as
editor of the number, Alain Locke sought to distinguish the
"new" from the "old" Negro. The "old" Negro, a stock figure
of subservience, was always more of a myth than a man but the
myth had force in determining the position the Negro had to
assume in American society. But now, the Negro was beginning
to shake off this "implied inferiority"; he was now an "integral
part" of "present-day democracy"; and he was beginning to find
new self-respect, new self-dependence, and freedom "both from
self-pity and condescension." In Harlem, he was finding his way
toward a new "belief in the efficacy of collective effort, in race
cooperation. This deep feeling of race is at present the main-
spring of Negro life." Until recently, Locke continued, the
American Negro had to choose "between the alternatives of
supine and humiliating submission and stimulating but hurtful
counter-prejudice." But now in "Harlem: Mecca of the New
Negro" he was finding a new sense of common consciousness
and discovering a new opportunity to be "a collaborator and
participant in American civilization." Now the American
Negro could turn from "controversy and debate" to "creative
expression."[30]

The *Graphic* sold over 40,000 copies of this special issue, a record which it did not surpass until the years of the Second World War, and in the fall of 1925, it appeared in expanded form as a book, *The New Negro*, with an introductory essay by Paul Kellogg. Its impact is impossible to measure, of course, but whatever consequences were claimed it is clear that it was a pioneering publishing venture unequaled by any other periodical in that era. For the first time a major publication with national circulation turned over its pages not to a discussion of "the Negro problem" (usually as portrayed by white authors), but to an exploration of the dynamics of cultural life in the Negro community as Negro leaders themselves perceived it. (It is significant in this regard that the only piece conjuring up old stereotypes was an account of Negro crime and vice written by a white penologist, Winthrop D. Lane.) In focusing on the contributions rather than the problems of the American Negro, in stressing the constructive cultural advances emerging in Harlem, in using Negro authors and critics to set forth the truths of the Negro renaissance, the *Survey Graphic* was far ahead of its time. Other journals might publish sympathetic articles now and again, but the *Graphic*'s adventure stands alone as a classic account.

This is not to say that the *Survey* was done with "social problems" and "reform." The *Graphic* had less of the crusading tone in the 1920s than the journal had exhibited in earlier years, but its role of advocacy was not completely subdued, of course. The *Graphic* followed sympathetically the development in these years of programs of vocational guidance and child guidance. It carried news and editorials on labor arbitration, the rehabilitation of criminals, the conservation of natural resources, the outlawry of war, the international control of opium through the League of Nations, the protection of women workers, the fight for ratification of the child labor amendment, the advance of mother and child health under the terms of the Sheppard-Towner Act, and the social costs of health care. But most of those issues dated back to the years before the war, not that they were not vital concerns in the 1920s but they were rooted in prewar progressivism.

Paul U. Kellogg and the *Survey*

Employment insecurity was another pressing social concern that the *Survey* had busied itself analyzing and publicizing for many years. Of major significance for the decade of depression that would follow the decade of hectic prosperity, the *Graphic* (like the *Midmonthly*) began to play up stories of widespread unemployment many months before the stock exchange crashed in the fall of 1929. In the winter of 1928, struck by the "unexpected picture of unemployment" that came to the *Survey* offices from many observers throughout the country, Paul Kellogg shaped a special number of the *Graphic,* published 1 March 1928, which set forth answers to the question "Is Unemployment Here?" The answer, of course, was a resounding "Yes"; the nation was on the edge of "a real crisis—the worst since 1921."[31] Beginning with that number, the *Graphic* (and the *Midmonthly,* too) followed the story of economic troubles and uncertainties: the precarious nature of prosperity that rested on installment buying, overextended consumer credit, and stock speculation; the impact of changing technology on job displacement; the need for long-range planning of public works; human-interest stories detailing what happens when a worker is let go; accounts of the study launched by the National Federation of Settlements into the extent and the human consequences of unemployment in times of prosperity; exposés of underemployment in contracting industries and unemployment among middle-aged workers.

In taking this tack in the winter of 1928 Kellogg drew information and support from his allies in the settlement movement who were beginning to see evidence in their neighborhoods of growing unemployment. He drew inspiration, as well, from his old friend Justice Louis Brandeis who wrote to "my dear Kellogg" in March 1928: "would it not be possible for the *Survey* to take up vigorously and persistently the musts of Regularity in Employment? That is the fundamental remedy. All others are merely palliatives. The right to regularity in employment must be raised above the right to dividends. It must be given equality with rent, interest and taxes. Regularity of employment would go far toward eliminating business cycles—in this country. It is essential to the emancipation of labor."[32] Brandeis's advice to Kellogg not to wait upon "the paternosters of princes and politicians," but to awaken the "moral sense of the social minded intelligentsia," and to arouse the "economic sense of organized labor," was, of course, entirely congenial to the editor's own progressive predispositions, and it was along these lines that he proceeded.[33]

The *Survey* did not predict or prophesy the panic and depression. It did, however, read the signs of economic insecurity more accurately than most other journals and newspapers. And it did stand on the natural right that Louis Brandeis had publicly enunciated before the war and renewed in personal correspondence in 1928—the right of every man to a steady job. Unemployment, the *Graphic* proclaimed in the spring of 1929, is "no longer to be endured in our common life." When we know that, Beulah Amidon, writing for the *Graphic* staff, continued, "economic and social invention will quickly derive means for making that opportunity secure."[34]

As usual the *Survey* was both prescient and utopian. It read the signs correctly: the nation was headed for hard times; but it was unduly hopeful of what response society might be expected to make. In months the panic struck and the downward slide into depression began. It proved a long, long slide indeed before the nation was prepared to act. When it did gather itself for constructive action, it was much along the lines that the *Survey* set down that it moved, with Roosevelt, toward a New Deal.

{VIII}

Depression and the Coming of the New Deal

THE NATION prospered mightily in the 1920s; so too did the *Survey* expand and grow in these years. Some of its gains in circulation in the postwar decade recovered ground lost during the war years, for the *Survey* which had gone to some 20,000 readers in the first year of the European war, 1914, reached but 14,000 in 1920. From that low point it began to grow and, after the separation of the two journals in 1923, to move ahead steadily. In mid-decade readership was back up to 20,000 and by decade's end over 8000 readers subscribed to the *Graphic* alone, and another 18,000 held joint subscriptions to both the *Midmonthly* and the *Graphic* editions, making a mail circulation of about 26,000 with another 4000 copies or so being sold from newsstands. For purposes of rough comparison it might be observed here that although the circulations of the *New Republic* and the *Nation* were erratic from year to year—far more erratic than the *Survey* journals which held to a relatively steady clientele—their readerships on the average during the interwar years were much the same size. Membership in Survey Associates, at ten dollars or more a year, exceeded 2000 for the first time in 1929. Circulation and advertising revenue, reflecting these trends, had steadily increased, and large donations and special foundation grants continued to fatten the *Survey*'s income during these years, so that the journal had more substantial and more reliable revenues with which to work. The momentum gathered carried the *Survey* to 1932-33 before circulation began to decline and revenues to fall off precipitously. The two journals enjoyed a sound financial position in the early years of the Great Depression, and with this assured strength they were able to cover the welfare front effectively when the nation and the serving professions confronted a most serious crisis.

The depression was the big story, but the *Survey* did not neglect other interests and concerns. A typical issue of the *Graphic,* 1930 and on into 1931, might include articles on the politics of Gandhi in India, the prison reforms associated with the career of Thomas Mott Osborne, famine relief in China, the textile worker strikes in the Piedmont South, Mexican art, sexual fulfillment in family life, flood control, and international congress on women's rights, art and culture among American Indians, the trials of a caseworker on her rounds, the burden of medical costs upon the poor, movements to preserve the wilderness and save the redwoods, continuing processes of adult education. A typical number of the *Midmonthly* might contain pieces on how a community proceeds in the establishment of a psychiatric clinic, benefits to which veterans were entitled, provision of dental inspection for school children, street sanitation, traffic accidents, special work with retarded children, mental hygiene for disturbed children, counseling for families struck by divorce, or labor-management bargaining in the anthracite coal industry.

Unemployment was the big story, however, and hard times soon dominated the pages of both journals. The *Survey* staff, as noted in the preceding chapter, had seen it coming a year and a half and more before panic rocked the stock market. Early in 1928, Beulah Amidon, who had come to be the *Survey*'s chief expert on all matters pertaining to industry and the economy, circularized experts in the field seeking evidence from them that would either confirm or deny the sense she had that prosperity was beginning to break. The replies she received were not reassuring; something more serious than seasonal readjustment or simple technological displacement of jobs seemed to be

underway. The series of articles she wrote on the subject, 1928-
30, did not, apparently, create much of a stir probably because
even the readers of the *Survey* had been persuaded that prosperity was in the very nature of life in the United States; she did,
however, receive encouragement from such students of the economic scene as William Leiserson, at that time a professor of
economics at Antioch College in Ohio, who wrote early in 1930
to urge that the *Survey* continue its revelations because other
newspapers and journals were failing to report the bad news
of economic slump.[1]

By the summer of 1930 staff members had the evidence of
hard times before their eyes every day as they came to work:
across the street from the *Survey* offices an apartment building
had been under construction for some months, the steel frame
was up, the concrete poured, but now, as Paul Kellogg told his
readers, "with the brick delivered, the block is full of idle men
with trowels under their arms, waiting patiently in the hope of
a chance at the bricklaying in spite of the sign 'No help wanted.' "[2]
What disturbed him most was the human waste and the need-
less human suffering that unemployment entailed; industry
set aside capital funds to replace worn-out and obsolete machinery, it set up reserve funds against many contingencies but
not against unemployment—that burden had to be assumed by
labor itself alone. If industries acted toward their physical plant
as they did toward their labor force, Kellogg complained to a
friend, they would be left "with roofs caved in, wires unstrung,
lathes and presses rusted and raw materials in a mess."[3] To
another friend a bit later, he needled those social agencies that
continued to deal with "psychiatric behavior, health, and character building"; such social workers were living in "a fool's
paradise. . . . you cannot deal effectively with an inferiority
complex on an empty stomach."[4]

The *Survey* journals did not confine their attention to unemployment in the great mass industries alone, although some of
their most dramatic stories detailed the extent and the significance in human terms of workers let go in such mass-production
centers as Detroit and Toledo. They carried news items, as
well, on unemployment among clerks, stenographers, office

workers—the "white collar poor" who were even more reluctant than factory employees to seek financial assistance from private or public agencies.[5] They carried feature stories on unemployed veterans, on the little armies of cast-off young boys who drifted aimlessly across the country not even bothering to look for jobs which they knew did not exist for them, and on unemployment among professional workers—executives, lawyers, engineers—whose services were no longer in demand. The right to a job, the right to steady employment, the right to a decent and reliable income—these were the principles to which the *Survey* returned again and again. It is not enough, Kellogg wrote in the early months of the depression, that wages be "high," they must be "long" as well, and "broad," that is, uninterrupted by seasonal layoffs, and "broad" across the whole community. Steady work and steady wages were essential "to hold up a home, sustain a community and help assure us continuous business prosperity."[6]

To the slogan, heard in different forms from the business community, that the unemployed needed jobs not the dole, the *Survey* responded that there were no jobs, and until such time as private industry could take back the jobless obviously the unemployed needed financial assistance in some form from any source.

The depression was not many months old before the *Survey* staff began to inquire of private agency executives around the country how hard times affected caseloads. They gathered data from other sources, as well, because nowhere in the country were statistics systematically being gathered. The reporting, under these conditions, was necessarily haphazard and episodic. From directors of community chests, from executives of family service agencies, from mayors and county commissioners, from professors of economics, from union leaders, from church leaders, and from liberal businessmen the journals pieced together articles which offered abundant proof that the extent of unemployment was substantially greater than official (and for the most part optimistic) estimates of the federal government indicated, and that the total sum being paid out to the needy unemployed was very much greater than anyone guessed. There was no need to tremble at the word "dole," as so many well-meaning citizens did; under whatever name, vast amounts of money were in fact being doled out, but not in systematic or orderly fashion, not according to need, and not with fairness to either donors, recipients, or community.

Long before the general public became aware of the problem, even before practicing social workers themselves really understood its dimensions, the *Survey* reported incontrovertible evidence that community chests, private agencies, and church-related relief operations would be unequal before many months passed to meeting fully the ever-increasing (and staggering) demands for financial assistance. Before 1930 had passed into history, the *Graphic* and the *Midmonthly* documented the ways in which casework agencies were beginning to abandon their traditional services of counseling, character building, and rehabilitation before the mounting pressure of the hungry and the homeless for food and shelter. Attempts in many cities to co-ordinate employment services, to increase the sums raised from voluntary charitable drives, to find new sources of revenue for public programs of assistance were related in the journals' pages in order that civic leaders in different parts of the country might learn from the experience of others. But the recurring theme was that of futility: the measures were too little, too late; and however great the efforts, need always outran response.

In the face of mounting relief needs, the *Survey* called on welfare leaders to set standards relevant to new conditions in granting assistance. In issue after issue the journals printed the guidelines that leaders in different branches of social work were seeking to follow: relief in cash was preferred to relief in kind; work relief, if it involved no work test, and if the work were carefully planned to match the skill and condition of an unemployed worker, was preferred to a cash handout; clear and simple ways of determining need had to be evolved if bureaucratic busywork was to be avoided, the kind of busywork that so frequently sapped the self-respect of the client. When private sources could no longer provide relief, the *Survey*'s was one of the first voices to call for government programs of direct cash assistance and work relief, and when local and state units of government proved fiscally unable to act, it demanded that the federal government take up direct responsibility for what was beyond a shadow of doubt a national problem of human want and misery. In this latter instance the *Survey* followed the lead of William Hodson, at that time executive director of the Welfare Council of New York City, who had publicly appealed to President Hoover in October 1931 for a federal grants-in-aid program which would channel the strength of the federal treasury back to local communities where the funds would be spent by a partnership arrangement between local and national government.[7]

Paul Kellogg joined other national leaders in testifying in December before a special subcommittee on unemployment chaired by Senator Robert M. LaFollette, Jr. The country was in "a national emergency as truly as any war," Kellogg began, employing an analogue the New Dealers would use to justify emergency measures in 1933; private agencies had not been able to provide assistance to the needy for many months and the resources of local government were exhausted. Local responsibility for relief was deeply rooted in the American experience, he admitted, but "the time has come when we need resourceful national leadership and action to stiffen and organize public responsibility through Government all down that line." In the long run unemployment insurance would be needed to stabilize purchasing power along rational lines, but until then the federal government would have to step in with a program of direct relief.

The impact of his testimony that day he reported by letter to Arthur. Senator Edward P. Costigan had asked him how he would define the dole; because he had never liked the word, he stumbled in his reply and then blurted out, "I'd define the dole as a catch word employed to confuse the public." "The newspaper men all snickered," Paul continued to his brother. "Costigan looked at LaFollette; they nodded. No further questions. They didn't want to take the edge off."[8]

On all these points the *Survey*'s views ran very much ahead of public opinion, ahead of public officials especially President Hoover and representatives of his administration, and ahead of the main body of social workers who clung to roles and functions as traditionally defined; Kellogg's own views on such matters were informed by the concerns of the settlement leaders whose views on unemployment he had sought in 1928. The *Survey*'s task of interpretation lay not only in arousing the concern of community leaders in general but in informing and educating welfare leaders upon whom a special obligation rested.

The *Survey* knew, however, that relief from whatever source in whatever form, however fairly and generously provided, was no more than a palliative. Security—the security that only a comprehensive system of social insurance could provide—constituted the only effective preventive and constructive measure that society could devise. So the *Survey* had proclaimed back in the days of Bull Moose progressivism before the war. So had it insisted throughout the 1920s, although during the decade of prosperity it had been largely content to analyze private industrial plans for employment regularization or labor-management agreements (as in the garment industry, for example) which built in provision for unemployment compensation out of industrial reserves. When, in the early depression years, several states (New York, Wisconsin, Ohio most notably) began to consider state systems of unemployment insurance, the *Survey* dutifully recorded the arguments pro and con, but in doing so it never lost sight of the ultimate need for a compulsory, comprehensive, national system of insurance to cover the risks of unemployment, sickness, and old age.

The *Survey*'s tone throughout its history, even on issues of great moment in which ignorance and self-interest frustrated the public good (as by the *Survey* perceived), had been even-tempered, reasoned, and nondogmatic; it was often insistent but never shrill, self-certain but always open to other and even contrary views; it was often disappointed but rarely bitter in its expression of despair. This is not to suggest that the *Survey* was ever bland or lacking in bite (although some of the *Midmonthly*'s social work pieces were couched in the awkward jargon and thick prose which Paul Kellogg himself called "social-worky"); it is merely to observe that the *Survey* was "liberal" in that old-fashioned progressive sense—it believed in man's essential rationality and good will; it believed that in the long run reasoned and free debates were the only way the truth could be discovered and put to work for the betterment of the human race. The bitterness of some of the articles printed in these years of frustration, when it seemed that nothing would ever be done to face up to hard times, is all the more notable therefore. A piece by William Leiserson, "Who Bears the Business Risk?" published in March 1931, is a case in point. To say that unemployment was caused by overproduction, by technological changes, by seasonal and cyclical changes that were part of the natural order of things, Leiserson began, was not to explain but to describe. The need, rather, was to understand the basic failure of business management to act responsibly and intelligently in regard to all the factors of its activities. Corporations set aside reserves out of which dividends could be paid to stockholders and interest to creditors in slack years; they set aside funds for depreciation and obsolescence; through trade associations and other arrangements they could curtail production to their own advantage. Every device was employed to stabilize income and guarantee security for industry and capital, but their employees were expected to care for themselves and to await re-employment at their own costs. It was not management or stockholders but labor alone that assumed the risks of business.[9] Other articles slipped into the same kind of bitterness: everyone, it seemed, took elaborate precautions to protect his interests; only poor workers and poor farmers, who had no means for self-defense, suffered from basic insecurities in the system which were no fault and no responsibility of theirs. Therefore both logic and justice demanded social insurance.

The *Survey* had no blueprint for social insurance. Different contributors had different concepts of what ideally should be the shape of a social security system. Some like Frances Perkins (who reported in the *Survey Graphic* on her visit to England in the summer of 1931 to study its system) preferred that industry should foot the entire bill of establishing unemployment reserves; to her the claim that insurance would "mean more" to the workers if they made contributions out of wages seemed a "sentimental consideration."[10] Others, however, believed in mixed funding, with compulsory contributions coming from both employers and employees, and (in some proposals) out of general tax revenues as well. By 1934 Kellogg had come to endorse such a form of balanced financing. Some wanted a centralized national program, others favored varied forms of federal-state partnership, and until 1934 and 1935 still others wished the states alone to keep the initiative in this arena of social policy.

Paul Kellogg set forth his own views on the subject in December 1931, in an editorial statement he headed "Security Next." He began, typically, by stressing what insecurity of work and income meant in the human terms of those who suffered: "Homes are wrecked; health is damaged; child nurture scamped; the whole range of constructive social work threatened; bitterness engendered." Unemployment relief was hit-and-miss and inadequate when measured by any standards; local units of government lacked the tax base ever to provide sufficient funds. The loss of a job always precipitated a family emergency, savings were quickly exhausted, family spending was pared back at the sacrifice of diet and health and well-being. What use to preach thrift when "savings are scrapped in a single hard winter!" A system of contributory, compulsory unemployment insurance was surely the next essential step, for even if it would not by itself move the nation out of hard times, it would help to secure purchasing power and it would provide effective relief to needy families.[11]

Such national leaders as Harry L. Lurie and William Hodson spoke to the same essential points in the pages of the *Midmonthly*. Social work could not do its job as long as families were in dire financial need; until family security was guaranteed traditional casework was mere palliation. The moral was clear: social workers should join with other community leaders to encourage the establishment of minimum wages, economic security, community planning, public health and recreation programs.[12]

All these measures implied the need for over-all economic planning, and given the passion for city and regional planning which had marked the *Survey* in the 1920s, it is not surprising that Paul Kellogg would revive that concept now that a desperate economic emergency had rendered traditional piecemeal proposals obsolete. In the summer of 1931 Kellogg began to seek advice from many sources on how the *Graphic* might best present the case for planning and by the spring of 1932 he was ready to go to press with a special number devoted entirely to that subject. In his prefatory remarks Kellogg referred to the world conference on planning held in Amsterdam in the previous summer. There the nations of the West had been forced to confront the challenge of the Soviet Union that in that socialist republic there was no unemployment. Soviet delegates to the conference held to the position that without common ownership of the means of production and the elimination of the system of private profit there could be no planning. Conservative representatives from capitalistic countries on the other hand, clinging to the traditions of classical economics, had warned that there was no way to plan without sacrificing individual liberty and personal initiative. It was Kellogg's obvious hope that in the United States ways might be found by which consumption could be increased and living standards raised without regimentation, without setting in motion "a huge mechanism of corporate control."[13]

As in other special numbers, this one drew on leading experts from many different specialties. Sidney Hillman was on hand to testify from his experience in union-management cooperation in the clothing industry to the efficacy of planning from the bottom up. The plan for industrial stabilization put forward by Gerard Swope, many of whose ingredients would be incorporated into the National Industrial Recovery Act the following year, received sympathetic appraisal. Stuart Chase rang the changes on popular themes—with the end of the frontier the need to plan, insecurity of employment and income the true threat to individualism, the vast resources which in America could be mobilized for plenty. Lewis Lorwin's contribution, however, was probably closest to the heart of all the *Survey* had been saying. "The laissez-faire of the nineteenth century was based upon a metaphysics of the providential guidance of natural law," he wrote. But "the *planning* of the twentieth century rests on a philosophical faith in the power of man to promote orderly economic and social change through scientific research and constructive imagination." The institution of effective planning in America, he went on, would require no sudden jump in outlook or procedure, for both the economy and the government had been evolving in that direction for a generation. Americans would naturally reject dictatorial methods but planning would require "some central unifying agency" through which the natural interdependence of all parts of the economy could be coordinated. Successful planning would require democratic participation at every level and by all concerned groups—management, labor, technicians, scientists. The key was for all groups working together "to learn the art of making social revolutions peacefully."[14]

It had been the fear of Evans Clark, director of the 20th Century Fund, and one of those experts whose advice Kellogg had solicited when planning the special number, that economic planning was "rapidly becoming a Cause which will stir the emotions of those who are not in a position to do anything about it, and scare those who are."[15] In retrospect it seems unlikely that either runaway enthusiasm or fear could have been aroused by this number. It undoubtedly confirmed the prejudices of many readers who were searching for some constructive way out of the emergency short of revolution; citizens who could have been made anxious by the proposals were, in all probability, not numbered among the regular readers of the *Survey*. Its significance lies less in the impact it had (or did not have) than in the position it represented, a position entirely consistent with the old Theodore Roosevelt New Nationalist version of the progressive faith. The *Survey* may have been "ahead of its times" (that it was ahead of the Hoover administration would seem beyond question), but its central precepts were still informed by the advance-guard positions of the prewar reform movements. However creative in program it was in the 1920s, it still longed for rationality, order, equity and justice, and social efficiency.

Paul Kellogg's position, moreover, was also in response to the concrete human condition. "Last night when I must have passed a score of men sleeping on the doorsteps of office buildings in our part of town, with old newspapers for blankets," he wrote to a friend in the early autumn of 1932, "it brought home to someone just returned from the woods how outrageously out of gear our industrial set-up is."[16]

Although the *Survey* rarely took a partisan position, and in both 1928 and 1932 the journal meticulously avoided a discussion of political affairs, loyal readers of the *Survey* must certainly have been able to deduce where Kellogg and other staff members stood. In 1924, an unsigned editorial (obviously written by Paul Kellogg) stopped short of endorsing Robert M. LaFollette, but its guarded words which praised the movement he led "for bringing economic and social considerations, which lie close to the life and labor of the common lot of Americans, clear through into the arena of searching public discussion" could hardly have been misunderstood as anything but an endorsement for the Progressive candidate and party. Just to make certain, Kellogg added a brief signed piece declaring simply his intention of voting for LaFollette.[17] Like many other welfare liberals Kellogg had been torn in 1928 between his loyalty to Governor Alfred E. Smith of New York on issues of water power, public health, child welfare, and education and his admiration for Hoover's role in the administration of overseas relief during the Great War and for his administrative skills as evidenced in his career as secretary of commerce and in his supervision of relief during the great Mississippi River flood in 1927; and Smith's stand on prohibition made him, like so many social workers, a bit uneasy. The *Survey* remained strictly quiet in 1928, but Kellogg himself voted for Smith and sported a "Smith for President" plate on his car, this choice (as he justified his vote to Jane Addams) essentially on the ground that Smith's stand on the public development of water power resources tipped the scales in his favor— "water" not "liquor" was the test.[18]

The 1932 election found Kellogg importuned from all sides. He kept the pages of the *Survey* entirely free of any partisan note whatsoever, although the bitter opposition aroused in welfare circles by Hoover's failure to act aggressively to meet the challenge of hard times was reflected in many articles. Kellogg's own frustrations may have been compounded by his inability to provoke a positive response from E. E. Hunt in President Hoover's Department of Commerce with whom he had a lengthy private correspondence on the subjects of unemployment, relief, and public works during the Hoover years.[19] He had enjoyed no more luck with the president himself—his letters to Hoover received perfunctory and evasive acknowledgments, or none at all.[20] It was a disappointment, for Hoover too had been a Bull Mooser in 1912, but Kellogg came to the judgment by 1930 that what Hoover had "missed in all those years he was off in China, Africa and elsewhere, dealing with corporations on the one hand, and coolies on the other, was that very give and take among the rank and file of folk in a democratic society which is such a handicap to him now in acting as its chief." Furthermore he had "surrounded himself with political advisers who insulate, inhibit and short-circuit him."[21] He saw no reason to change his judgment in 1932.

Kellogg did not lend his name to declarations for any candidate in 1932. For a while he was tempted to support a move on the part of old insurgent Republicans to seize control of the party from Hoover and nominate some such candidate as Gifford Pinchot. "If you can really build up an insurgent Republican movement of calibre," he wrote to Harold Ickes, " a lot of old time Progressives like myself would be more than interested."[22] But there proved to be no mileage in that tactic. He was tempted to declare for Franklin Roosevelt who, almost alone of prominent national political figures, stood for exactly those measures that Kellogg and the *Survey* embraced; but finally he let it be known to a few close friends that lacking assurance in the "mixed assemblage which is the Democratic party as the vehicle for change," he was voting for Norman Thomas on the Socialist ticket, believing "that as in the Progressive movement of 1912 there is chance for more effective leverage on the outside."[23] Kellogg remained far more committed to the democratic left than so many other old progressives who veered to the right or turned sour during the interwar years.

When the votes were counted, Kellogg's old friend Frances Perkins, in whose company he had fought side by side for so many years in securing welfare measures in the state of New York, wrote gently to chide him: "I have long ago forgiven you for not voting for Franklin. Your vote wasn't needed, you see, and didn't do the third party movement much good, did it?" Kellogg replied in kind: "Of course I want to help now and in the years ahead any way I can"; could he be of any help in securing her appointment as secretary of labor?[24] The friendly exchange indicated the kind of relationship Kellogg would enjoy with the Roosevelt administration, especially during its first term, and anticipated the political line the *Survey* would follow in the early years of the New Deal.

The only notice taken at the time of Roosevelt's election was a brief news note under the headline "Survey Contributor Promoted" which stated, in full: "Franklin D. Roosevelt, the author of Growing up by Planning in the *Survey* of February, 1932 (page 483), was elected president of the United States on November 8."[25] During the long period of the interregnum, from election to inauguration, the *Survey* held back from speculating on the policies Roosevelt would shape as president, although during this period Kellogg was in correspondence with Frances Perkins in regard to her selection as secretary of labor.

Once the New Deal got rolling, however, it proved almost impossible to find enough space in the pages of the *Graphic* and the *Midmonthly* to detail all the new welfare measures that poured out of Washington. For months there was room for little else than accounts of programs so long delayed and of programs whose day had finally arrived. One chief function, especially of the *Midmonthly,* was merely to inform professional welfare workers of how their own services should adapt to new federal programs, especially in the field of relief. Beyond that the journals held true to their line of providing quick analysis, interpretation, and evaluation. And throughout 1933 and on into 1934 the evaluations, except for an occasional small caveat, were all sympathetic and favorable.

The *Survey*, indeed, was enthusiastic —after so many dreadful years of delay, lethargy, and inaction the nation was on the march again. Direct federal grants for relief of the unemployed and for public works, the labor clauses of the NRA, creation of a federal employment service, regional planning in the TVA, the elimination of child labor—these were accomplishments designed to please reformers. As the great mass of the American people responded affirmatively to Roosevelt's militant leadership, so too did the *Survey* take on a new spirit, buoyant, optimistic, and confident.

The private assessment Paul Kellogg made of the New Deal, in the fall of 1933, to his friend Margaret Bondfield, an old stalwart of the British labor movement, provides a sharp insight into how he and the journals he edited judged Roosevelt's leadership. "My feeling is that something affirmative has been started in the Recovery program, in spite of hitches and haws and ballyhoo; that it is a stroke of fortune to have such a piece of team play by Roosevelt, Johnson, Richberg, Ickes and Frances Perkins; and that the months ahead are going to bristle with all sorts of fighting issues on which will hang the outcome not merely in the matter of revival, but in the long run evolution of American industrial life. The very fact that things are so experimental, so at loose ends, so lacking in a rigid program, seems to me to offer the chance for a real swing to the left."[26] The formless quality of the New Deal, its intense pragmatism, its willingness to move quickly in practical ways to meet pressing needs, its lack of dogma, its openness to many different ways to recovery—these were the qualities that constituted its chief virtue.

The frontispiece cartoon by Van Loon which set the tone for the August 1933 number of the *Graphic* was probably the first hopeful drawing of his the *Survey* had published in more than four years. It depicted two factories, one belching smoke, the other still idle. The caption affirmed the reality of recovery: "Do you mind my smoking?" queried the one. "No. Go ahead. I'll be smoking in a moment," replied the other.[27] It was not Van Loon's best effort—he was generally better at spoofing than at affirmation—but it caught the upward tending hopefulness of the moment. In the same issue the *Graphic* published an extravagantly exuberant essay by Harry A. Overstreet, whose earlier articles in the *Survey* had been largely devoted to a popularization of positive developments in mental health fields. Now he came to examine and to rejoice in the new spirit of adventure that was loose in the land. Now the nation had put considerations of common welfare paramount; now there was the assurance to all people of "the right of a secure and wholesome life." The reconstruction lay not alone in politics and economics but in the central stuff of human values—a "new era of leisure" was being born; the dividing walls of nationality, race, and religion were being torn down; the employment of military force was in decline; women's place in society was now more "generously conceived." Everywhere, in America and in other countries, the "individualistic state" was being transformed into the "social state." Humanity was moving toward a "promised land."[28] In every issue this new-found confidence was expressed; beyond all the specific acts of the New Deal the *Survey* hailed the use of the law as a tool of constructive social revolution, the harnessing of production to the goal of plenty, the advance from poverty and want to security. The moment must have seemed almost as exciting as 1912, and the name was still Roosevelt.

It was symbolically appropriate that Paul Kellogg selected Harold Ickes, another old Bull Mooser like himself, to address the annual dinner meeting of Survey Associates in March 1934. The Old Curmudgeon was in great form that night, and his audience responded with friendly cheers and enthusiastic applause. We know now, he began, that 1932 wasn't just another political campaign but a response to "a far-reaching and fundamental political revolution." It was a crusade, a "bloodless revolution," in which the *Survey* had been a pioneer fighter for social justice: the rights of labor, the protection of women, the abolition of child labor, slum clearance, workmen's compensation and mothers' pensions, unemployment and old-age insurance, "correctional instead of punitive handling of juvenile delinquents." "We are blazing new trails," he proclaimed in a metaphor that Paul Kellogg himself employed over and over again, "just as surely as our ancestors did when they felt their way cautiously through the untrodden forests." The New Deal, "neither reckless nor foolhardy," had set its heart on turning out "wealth and privilege" and ushering in a world that would be a better place for all. The day was being won not by indulgence in idle daydreams but by sweeping and practical measures for the common welfare.[29]

Throughout 1934, not content alone to publish staff analyses of New Deal measures, the *Graphic* opened its columns to prominent New Dealers to explain the ways in which the Roosevelt administration was advancing the common welfare. Arthur E. Morgan described the TVA; Harold Ickes explained soil conservation measures; Frances Perkins contributed two long articles on the steps being taken toward security; Arthur C. Holden, of the Division of Economic Research and Planning in the NRA, defended the administration's housing proposals; Henry A. Wallace not only justified the New Deal's farm policies but spread out all its varied programs for admiration.

Members of the *Survey*'s board responded to these developments with much the same enthusiasm as the staff, and the minutes of board meetings, during the first couple of years of the New Deal, are sprinkled with words of praise for the *Survey* because it had anticipated in broad outline, and often in specific detail, the breakaway of reform now being initiated by FDR. Agnes Brown Leach, for many years one of Kellogg's staunchest (and most generous) friends on the board, summed it up in a little note following a board meeting in the fall of 1934: It must be "exhilarating for you to see the ideals you have written for a generation and a half actually being daily put into execution by the Federal government."[30]

The answer was yes, it was exhilarating to see promise realized. The beginning of the Tennessee Valley Authority was perhaps the biggest satisfaction to Kellogg for it represented better than any other New Deal measure the hope for democratic planning. Federal aid to relief, public works programs, labor's rights—these were essential, but they were more palliative than positively constructive. But in the TVA the engineer and the public administrator could form a partnership for progress; by democratic processes out in the grass roots men working together could control their own destinies through cooperative efforts; through the instrumentality of an autonomous regional authority the good earth could be conserved by flood control, soil conservation, and reforestation; through the availability of cheap electric power the burden of household tasks would be lessened and light industry attracted into a depressed area. In the series the *Graphic* ran on the TVA in 1934, Arthur E. Morgan touched the point so dear to Kellogg's heart: the TVA substituted "order, design and forethought" for "haphazard, unplanned and unintegrated social and industrial development."[31] Democratic social planning, social invention, the engineering of society—these promised, for Kellogg, the highest social good, and the TVA seemed to embody them all.

Of planning in the NRA Kellogg was not quite so sure. The codes prohibited the employment of child labor and promised recognition of the right of labor to organize and bargain collectively through agents of their own choosing, and they brought some order where chaos had reigned; but it did seem that the old restrictive trade associations were given too much power, and the public, that is the consumer, was not represented effectively in the councils at all. When in the late summer of 1933 the administration permitted company unions to satisfy the requirements of Section 7a, he was further disappointed. Not many of these reservations found their way onto the pages of the *Survey,* but when the NRA was killed there were no lamentations from the journal.[32]

The honeymoon between the *Survey* and the New Deal lasted for a year and more, but already by the spring of 1934, Kellogg's misgivings led him to join with other notable welfare leaders critical of certain tendencies in the Roosevelt policies and critical particularly of what seemed to them serious omissions in its over-all programs.

Exactly at this juncture events in his private life preoccupied his attention. In June of 1934, after twenty-five years of marriage, he and his wife Marion were divorced. A month later his brother died suddenly of a heart attack, leaving a hole in Paul's life and in the *Survey* neither of which could ever be filled. Arthur's untimely death, in turn, required a major overhauling of the *Survey* staff and of its entire operation. At age fifty-five Paul Kellogg faced an entirely new chapter in his life.

{IX}

Years of Crisis

FROM the beginning most of Paul's energies had been consumed by the *Survey*; he had worked late and brought his work home with him. Even during the summer, Paul carried his office responsibilities along with him to the camp on Lake Memphremagog where he spent two months with his family. It was only during the second month which he took as vacation that he was able to take part in family activities without distraction. The success of the *Survey* was his persisting passion.

On extended professional trips, in part because of a restricted family budget, Paul traveled alone. There was, for instance, a journey through England, France, and Germany in the summer of 1928 while he was in Europe for the International Conference of Social Work. In Paris he went to a café "where nude girls walk about your table. . . . One of them had an intelligence that would have won her honors had she a chance at college and another . . . was as beautiful as any woman at the conference. She was earning she said ten times what she had earned in a shop." So he wrote to his secretary back home in New York as though he were reporting an event for the *Survey*. "Most of them left me cold but these two made me mad," he concluded in the best style of a progressive of social conscience.[1] In the summer of 1930 after leading a seminar for the Committee on Cultural Relations with Latin America, meeting in Mexico City, he seized the opportunity to travel the back country in the company of Frank Tannenbaum, a contributor to the *Survey*, where he saw with excitement the rural education program of the Mexican government which was seeking to make village schools centers for social change in the countryside.

Circumstances and Paul's professional preoccupations led gradually to a drifting apart of Paul and Marion. Following a trip to Mexico in June of 1934, where a divorce had been secured, Paul sailed out of New Orleans for Havana, Cuba, where he joined a special commission of the Foreign Policy Association investigating Cuban-American relations. The trip was designed to be a much-needed break from family and office troubles. It was on the high seas while returning to New York, after several relaxing if busy weeks in Cuba, that he learned of Arthur's death.

Arthur's death "pretty much knocked my world to pieces," Paul confided to a close friend.[2] More than two years later, to the board, confessing how terribly difficult it was to function without Arthur's support, Paul said that Arthur had been "the hub of our staff operation, I the rim; and we have yet to make good his genius for integrating and inspiriting the round of our work."[3] All the staff members suffered, with Paul, a sense of irrevocable loss. "Without him we are just not as good as we thought we were," wrote Gertrude Springer, the chief of the *Midmonthly*. "He complemented every one of us without our knowing it."[4]

Paul, a genuinely warm and compassionate person, who was generous to his friends, had about him a certain natural grace of manner. He could "talk the birds out of the trees," one who knew him well later commented, adding a bit ruefully: ". . . when he wished to." He quickly set others at ease, whether they were young stenographers, social workers, laborers, or prime ministers, but he never talked much about himself—it was the other person's story he was interested in hearing and having told. In letters to intimate friends and to family, he wrote of what was happening about him, the interesting persons he met, the exciting ideas he heard, the places he saw—only rarely did he write a sentence about himself, his longings, his anxieties, his joys. In part this quality came from the reporter's habit of writing about persons and events external to himself, and in part perhaps from his admiration of his mother's talent for drawing people out. It seems likely that if he could ever unburden himself it was only to Arthur, and that it was Arthur alone who really knew and understood Paul. With Arthur's death, Paul had no other man to whom he could turn to share his joys and his sorrows or to talk out his anxieties.

Much of this sense of utter loss was redeemed in his second marriage, in 1935, to Helen Hall, a woman of charm and substance, thirteen years his junior, whom Paul had met at a settlement conference some years before and with whom he had come to share a friendship based on both mutual social interests and personal compatibility. Miss Hall (as she continued to be known after her marriage to Paul) was one of the second generation of settlement house leaders who showed that same flare and compassion, intelligence, quick wit, and vitality which had been the mark of Jane Addams, Lillian Wald, Mary McDowell, and so many others; like them she was both a patrician and a democrat. A career woman, successor to Lillian Wald at Henry Street, utterly independent in spirit, Helen Hall was a loving wife in the twenty-three years they shared before his death. A close friend of the Kelloggs observed of their marriage, many years later, that however close Paul and Helen became—and it was a relationship marked by intense intimacy, shared interests, and fierce loyalty on both sides—Paul remained "married" to the *Survey*. It was always a *menage à trois,* he concluded. A *menage à quatre* might be closer to the truth, for Helen was as devoted to her work as Paul to his. The *Survey* and the Henry Street Settlement were both demanding and jealous commitments—but that was part of the strength of the marriage: each partner had a consuming career commitment, each respected the professional rights of the other.

With Helen, Paul found new ease and comfort and joy. She was a lively, tender, and thoughtful companion; the skill with which she presided at Henry Street, the affection the neighbors had for her, and her influence in civic affairs were all sources of pride to him. With Helen he learned to have a good time. Her spontaneous sense of humor, Paul once confided, was a "good counter" to his own "sober sides."[5] Life at Henry Street proved a counter to Paul's absorption with *Survey* affairs. After his remarriage he was no less the devoted editor in chief, but he no longer needed to be as compulsive in his attention to the journal as he had been for a quarter century. For the first time he was able really to shake free of his (sometimes oppressive) burden of responsibility.

The good fortune of this fulfilling relationship so late in life compensated to a substantial degree for Arthur's loss. At the *Survey* no such compensation was to be found. Whatever title he had carried—associate editor, business manager, managing editor—it was Arthur who saw that the *Survey* got published on schedule. When Paul was out of the office, which he was a great deal of the time, his home office responsibilities were carried unobtrusively, by Arthur. Arthur bought the newsprint, hassled with creditors, negotiated with printers, laid out the pages, cajoled disgruntled staff members, smoothed the ruffled feelings of sensitive contributors.

Arthur was a no-nonsense kind of person, the least sentimental of souls, impatient chiefly with anything shoddy, but accepting of human foibles. Sitting for official portraits, Paul could look solemnly thoughtful or philosophical and even dreamy (eyes fixed on the middle distance); Arthur's photographs almost invariably showed him smiling. When the two brothers had to learn late in life how to drive a car, it was Arthur who advised and taught Paul, but the kid brother remained an absent-minded and awkward driver, easily distracted from street or highway and surrounding traffic; Arthur drove skillfully and with a certain gay élan, even under the worst of conditions. (On one auto trip he wrote to Paul of the trouble he was having with his old Model T which, when he throttled down for a stop, emitted "a series of obscene little plops, like gentle farts, that were hailed with delight by any of the younger generation of males who happened to be around when I drew up at a hotel or gas station.")[6]

Leon Whipple, professor of journalism at New York University and editor for many years of the book review section of the *Survey,* came to know Arthur well. On weekend expeditions and vacation trips he and his wife Katherine were constant companions of Arthur and Arthur's second wife, Florence. (After twenty-three years the marriage of Arthur and Augusta Kellogg had gone on the rocks; they were divorced following several years' separation, and Arthur had later married Mrs. Florence Loeb Fleisher, who had been divorced from her first husband. A vivacious and talented young woman, Florence was art editor for the *Graphic,* a position she retained after her marriage.) Whipple summed up Arthur's quality: "He was no 'joiner' but having joined the human race, he worked for the good of the order, with pungent comments on most of the ritual." He enjoyed camping, tramping, canoeing, and loved "the earthy and salty people who live outdoors." He had an "everlasting zest for life," but to this enthusiasm "was mated a hard cool sense of reality and of the sadness of life. But for them the decent reticence. Then the quick flash of humor . . . and on down the road."[7]

Quiet and modest in manner, Arthur was a sound reporter but stuck to managing the journals, for if he had not, no one else would have. He was chief of staff, and his death "left empty the desk across which passed all manuscripts for the two magazines in every state of acceptance, editing, illustration, lay-out and proof-reading."[8]

Ten years before his death, Arthur had written out instructions for his survivors. He wished to be cremated, the ashes sprinkled somewhere "on the surface of the earth, preferably under a tree. . . . And if anyone should propose a memorial meeting I feel sure I should come back to life and break up the meeting."[9] The wishes were honored: Florence, Paul, and Pat (who had been with his Uncle Arthur the night he died) sprinkled his ashes beneath his favorite willow tree at his weekend retreat up the Hudson. For Paul the task, then, was trying to fill the vacant place in his own life and the vacuum in the *Survey* which had been for so many years their life together.

The *Survey*'s finest asset from the mid-twenties on into the late 1930s was an office staff and associate editors who were intelligent, lively, and loyal. Ann Reed Brenner, after joining the staff in 1917, was a regular member, except for a brief leave of absence in 1926, until after the Second World War. Buoyant, emotional, sometimes explosive in personality, she was out of the office seeking large financial contributions a great deal of the time. Of the women on the staff, most of whom felt a deep attachment to Paul, Ann Brenner was probably the most affectionate toward him and the most protective. Florence Loeb Fleisher came on the staff the same year as Ann Brenner and in time became the person chiefly responsible for the art work and the layout of the *Graphic*. Although she inherited, in later life, a good deal of money, she lived simply and unostentatiously, and quietly supported a number of political and social causes. In a staff often volatile and sometimes contentious, hers was a steadying influence. Year after year she upheld high literary and artistic standards on the pages of the journal. Although Ann Brenner and Florence Loeb Kellogg each had her own special sphere of responsibility, they were both generalists as well and picked up different writing and editorial jobs as they needed to be done.

Two other women—Beulah Amidon and Gertrude Springer—carried heavier editorial responsibilities. Daughter of the noted liberal and prairie judge Charles F. Amidon of North Dakota, Beulah came naturally to radical politics. Before joining the *Survey* at age thirty in 1925 she had done publicity work for the Nonpartisan League and for the National Woman's party (and claimed at the time she was being considered by the *Survey* that if she could get along with Alice Paul, chief of the National Woman's party, she could get along with anybody). She had married a man by the name of Ratliff in 1919, borne two children, and by 1925 was on her way to a divorce. Tall and dark-haired, she was quiet in manner but a woman of forceful ideas and strong will. Her beat, from the beginning, covered the fields of industry and education on which subjects she made herself an expert. She wrote in a crisp and crackling style and wielded an editor's blue pencil ruthlessly on the manuscripts of others. Gentle on the surface, although in her later years she became more acerbic and sometimes bitterly sarcastic at staff meetings, she was always direct and straightforward in her letters and her articles. Of all Kellogg's office harem (as some friends teasingly accused him of keeping), Beulah Amidon came over time to be the editor's most caustic critic.

In politics she was, like most members of the *Survey* staff, to the left of the New Deal, but it was a mildly radical position rooted in the agrarian protest of the Middle West, not in the

141

ferment of the urban East. She instinctively hated pretense of any sort and was uncomfortable in the presence of the rich philanthropists who subsidized the *Survey* and kept it going. In 1937, sitting in the Supreme Court chamber listening to the arguments in the labor cases when the constitutional fate of the New Deal hung on the judgment of nine men who held such "ultimate power," she wrote: "I wish some cartoonist would draw the vast new S. C. chamber with the Justices on the bench. It's an incredible scene! Such vast marble splendor—such small gnarled men."[10] She always suspected men and institutions who held great and unaccountable power—philanthropists, industrialists, labor leaders, welfare executives, government officials, Supreme Court justices. She had interviewed them all and had come impartially to distrust them; they all had something to conceal. Frustrated in her attempts to garner simple facts on a crisis in the WPA from either government or labor leaders, she confided in Paul Kellogg: "Tomorrow morning I think I'll follow my old practice—which is to go over to Stuyvesant Square and chat with men standing in line waiting for a job assignment."[11] Most of all she distrusted communism, both foreign and domestic varieties. Unlike many of her associates she never bought the Popular Front line during the 1930s and never could quite persuade herself during the war years that the Soviet Union was a democratic comrade in arms. A staunch civil libertarian, she had been convinced by her experience that Communists had "no regard for civil liberties which they ridicule as 'bourgeois softness' " but "are unfailingly vocal when they feel that a cry of academic freedom and civil liberties is to their own advantage."[12]

Beulah Amidon's innate skepticism never turned to cynicism. She did not believe in the inevitability of progress, but she knew the battle for social progress and social justice was its own justification and threw herself into movements for better schools, medical care for the poor, better working conditions, more wholesome recreation, civil rights and civil liberties as though they really had a chance of success. When she witnessed the failure of Congress, in 1938, to pass the simplest amendments to old-age insurance legislation she despaired that "we are civilized enough in this country to make democracy work."[13]

All these qualities lent a salutary balance to the *Survey* staff. A conscientious mother, she never remarried and her energies and loyalties were consumed by her career on the *Survey*. The journal became her whole life; when it folded, in 1952, so did she; she died six years later.

After Arthur's death it was Beulah Amidon who kept the *Graphic* in hand from month to month; Gertrude Springer did the same for the *Midmonthly*. Like Miss Amidon and the Kelloggs she was a native midwesterner; after graduation from Kansas State University, she worked on several newspapers until the First World War afforded her the opportunity of joining the Red Cross in Italy. That experience converted her to social work and alerted her to the only justification for welfare services— what happened to "the little people at the end of the line of command." "My job took me out into the field," she recalled years later, "and I saw what a struggle it was to reconcile the rules laid down in the Rome office with the conditions prevailing in the little towns and villages. From then on I've never been too at ease with the big brass."[14] After the war she worked for a while for the Bureau of Advice and Information of the New York COS, and then as managing editor of one of the best welfare association house organs, *Better Times,* before joining the *Survey* in the fall of 1930.

For the twelve years she ran the *Midmonthly,* she labored under the handicaps of insufficient budget, too few assistants, and a home life that centered about a hopelessly invalided husband. The *Graphic* could offer its authors an honorarium for the articles they contributed; the *Midmonthly,* Mrs. Springer bemoaned, was unable to recompense its authors "with anything more substantial than appreciation."[15] With no budget for authors, she had to fall back upon cajolery, appeals to social conscience, and good-humored needling. That she came to know all the prominent social work leaders in the country on a first-name basis helped; that she won their profound respect for her skill in interpreting complex technical matters without falling into "popularization" encouraged them to cooperate in every way they could. Still, the job of inveigling busy welfare leaders to send in manuscripts was neither easy nor pleasant. "I know I'm a pest," she once wrote to Grace Abbott, "but it goes with the job. In private life I'm really quite a nice person."[16]

There was one overriding prejudice in her professional life—an abhorrence for abstraction. "I don't think statistics alone tell us much. It's the people behind 'em we're trying to see," she admonished Harry Hopkins.[17] And to Ann Brenner she declared that social work would get along farther "if we talk about people and not about problems and processes."[18] Professional do-gooders who loved people in the abstract when there were millions of human beings in terrible need she dismissed as a "lot of good people" running around "protecting bird-life on a raging battle field."[19]

It was her quick and sympathetic understanding of both the client and the social worker that made the long series of chatty articles she wrote under the name of "Miss Bailey" the most popular feature of the *Midmonthly*. Through the person of "Miss Bailey," who posed as a casework supervisor in public assistance, Mrs. Springer sought to give the kind of down-to-earth practical advice that untrained social workers in the depression so desperately needed: how to handle a drunk or abusive client, how to gather essential family data without offending its members, what to do in the face of emotional outbursts, how to keep the office running smoothly when welfare recipient pickets patrolled the corridors. The columns, which appeared (with but a few breaks) every month from March 1933 until the end of the decade, bubbled with wit. Designed to reach newcomers in relief work and to advise them on human relationships in their day-to-day rounds, the pieces featured one recurring theme above all others—that social workers must hold to their own humanity and must respect absolutely the right of their clients to direct their own lives. Thus, social workers were admonished never to use the granting or withholding of relief as an incentive to impose their own middle-class standards on others. The family's life style was its own business and its moral standards and values were to be accepted and respected unless, of course, they overtly interfered with the purposes of assistance. The sexual and drinking habits of a client family were to be held irrelevant unless, for example, the heavy drinking of a father deprived the children of food or clothing. In eliciting the essential data required by law, the social worker should treat heads of families with courtesy, tact, and consideration, and never seek out information by pumping the children or the neighbors. If a desperately poor mother greeted the social worker with a freshly baked chocolate cake, the hospitality should be accepted graciously even if the extravagance was likely to skew the meager budget for that week. Hard times frayed the steadiest of nerves, and emotional outbursts were therefore to be accepted as part of the expected reaction of men and women down on their luck.

By immediate popular demand "Miss Bailey's" columns were gathered together in a series of pamphlets which sold by the tens of thousands throughout the depression years. Nothing the *Midmonthly* ever did aroused such a favorable response and the pamphlets became the chief required reading in on-the-job training courses for new recruits in public assistance. Everywhere she went, Gertrude Springer wrote back to Arthur Kellogg from the field, "people fall on me with loud screams, and I am called Miss Bailey about as often as anything else."[20] In 1937, the line on public relief having been played out, Mrs. Springer launched a second series which offered practical advice to workers in the newly established social security offices throughout the country.

The *Survey* office was not a solemn place but a certain serious tone did pervade its daily work. Mrs. Springer's light touch often gave a lift to the day, especially after Arthur's gentle wit was gone. Her letters from the field were a delight to the staff when read aloud at teatime. During an expedition to Boston, for example, she wrote to say that her return home had been delayed because "the dam R. C. Bishop and the labor boss" had stalled her off another day. "I've lunched with Bordens and Braytons, driven about with the Historical Society, smoked and told dirty stories with the mayor, the Chamber of Commerce and the newspaper boys, trailed through a mill, visited a public school, boys club and settlement—and I'm good and ready to come home."[21] Or there was the account she wrote back of spending a weekend with two of the most distinguished social workers alive, Edith Abbott and Neva Deardorff, when they were confronted with a family crisis by the cat's delivering three kittens. We had a "case conference on the disposition of the three children," she wrote. "Miss Abbott insisted on placing out, but a pail of water got the lot just the same. Here we had all the hot experts and then did as we pleased. Just like social work!"[22]

To keep her spirits in the face of persisting human need, as the years went by and millions of Americans remained unemployed, and to return home in the evening to be with her husband whose "vigorous, well furnished mind" was going to pieces and whose "strong, disciplined body" was losing its "dignity," were challenges that somehow she survived.[23] When war came to America on 7 December 1941, it was a blow which, taken together with the others, proved too much. The other staff members, her colleagues and friends, welcomed the relief of tension that Pearl Harbor brought, but she could not share in the elation. "I 'did' the other war up to the hilt," she wrote to Edith Abbott several weeks later, "and I have nothing for this one but sorrow, and that doesn't win wars."[24] She resigned and left for the little cottage on Cape Cod that she and her sister had bought as a retreat. "We only get a newspaper if we go to the village for it, and the radio doesn't work very well. Escape? Sure. I knew it first." That to one of her dearest friends in public welfare.[25] And when another friend tried to persuade her that everything would turn out all right, that evil would destroy itself and a better world would emerge from war, Mrs. Springer retorted that she did "not give a very big damn about living in the kind of world this is." She did not belittle others who had found faiths to cling to, but for herself she'd just have to try "to find comfort in raising petunias."[26]

Differences in temperament there were among the *Survey* staff, but a common commitment and a common loyalty to the *Survey* as an institution and personally to Paul and Arthur Kellogg kept them together. They were strong-willed and independent-minded women, the kind of women Paul Kellogg had attracted and surrounded himself with ever since the days on the Pittsburgh Survey in 1907. Ann Reed Brenner, Florence Loeb Kellogg, Beulah Amidon, and Gertrude Springer were crucial to the *Survey*'s success and survival. And there were others—Mary Ross Gannett who assisted in the health department; Loula

Lasker of the wealthy New York family, who lived in a penthouse in an exclusive residential hotel but put in a regular workday like everyone else, and who devoted her time especially to the field of housing reform; Mollie Condon, who managed the circulation department; Martha Hohmann, whose tenure dated from 1910 and who kept the financial records; Hannah Gallagher, a dependable, sweet Irish girl, who came on the staff as a stenographer and clerk in 1913 and was the one to lock the door on the *Survey*'s last day in April 1952; and Janet Sabloff, Paul Kellogg's personal secretary from 1925 to 1952, a slight, intense, shrewd Russian-born woman who had been caught up in Jewish Socialist circles as a young girl in New York.

Contributing editors in these years included Leon Whipple, who edited the book section of the *Survey* from 1924 to 1934, after which time he still took on occasional assignments. "Whip," as he was known, was an expert on the relation of civil liberties to the working press, and he was a source of sound advice on any number of editorial issues. Michael M. Davis, a sociologist by academic training, had made himself one of the leading experts in the field of medical economics and it was on the subject of provision, distribution, and costs of health care that he contributed to the *Survey*. John Palmer Gavit, who began his journalistic career in the 1890s as editor of *The Commons,* held reporting and editing jobs on a number of different newspapers at the same time that he wrote a monthly column, "Through Neighbors' Doorways." Gavit, like Whipple and Davis, was only part-time and sometime in his commitment, but his advice on general editorial matters, although frequently erratic and opinionated, often contained useful nuggets of counsel. Harry Moak, a summer neighbor of the Kelloggs in Quebec, took intense pride in his craft as printer and his advice on such technical matters as type, layout, and printing techniques was regularly solicited.

These were the assets the *Survey* enjoyed in the crisis it confronted in the mid-years of the depression. Whatever troubles it had to surmount—and there were problems in abundance—it had on its side a loyal, experienced, and talented staff. It would need whatever strengths it could claim.

{X}

The *Survey* and the New Deal, 1935–41

ARTHUR'S death in July 1934 precipitated a crisis that had been on its way for several years. The prosperous years of the 1920s had carried the *Survey* into the depression with a reserve of working capital and good will but by 1931-32 that momentum began to falter. Circulation gradually began to fall off as social workers and their allies, who needed the *Survey*'s services even more now that hard times had exacerbated social problems, could not afford the modest fee. Many persons of substantial means, who had given generously during the years of prosperity, found themselves unable to continue their gifts not only because their own financial positions had been rendered precarious by the stock market panic but also because there were now so many other worthy demands competing with the *Survey*'s claim for support. The *Survey* always operated with a high rate of fixed costs and always along the margin of survival, so making internal economies proved difficult.

In 1932 the *Survey* retained a management consultant to advise the editors on what they might do to overcome these obstacles, but the reports that John Hanrahan turned in, however accurate they were in analysis, offered little that was helpful by way of practical counsel. Noting that "very few publications last more than two generations" in any case, he urged that the

Graphic and the *Midmonthly* be made even more autonomous of each other than they were and that each be allowed to find its own natural market. He warned that to invest money in a sales campaign would bring in few subscriptions that would stick into a second year of renewal; better, he suggested, to invest money in turning out improved journals and thus attract a larger readership. The journals were, in fact, cut further apart administratively at this time, but lacking capital to pour into the editorial budget there was little that could be done to improve quality.[1]

Friends and patrons offered kindly advice. The "tired social worker" just couldn't wade through all the facts the *Midmonthly* threw at him, one suggested. Another reported that his students felt the *Mid* was too sentimental and "often sicklied o'er with the Christian Science smile and the Y.M.C.A. glad hand"; it lacked "reserve" and "austerity" and "cautious understatement"; it lacked real humor and ran "consistently bad pictures." A friend from the *Nation* volunteered that the *Graphic*'s cover was dull, and too many of its articles "heavy, laborious . . . and too academic in tone." A faithful reader (and frustrated contributor) complained that the *Survey* never printed anything about "just average middle-class people. So far as I know, not one of them has ever defiled your pages," although there were enough of "the soviets, the strikers, the sharecroppers, etc. etc." A newspaperman suggested that no one liked to read long articles any more; the *Survey*, it followed, would do better if it read more like the *Reader's Digest*. A board member observed that there hung about the *Survey* "a certain dead weight. It comes as a symbol of duty rather than a temptation to excitement."[2] But these free-will criticisms provided no more helpful specifics for change than Hanrahan's prescriptions.

Leon Whipple offered in June 1935 an extended analysis which carried weight both because of his expertise in the field of journalism and because he knew the *Survey* so intimately from the inside. Its troubles were more philosophical than technical, he claimed. It saw the world from the point of view of an old "democratic-scientific-humanitarian liberalism" which was no longer relevant to an age of mounting crisis. The *Survey* had gone on living in a "fool's paradise, offering stop-gap remedies and sops under a dying capitalism, playing with case-work techniques when what is needed is the re-creation of society." It had been concerned with relief, well and good, but what "of organizing security in a surplus economy . . . what of health care in a profit-seeking economy"? The *Survey* had "been interested in serving by factual research investigation of remedies for specific evils; now the challenge is to remedy root evils. I do not see how we can speak clearly on housing, taxes, relief, and above all on social planning unless we give some notion of what kind of state and economic system we think will make progress in these fields possible." Furthermore, he continued, other journals had jumped into fields of social investigation that once the *Survey* had all to itself. In the twenties and in the early thirties, the *Survey* had scooped all other journals on medical care, social planning, industrial disorder, and unemployment; but lately it had been "caught in the net of the immediate and the seemingly urgent." It had failed to see the true significance of the NRA; it had neglected to explore the constitutional and social implications in the assumption of a general police power by the federal government.

As for the administrative tangle into which the *Survey* had fallen, especially since Arthur's death, Paul would have to redefine his responsibility. In Whipple's opinion the editor was trying to play entirely too many roles—he was chiefly responsible for raising money, he shaped the over-all policies of both journals, he directed the details of editing and publication, he represented the *Survey* to the public. No one man could do all those jobs well. Kellogg should think of cutting back to what had always been his most creative act—keeping "a fresh stream of exciting and vital articles coming forth monthly"; there should be "no other drains on his energy and time." The immediately pressing need, then, was to find an able managing editor and to delegate to that person clear power and responsibility.[3]

Whipple's extended critique, clearly from a position to the political left of that occupied by Kellogg, Amidon, and Springer, provided shrewd analysis and sound counsel. In 1933 and 1934 the journals had fallen into the habit of accepting the New Deal pretty much at face value, a charge that was particularly true of the *Graphic*. A disproportionate amount of space had been turned over to description and praise of the Roosevelt relief programs, often to the neglect of other critical matters. The *Graphic* invited members of the administration to use its columns, or it printed essays from authors representative essentially of the New Deal position. The *Midmonthly* in these years undoubtedly played out its traditional role more effectively than did the *Graphic*. When compared with the *New Republic* or the *Nation* in the same years, the *Graphic* appears relatively stodgy, where in its near-recent past it had been lively, critical, and a jump ahead of social and economic events. As Leon Whipple noted a year later: "The middle of the road is certainly where the load is hauled, but it's a dull place."[4]

No one knew better than Paul Kellogg himself how very accurate Whipple's criticisms of editorial administration were. He was spread too thin. He had to administer the budget, write financial appeal letters, solicit large donations, coordinate the staff, work with the board, solicit manuscripts, edit, write, and rewrite. Clearly it was too much, and his first executive priority throughout 1934 and 1935 was to find someone to take over as managing editor, someone who could pick up some of the responsibilities that had fallen on his desk with Arthur's death. And it had better be someone with high diplomatic skills, John Palmer Gavit warned Kellogg, for "to keep a staff, mostly of women each characterized by real genius and the temperamental qualities that go with it, cheerful and cooperating with him and with each other, is no small job."[5]

Victor Weybright, who had been hired as managing editor before Gavit had offered his advice, was such a person, and just the kind of man Kellogg loved—capable of sustained intelligent effort but with a certain gaiety about him. Legend has it that Kellogg first met Weybright in the 1920s as the young man was escorting a troop of Gypsies into Hull House. If the story is true (and it is surely plausible), Kellogg must have welcomed the young Weybright as a soul companion even then, and when the *Graphic* assembled a special issue devoted to the Gypsies, in October 1927, Weybright's was one of the most lively and astute of contributions. He had been born of patrician stock in Mary-

land, and with a happy and secure childhood behind him he
attended the Wharton School of Business. He was too untram-
meled to consider a career in business, however, and spent
several apprenticeship years, instead, at Hull House before becoming managing editor of the magazine *Adventure* and a free-
lance contributor to other popular journals. It was during his
free-lancing days that he wrote a highly readable biography of
Francis Scott Key.[6]

His letter of application to Kellogg was fresh, breezy, and self-
knowing: "My experience has been versatile; my industry is (in
all modesty) great; my range of interests wide; and my point of
view liberal."[7] That he knew next to nothing about social work
or social welfare really didn't matter; his heart was in the right
place, and after all, of the entire staff only Gertrude Springer had
experience in social service; all the rest were out of journalism.
He knew how to write, he had boundless energy, he had a quick
instinct for a good story, and what he needed to know about
welfare he could learn as he went along, as every good reporter
must. Even Gertrude Springer applauded his selection: "He is
young and enthusiastic, knows the technical aspects of the job
but not our subject field," she cheered. "He is Paul's pick and
Paul likes him, as we all do."[8] Dark-haired, with snapping eyes
and the ruddy complexion of one who lived in the out-of-doors,
Weybright had a brisk and candid manner which endeared him
to the staff; he brought a breath of vitality, a sense of engagement with the world that the *Survey* so desperately needed at
that moment. He was quickly at home with the *Survey,* the causes
it espoused, the friends it enjoyed. As managing editor of the
Graphic he had entry into all the circles of government, industry,
and labor which were on the move and on the make in those
years. He made friends quickly and found not so much satisfaction as real joy in being in the midst of what he called "a free
masonry of interest" that had sprung up "among progressive
folks, often strangers, in the United States in the past ten years."
It was good, he wrote in 1939 to Richard Neuberger, then a
young Oregon newsman and budding politician and a person
who shared many of Weybright's enthusiasms, "to feel on the
inside of such a crowd."[9]

The *Survey* and the New Deal, 1935–41

Many friends, on the staff and on the board, undoubtedly looked on Weybright as the logical successor to Kellogg when the time should come for his retirement. Perhaps Paul Kellogg did so himself, for he delegated a great deal of responsibility to the younger man during the seven years Victor worked as his associate. When he went off to the wars in 1942 as a member of Wild Bill Donovan's Office of Coordinator of Information attached to the American Embassy staff in London, no successor was ever named, even though Weybright had made it clear that he didn't intend to return to the *Survey* when the war was over. Whether he could ever have become the "heir apparent" and taken over as editor of the *Survey* empire in his own right is a question for speculation; that he helped to make the *Graphic* a more vital, relevant, and critical journal in the years he managed it is beyond dispute.

Before Victor Weybright joined the *Graphic* staff, Paul Kellogg had counseled the Roosevelt administration on its social insurance proposals and had come out with his enthusiasm for the New Deal subdued. It was fitting that Kellogg should have been asked to serve on the Advisory Council on Economic Security which Frances Perkins had appointed in October 1934 to advise the Committee on Economic Security, the small group of cabinet officers Roosevelt had asked to draw up recommendations on social insurance which he could then submit to Congress. It was fitting because the pages of the *Survey* had followed the social insurance story for as many years as Kellogg had been attached to it and in no other journals had the coverage been so regular, so persistent, and so deep. All the great names in the pioneer social insurance movements found their best outlet in the *Survey*—Abraham Epstein, Isaac Rubinow, Paul Douglas, William Leiserson, Michael M. Davis, and Frances Perkins herself.

Paul Kellogg had been one of the prime movers, together with other prominent social work and reform leaders, of an open letter to President Roosevelt (carried to him in late April 1934) which petitioned FDR to move far more rapidly on a whole range of labor and welfare legislation than the administration had found expedient down to that time. The preamble to their four-page printed statement cited the need for the nation to move at once toward a more equitable distribution of national income. "We believe that higher wages, higher purchasing power, higher living standards, can, short of government dictation, come only through the bargaining power of labor so well organized that it has an effective voice in determining working conditions." The NRA had not worked to that end, the ad hoc committee maintained, and concluded that an independent federal labor board must be created to guarantee the rights of labor. From that declaration the letter went on to list some of the conditions the committee felt essential to the formulation of a new program within the New Deal: the upgrading of minimum wages in NRA codes; consumers' protection in the NRA; an orderly system of unemployment relief which looked beyond emergency measures to long-range planning; a federal housing authority with power to grant low-interest loans over long amortization periods; a larger degree of "planning and cooperative control" in basic industries (coal, oil, electric power, transportation, communications); progressive income and inheritance taxes; and a national system of unemployment compensation, old-age pensions, and sickness insurance.

Paul Kellogg served as secretary of the drafting committee and replied to several critics of the letter that he had been "responsible for the thread on which the statement was strung rather than the beads." He himself, he privately told several correspondents, did not believe in the details of every specific item but he did stand by the statement as a whole because it provided the outline for constructive action to fill a vacuum in national social policy.[10]

Kellogg's leadership in establishing the committee and being the chief author of its letter marked a shift of position to one critical of the New Deal, less for any wrongdoing than for its sins of omission. Roosevelt had gotten the nation on its feet and going again, but his programs had not gone far enough fast enough to meet the drastic challenges of the times, nor had he fully utilized the unique opportunity which had been his, as Kellogg judged it, in 1933 and 1934 to create orderly procedures for the rational planning of society; he had deferred too often to politics, ignored too frequently the dictates of planning and the expert advice of the planners. Of all the pressures on Roosevelt to move in the directions outlined in the letter, this particular petition may have had relatively little impact, but it provided evidence of discontent among welfare and reform leaders of some note, and it was one factor among many others that made it logical for Kellogg to be appointed to the Advisory Council on Economic Security.

Kellogg came on the council with more than two decades of experience in the social security field to his credit. He had helped to write the clauses on social insurance that became part of the Progressive platform in 1912; in the 1920s not only had he opened the pages of the *Survey* to the subject, but he had often spoken publicly at conference and convention in support of America's joining all other industrial nations in providing some form of security. Generally he had sided with those proponents of unemployment insurance who wanted premiums related to the employment record of a given industry (not a particular firm) in the expectation that such a sliding scale would act as an incentive to industry to regularize and stabilize employment just as workmen's compensation, presumably, had acted as an incentive to industry to accelerate accident prevention programs. Generally he had believed that workers should contribute, along with the employers and the public, to unemployment reserve funds in order that the worker could feel that he had an investment in the program and that he was entitled to compensation as of right. But Kellogg had always been a pragmatist, and on none of these points was his mind irrevocably set.

Events in the shaping of what came to be the administration's proposal for social security legislation moved fast in the autumn of 1934 and the winter of 1935, and the pressure was on within the administration to get a recommendation from the Committee on Economic Security early in 1935 in order that Congress might be able to begin its own deliberations and act before the session had ended. It was probably not conceived that the Advisory Council, to which representatives of management, labor, and the public had been appointed, was to serve much of a function beyond that of broadening the political support the president could manipulate to his own advantage when the time came.

Paul U. Kellogg and the *Survey*

But Kellogg and several others had their own opinion of the council's function, and their own expectation of what the president was prepared to support. Kellogg had been present at the 27 April 1934 meeting in the White House when the ad hoc committee's letter had been presented to Roosevelt personally. "At one point," Kellogg wrote to Frances Perkins of that meeting, FDR "told us of his project of a blanket scheme of social insurance from the cradle to the grave; and we came away feeling that history might be repeating itself; and that just as Lloyd George put over the social insurances in England a quarter of a century ago, so F.D.R., with his personal appeal to the country, with his dramatization of security as a national asset, might put such a rounded scheme through the next Congress, and do in a year what might otherwise take a generation."[11] Among other hopes, Kellogg expected any national comprehensive security scheme to include health insurance which was, in his mind, of equal importance to coverage against the hazards of unemployment and old age.

Kellogg agreed to join the Advisory Council (as did his wife-to-be, Helen Hall), in the conviction that it was *advice* the Committee on Economic Security wished and not some kind of ambiguous support for what the committee itself might deem expedient. The council was chaired by Frank P. Graham, president of the University of North Carolina. Kellogg attended thirteen full days of hearings in November and early December 1934, and before many sessions had passed had begun to criticize several phases of the outline the council had been given to study. He found, for example, that the benefit terms under unemployment insurance toward which the committee was tending were thoroughly inadequate. To insist on a four-week waiting period before benefits could be claimed, and to limit the weeks of coverage to fifteen, just wouldn't do, in his opinion. He objected as well to the preliminary provision of a 3 percent payroll tax on employers alone on the ground that it would not provide an adequate reserve base out of which benefits could be paid. He also objected strenuously to the proposed administrative mechanism for implementing the unemployment insurance provisions of social security because it gave (as he saw it) entirely too much power to the several states; rather than a cooperative relationship that reserved to the states a major role in setting standards, Kellogg preferred a procedure through which the federal government could effectively establish national standards to which all states would have to adhere. To the embarrassment of Frances Perkins, and other administration spokesmen on social security, Kellogg drafted a minority supplementary statement setting forth these reservations which was also signed by Frank Graham, Helen Hall, Henry Ohl, and William Green. It was known on the Advisory Council that three other labor representatives agreed essentially with the Kellogg statement, but they did not add their signatures, primarily for fear the reservations might be taken as opposition to the whole proposal for social insurance.

In his subsequent testimony before the Senate committee considering the administration bill, Kellogg took publicly the position he had held on the council even though E. E. Witte, executive director of the Advisory Council and Frances Perkins's chief adviser on all substantive matters, had warned that administration forces would have a difficult time keeping the proposed standards from being diluted even further by unfavorable congressional action. To the annual meeting of Survey Associates in early February 1935, Kellogg praised Roosevelt for having broken with precedent by assuming a national responsibility toward unemployment, but repeated his criticism of the specific clauses on benefits and administration. "We are told that it is good sense to begin in a small way," he said, "but it is better sense to begin in a right way."[12] He pleaded for a 2 percent contribution from general federal revenue funds, to be added to the 3 percent payroll tax on employers, as a just way to let society share in underwriting a system from which the whole nation would benefit and as an effective way to increase reserve funds so that benefits could be expanded.

Kellogg was disappointed on many scores; he particularly resented the cavalier brush-off given to health insurance, which was not even discussed. But when the final bill was passed he threw his support behind it and called for the passage of enabling legislation in all the states, explaining that the questions he had raised "had to do with strengthening the bill, not with scuttling it."[13] In subsequent years, Kellogg and the *Survey* actively supported every proposed amendment which would strengthen the act, but at the time it seemed to him that the administration had been following the old tradition in social reform of getting "the nose of the camel under the tent," when what was required rather were "reverse tactics"—to drive hard at once for a strong law while interest was keen and the payment of benefits three years away.[14]

Forces combined in mid-decade to move Paul Kellogg and the *Survey* to the political and social left. First there was the disenchantment with the haphazard administration of relief which seemed, by 1934, to promise no long-run rational federal planning; then came Kellogg's unhappy experience on the Advisory Council on Economic Security. The failure of NRA to protect the consumer and truly to encourage labor unionization had been a sticking point from the beginning. The *Survey* did not take a partisan position in either 1936 or 1940, but Kellogg himself voted for Roosevelt both times. Together with many progressives Kellogg hoped that the Democratic party might be made a more liberal coalition, and he voted for FDR in 1936 rather than for any third-party candidate because, as he explained to Bruce Bliven of the *New Republic*, "the election may be close and every vote will count."[15] He backed Herbert Lehman over Norman Thomas for governor of New York in 1938, and Harry Laidler, of the League for Industrial Democracy, for the City Council in 1939 (when he won) and again in 1941 (when he lost reelection). In 1940 it was Roosevelt again (anxiety over the future of the TVA in Willkie's hands being one important factor), and his public endorsement was made through the national Committee of Independents for Re-election of Roosevelt, chaired by Senator Norris and Mayor LaGuardia. In 1944 the choice was easy—Roosevelt, win the war and win the peace. Landon, Willkie, and Dewey offered no alternative for an old progressive, but Kellogg's votes those years were cast without the enthusiasm he had felt in 1912 for Theodore Roosevelt and in 1924 for LaFollette.

Even before Arthur's death many staff members had been discontented with what seemed to them the failure of the *Survey* to keep pace with rapidly changing developments, and after his death the search for a new managing editor sharpened the self-examination and self-criticism among the staff and among some board members. Finally, it should be noted, there came in 1934 a so-called rank-and-file movement among the younger and more radical men and women who had been attracted into social service by the demands of the depression; they complained of how stodgy the *Survey* had become and how uncritically it supported the New Deal.

Mary Van Kleeck, who set the fires of radicalism among social workers ablaze with her stirring attack on the shortcomings of the New Deal at the May 1934 convention of the National Conference of Social Work, had written a stinging rebuke to Kellogg in early March. The *Survey* had obviously been persuaded that the New Deal marked a severe break with the past, she charged, when in fact it offered mild palliatives designed to keep the old system going. The *Survey,* she said, would be untrue to its heritage if it became "a supporter of the federal government rather than a reporter for the people—among whom the workers are the vast majority." Kellogg replied that the *Survey* held "open house" to those who promoted change—and to their critics—and when such a friend as Miss Van Kleeck tried "to nail us to the mast for espousing the New Deal as an American panacea," it was time indeed to take stock. Confessing that he felt "deskbound," and wanted to share the sense of her feelings, he concluded with a caveat of his own: "Mary, Mary . . . you seem so cocksure that you've got Truth by the tail, that you make me not only mistrust myself a lot—but you too."[16] The *Survey*'s coverage of the stormy Kansas City Conference of Social Work provided a balance between Miss Van Kleeck and those who wished to carry organized social work into a radical camp, on the one hand, and their critics on the other, most notably William Hodson, commissioner of welfare in New York City, who replied directly to the radicals at the convention with a defense of the New Deal as the best way to salvage what was good from the past and achieve orderly progress in the future. Kellogg, at that time, stood closer to Hodson than to Van Kleeck and so did the *Survey,* but Kellogg's role in petitioning Roosevelt to move farther and faster down the road of social reconstruction, and his subsequent experience with the social insurance hassle, inclined him to lean further to the left. When the rank-and-file movement in April 1934 established a journal of its own, *Social Work Today,* edited by Jacob Fisher of the Bureau of Jewish Social Research and guided by such big names in social work as Gordon Hamilton, Eduard C. Lindeman, Ira Reid, Roger Baldwin, and Mary Van Kleeck, the *Survey* faced competition on the left to which it remained sensitive throughout the rest of the decade until the radical journal folded in the early years of the Second World War.

Both the *Graphic* and the *Midmonthly* became more independent and lively once again from 1935 to the end of the decade. They sought to get out of the routine ruts into which they had fallen and to put a surprise into every number. With insufficient staff and insufficient budget, the journals, as Weybright put it, had become "gleaners instead of harvesters," so the staff tried to get out into the field again and report firsthand the major developments in welfare.[17] Weybright reminded the board and the staff that "we are not getting out a monthly report on housing, labor, health, government, conservation, etc.—but a challenging publication devoted to the things which good minds want to know about," and there did follow a kind of freshness of approach and subject, with more and briefer articles in each number, and fewer articles that sounded as though they were slightly revised versions of speeches and papers delivered before social work conventions.[18] Luncheon meetings at which invited visitors opened up new issues with members of the staff and provided them with background information for their own work became part of the regular office routine again. Under Kellogg's gentle and permissive but firm direction the staff's weekly meetings became, as Weybright recalled them, "slap dash seminars in social science," with Paul listening respectfully to every point of view, and prodding the discussion by searching questions, at the end of which the staff knew better the week's and the quarter's plans. That strong personalities often clashed did not detract from the usefulness of the meetings in defining the direction the *Survey* would take.

The two journals continued to serve their long-held function of keeping their constituencies well informed on the details of all developments in welfare, both public and private. As social security came into existence both the *Graphic* and the *Midmonthly*, but the latter journal particularly, carried many inches of print explaining exactly how the new programs were being implemented. Social workers, bedeviled by complicated instructions from Washington on old-age pensions and aid to dependent children, aid to the blind and the handicapped, must have been relieved to have the guidance that the *Midmonthly* offered in simple, direct, functional prose. Social security, for example, had immediate impact upon traditional means of caring for the dependent aged out of county funds, and the *Survey* was quick to point out the need for effective regulation of private boarding houses as the old-fashioned county poorhouses disappeared.

As it had in the teens and the twenties, the *Survey* covered in depth labor-management relations, unionization, strikes, and the relevance of new laws—the Wagner Labor Relations Act of 1935, the Fair Labor Standards Act of 1938—to the social scene. It followed what it came to know as the "muddle" of relief as year followed year without a clarification of complex bureaucratic rulings that often worked at cross-purposes with the execution of efficient and humane programs. As early as 1934 the *Survey* had called for the substitution of carefully planned long-range programs for the scattering of emergency measures, but it could report little effective progress in Washington, and when the recession of 1937-38 struck, the *Survey* found the nation little better prepared to meet the needs of the unemployed, still measured in the millions, than it had been in 1933 or 1934.

It was this persistence of widespread unemployment, year after year, that discouraged the *Survey* more than any other social problem. Congress failed to appropriate funds sufficient to cover the minimum needs of the millions of families for whom unemployment was still the basic fact of life and had been for six, seven, eight years of hard times. Attempts by the WPA to distinguish between employable and unemployable workers without jobs had proved to be a fiasco, as the *Survey* reported it, and although much that was good was being accomplished, the failure to lay long-range plans wreaked havoc with an orderly evolution of sound policies. The *Survey* documented the relative lack of concern for sharecroppers and migratory workers in the over-all development of New Deal agricultural policy, although it did, of course, carry stories on Farm Security Administration camps for drifting rural workers. Without immediate and thorough steps to overhaul all its relief and public works projects, an article in the *Graphic,* April 1936, warned, the national economy would be due for another drastic slump in 1937. The economic loss to the nation lay not in the accumulation of a public debt, which was after all a debt that the citizens owed to themselves, but in goods and services not produced; yet in the face of this obvious fact government policy continued to be characterized by "delay, confusion and waste."[19] And in the 1939 National Conference of Social Work, Kellogg (who was the organization's president that year) found a general mood of "tiredness and disillusionment" among social workers; a full decade of hard times had passed and organized social workers still had no means for effectively making known their views on public assistance, wages and hours, social insurance, and health. Both social work and public policy, it seemed, were stalled.[20]

The *Survey* did far more, these years, than play the role of friendly (though sometimes carping) critic of national policy. It highlighted, for example, the persisting scandal of the county jail system with its ill-treatment of inmates, its neglect of medical care, and its indiscriminate mixing of hardened repeaters and first offenders.[21] More than any other journal it publicized at length the persisting inequities that characterized provision of medical services in the nation. In the neglected field of housing the *Survey* provided sound reporting, not in occasional, isolated exposés, but in issue after issue of the two journals. And in 1936 it printed a long article on syphilis, "The Next Great Plague to Go," by Dr. Thomas Parran, surgeon general of the United States, which sold 55,000 copies reprinted by the *Graphic* and another 400,000 reprints circulated by the *Reader's Digest,* which had helped to finance and sponsor the original research and publication.[22]

Perhaps because of the new spirit in the *Survey* beginning

around 1935, perhaps because of the general (if slow) upswing in the economy that came in these years, the circulation of the journals gradually increased until by the decade's end it was back approximately to the level it had enjoyed in 1929: 25,000 regular subscriptions and another 5000 or so sold on the newsstands. This was hardly a magnificent showing, but it did indicate that the *Survey* had a constant, reliable subscription list of readers who remained loyal to the journals because they served a very real need in their professional lives.

Then history began to repeat itself. In the midst of unresolved social problems and uncompleted social reforms, clouds of war gathered. Nazi Germany and Imperial Japan began to move, and the world lurched from crisis to crisis: Manchuria, Ethiopia, Spain, China, Czechoslovakia, Austria, Poland. Once again, as in 1914, 1915, and 1916, the *Survey* was forced to turn its attention reluctantly from the domestic to the foreign scene.

{XI}

Reprise: War
and Reconstruction

THE SURVEY'S was largely a stay-at-home province; domestic reform not foreign adventure had to be its central concern. Yet nothing human was alien to its page, and human suffering abroad provoked the compassion of the journal almost as much as suffering in the native land. Wherever there were people in need— hungry, cold, unsheltered, driven from home by war, tyranny, or famine—there the *Survey* believed it had a mandate to go, observe, and report. When American social workers went abroad during the First World War and after, most often under the auspices of the Red Cross but through many other agencies as well, both secular and sectarian, the *Survey* kept track of their activities, and as the United States was thrust, willy-nilly, into playing the role of a great power the journal's general foreign news coverage increased. Furthermore, there were lessons to be learned for America in the welfare programs of other nations. From the day Paul Kellogg spent with Robert Smillie, Scottish leader of the British coal miner union, at the Nottingham convention in January 1918, the British labor movement was the model against which he measured the social policies of any modern industrial nation: an example of social democracy in action, a popular movement, firmly rooted in workers' power, that promised grass-roots social planning and honored the rights of the individual. So, too, as Kellogg saw it, did the experiments in social democracy which the German nation launched in the years of the Weimar Republic provide evidence which the American people might study to their own benefit.

Kellogg, as we have seen, had been the chief instigator in calling together in the spring of 1918 the informal "Committee on Nothing at All" that formally organized that summer as the League of Free Nations Association, whose mission was to build support among intelligent and concerned citizens for the Wilson ideals of self-determination, collective security, international cooperation, and peace. When the organization changed its name again in 1921 to become simply the Foreign Policy Association, Kellogg remained on its Board of Directors and on its Executive Committee, and for many years was one of its members in most regular attendance. In the mid-1920s, the organization became polarized between those who wished it to be action-oriented, as it had been since the days of its founding, and those who saw its function as research and education, objectives that could be served, as this group saw it, only if the association refrained from taking positions on controversial policy matters. Kellogg found his natural allies among those who preferred action to study, but at meetings of the Executive Committee he argued vehemently for a "rational and constructive" middle course between sterile research and deliberation on the one hand and hectic reactions to foreign policy crises on the other, a centrist position which he defined as "thought-out opportunism."[1] With the passing of time, Kellogg's insistence that research and action were not contradictory but necessarily interrelated functions, with study the intelligent guide to action, began gradually to lose ground, and when the association came to focus essentially on research and information, Kellogg gradually dropped from active participation. His withdrawal may also have signified Kellogg's gradual disengagement from some other outside commitments as he grew older and as the *Survey* came to consume more of his energy.

As for the *Survey*, in addition to printing special articles and news stories on events abroad it had established in 1927 a special Foreign Service Department under the editorship of John Palmer Gavit, who saw the world much as Kellogg did—"a very small place, in which nobody can do or be anything without its having an effect on somebody else. Nay, everybody else." Gavit wrote to Kellogg at that time that he hoped to make the regular feature "informal and personal . . . interesting . . . humanly appealing . . . responsible and accurate." He intended his column to be no regular news summary—readers could find that kind of information in any number of other journals; he would trace, rather, "the struggle of races and individuals toward free self-expression and self-control on the way to unity."[2] How many readers Gavit's department regularly attracted is, of course, impossible to estimate, but if *Survey* readers preferred the style that marked most of its other columns—concise, muscular prose —they must have found Gavit's vagaries difficult to tolerate. Surviving members of the *Survey* staff reported in numerous interviews that of several shortcomings as an editor Kellogg's chief liability was his inability to fire anyone: Arthur knew that it was not a favor either to the staff member or to the journal to keep a person on when he no longer fit; Paul didn't have the heart to let anyone go. The number of years that the *Survey* printed Gavit's discursive ramblings may be a case in point.

In the years between the wars, from the final defeat of the Treaty of Versailles in the United States Senate down to the Nazi-Soviet Pact and the attack upon Poland, the *Survey* held back from embracing editorially one position or another on the controversial issues of foreign policy. It was clear enough that the *Survey* approved control of the international traffic in drugs through the good offices of the League of Nations, that it smiled on movements for national independence everywhere (from Ireland to India to the Philippines), that it prayed for disarmament and the resolution of national differences by peaceful negotiation without resort to force (Locarno and the Kellogg-Briand Pact both received sympathetic accounts), but otherwise it did not publicly take sides.

For Paul Kellogg, private citizen, it was another matter. He tried, unsuccessfully as it turned out, to persuade the Foreign Policy Association to strengthen Secretary of State Stimson's hand during the Far Eastern crisis of 1930-31; he praised Roosevelt's recognition of the Soviet Union as a step toward peace and a boost to world trade and therefore to recovery; he supported Secretary Hull's hands-off policy at the time of the Italian-Ethiopian War; and he welcomed the revelations of the special Senate committee investigating the munitions makers and the international bankers who, presumably, had constituted the major pressure for America's intervention in the First World War.[3]

Kellogg's summer-long trip to Sweden and then through the Soviet Union in 1936 did much to open his eyes to the complexity of events abroad and made it that much more difficult for him to take an unequivocal stand on foreign policy issues in the several years that followed. He toured in the company of his wife, Helen Hall, John L. Elliott, director of the Hudson Guild, Helen Harris, another New York settlement leader, and other social workers; Louis Fisher, an enthusiast for Soviet experiments until disillusioned by what he saw on this trip, served as tour guide. The group traveled by private railway car from Leningrad to Moscow, Kharkov, Rostov, Baku, Tiflis, Batum, Sochi, Yalta, Odessa, and Kiev. The new Soviet Constitution had just been adopted and wherever they went they found workers and peasants hopeful that the democratizing clauses would in fact be implemented. But their visit also coincided with the beginning of the purges and they found widespread repression and fear among Soviet citizens to speak their minds freely. In Moscow it was arranged for Kellogg to visit in his hotel room with an old *Survey* employee who seemed to speak freely enough, but then Paul and Helen noted that his Russian wife was nervously patrolling the corridors to watch for secret service agents.

On the positive side, Kellogg was exhilarated by the drive that young Russians were putting into social and economic planning. Exploded in his mind, once and for all, was the idea, repeated by so many complacent Americans, that socialism would not work, for it was working in Russia. "You get an eager sense of a people who are throwing themselves into an adventure—one perhaps even more daring than the settlement of the American continent," he wrote home from Paris. Their "free handling of racial minorities, their rope to the nationalities, their security for all workers, their new and industrial centers set a pattern which will give us stiff competition to match."[4] And to Samuel B. Fels he confided that the Soviet Union might confront the United States "with a calibre of security, a standard of living with opportunity for the young, and mastery of the factors for economic and cultural progress that will show us up as back numbers."[5]

On the other hand, Kellogg was sobered by his "close-up of what life would likely be, its constrictions, inhibitions and cramp, under one employer and one landlord." The Soviets had "thrown so much emphasis on production, on the new technical class that there are big gashes and holes in their pretensions that the workers are central to the whole scheme. We found wages that were as bad as sweating under capitalism . . . and the new housing doesn't go around yet, and there's vile overcrowding."[6]

To many of his friends at home Kellogg concluded simply (and ambiguously), on his return, that the "Soviet Union stretches one's imagination as to what we should make of America—in our own way."[7] Kellogg's dilemma was all the more poignant because it was shared by so many reformers like himself: he and his associates were profoundly and equally committed to two ideals which they felt were fully compatible—social planning and preservation of the rights and liberties of the individual. In the United States a tradition of rugged individualism rendered effective social planning not only difficult to achieve but abhorrent to millions of American citizens on both pragmatic and ideological grounds. In the Soviet Union economic coordination and social reorganization meant regimentation and the destruction of personal rights and liberties. Later, during the Second World War when the Soviet Union had become an ally with the United States and Britain and others of the United Nations in the great crusade against German and Japanese tyranny, Kellogg (together with many others of his persuasion) tried to see democratizing tendencies emerging in Russia which would make possible a union of progressive forces throughout the world when victory was attained and mankind could turn to the role of reconstruction again. But Kellogg's hope was always laced with a certain skepticism: he could not shake from his memory the images of citizens intimidated by fear of the secret police.

In Spain the issue was more clear-cut for him: a legitimate and democratic government besieged by counterrevolutionary forces supported by German Nazism and Italian Fascism. Kellogg's sympathies were enlisted on the Loyalist side from the first shot. As an active member of the American Friends of Spanish

Democracy organization, Kellogg joined others in pressuring the Roosevelt administration to lift its embargo on the export of arms to both sides in the civil war. Their arguments were partly legalistic—the neutrality laws did not require an imposition of an embargo in this conflict which was not a war but an insurrection of fascist forces against the legitimate authority of the Spanish Republic; and partly substantive—a victory for Franco would constitute a setback to democracy everywhere and would weaken greatly the American influence for progress in the Western Hemisphere. Kellogg engaged in personal correspondence urging these points of view upon his friends in the Roosevelt administration—Adolf A. Berle, Jr., Harold Ickes, and Frank Murphy—and upon Senate leaders Borah, Nye, Pittman, and Pope.[8]

With the fall of Madrid in the spring of 1939 the American Friends of Spanish Democracy reconstituted itself as the Spanish Refugee Relief Campaign whose proclaimed purpose, as its name implied, was to raise funds for Loyalist refugees. It soon became clear, however, that presumed Communists and Communist sympathizers on the Executive Committee were intent on turning the campaign to their own political advantage, and at a testimonial dinner to Paul Kellogg sponsored by the Social Workers Committee of the Spanish Refugee Relief Campaign in February 1940, spokesmen for the left were granted precedence. There followed a fight for control of the organization between the liberals—Roger Baldwin, Bishop McConnell, Samuel Guy Inman, Jay Allen, W. W. Norton, Josephine Shane, Helen Harris, and Guy Shapler, for example—and spokesmen of the Communist line. It was typical of Kellogg that he tried, almost alone as it turned out, to hold both factions together and keep the campaign as a whole focused on its one goal of surpassing significance: to organize relief for needy refugees regardless of political considerations. When his efforts failed he lined up with the non-Communist majority, and was relieved when the dissidents withdrew and launched a rival organization. Long after these events Roger Baldwin, who was more sensitive in those days to the machinations of Communist-front groups than was Kellogg, recalled Kellogg's heroic efforts to get all factions to conform to "principle, not party": "I thought Paul a bit naive in his efforts;

he did not know the Communists as I did, but it was an eloquent try."[9]

Naive and eloquent his acts may have been, and stubborn too, for Kellogg clung obstinately to the central purpose of the campaign, the only purpose that mattered to him—relief for political refugees who, regardless of their own politics, had fought in a common front with all factions for the survival of Republican Spain. It was to this central ideal that the *Survey* adhered: partisan politics, in domestic or foreign affairs, it eschewed, but it could stand for the relief of refugees, and it did.[10]

The deepening European crisis, beginning with Munich, constituted a more complex sequence of events, as Kellogg saw them, and he was torn in several conflicting ways before Pearl Harbor resolved his moral dilemma. Trying to explain himself to John Palmer Gavit (and to himself), Kellogg wrote in February 1939 that "fundamentally my thinking goes back to the excruciating months I went through 20 years ago, prior to April 1917, when we were stripped of all choices but two: keeping out or going in." This time around he hoped that the United States might be able to find a "broad affirmative course" between "belligerency and neutrality."[11] Trying to stay out in 1917 hadn't worked, and negative efforts just to stay aloof wouldn't work this time either, he believed. American neutrality legislation, for example, while well intentioned, constituted an open invitation to aggressors to move ahead with no fear that the United States would ever act to stop aggression. He was reluctant, on the other hand, to see the United States line up with one group of powers, France and England presumably, without very clear assurances that these nations in fact offered constructive alternatives to tyranny or to drift. To apply the embargo provisions of the Neutrality Act just to the aggressor powers, "Japan first of all," appealed to him, but he realized that it was not always possible to distinguish when a clear-cut act of aggression had occurred.[12]

On some occasions he recognized the need for the United States to be strong if it were to be able successfully to follow an independent course of action; at other times, as in a February 1940 address to a convention of the Women's International League for Peace and Freedom, he attacked military spending as leading to militarism, exhausting American resources, and diverting funds from unemployment relief, social security, public housing, health care, and education.[13] By the winter of 1941, however, he had swung around to endorse the central philosophy of William Allen White's Committee to Defend America by Aiding the Allies, on the ground that such measures as the proposed lend-lease bill provided alternatives to choosing to go "to war (action of another sort) and doing nothing."[14]

Members of the *Survey* staff were as badly torn as Kellogg himself, all the members of the staff, that is, except Gavit to whom neutrality seemed both stupid and dishonest. In Ethiopia and Manchuria, he railed at Victor Weybright, "we ran like a scared rabbit from the responsibilities which Manifest Destiny laid upon us. . . . We deserve the contempt of the world. But then," he concluded ruefully, "so do all the rest of the 'great' nations, which piously deplore aggression, while continuing to sell oil and munitions to the aggressors."[15] Victor Weybright, on the other hand, was a convinced pacifist throughout most of the thirties but gradually swung to Kellogg's position that the victims of aggression deserved whatever material support the United States could provide; and after the invasion of Norway, he became an openly avowed interventionist. When, three months after Pearl Harbor, he resigned from the *Survey* to become an officer in the Foreign Information Service, he explained that in conscience he could do none other, for he had been "a convinced and conspicuous Interventionist, advocating conscription, lend-lease, and actual declaration of war, long before these active measures were taken."[16] Gertrude Springer knew nothing but sadness as the nation drifted toward war, and Beulah Amidon had to overcome the deepest scruples to accept the expediency of the Roosevelt policies. With Paul Kellogg out of the office sick most of the summer of 1940, Weybright described the tone of the *Survey*: "Our staff is divided on many issues of the day. I have to lean over backwards not to impose my personal feelings on what is, after all, a cooperative enterprise."[17]

The *Survey* was torn internally, then, from the days of Munich down to the attack on Poland, and through the fall of Norway, the fall of France, and the long agonizing months that preceded

171

the Japanese attack upon Pearl Harbor. But as early as the spring of 1938 Paul Kellogg felt that the foreign crisis was not one that the *Survey* could forever evade. He himself was deeply moved, more than by any other event outside of Spain in these terrible years, by the plight of the Jews in central Europe, which he described "as one of the most excruciating human situations in all time."[18] And so he began a canvass of persons who might bring insight to the problem of racial and religious persecutions in central Europe and who might counsel the *Survey* on what lines of investigation and analysis it might pursue: Felix Frankfurter, who feared the reaction that might be aroused if the *Survey* published a special number filled with articles by Jews about the plight of the Jews in Europe; Oscar Janowsky, who recommended that the Jewish problems be set forth in the larger context of the problems that all minorities faced in authoritarian societies; Morris Cohen, who suggested that the issue would be thrown out of perspective unless it included a survey of the world-wide recession of faith in democracy and an exploration of the state of that faith in America. He also consulted Joseph P. Chamberlain of Columbia University, chairman of the *Survey* board's committee on research. In the summer of 1938, Kellogg had raised enough money for this special number to retain Raymond Gram Swing, free-lance journalist, to be its editor, and Swing set out at once to survey the scene in Europe. By the time he got back late that fall, Czechoslovakia had been sold out at Munich and the climate of world opinion had changed—Swing now saw the Jewish problem as symptomatic of a larger and deeper crisis in the affairs of man and it would have to be on democracy and its survival that the *Survey* would focus.

Like the Harlem number in 1925, the "Calling America" number, published in February 1939, included contributions from many notable persons as well as articles by lesser known experts. Felix Frankfurter wrote a thoughtful essay on the contribution of the immigrant to American life and the "hospitality to the human spirit" for which America had stood; Dorothy Thompson recounted the plight of refugees everywhere and stressed the need for world-wide action; Archibald MacLeish proclaimed free speech as a right, not a privilege, designed not for the pleasure of the citizens but for the health of the state; Dorothy Canfield told the story of the United States as a haven for refugees of all sorts over the years; Lewis Gannett pointed up America's central failure in denying rights and opportunities to its own black minority; Arthur Feiler traced the denial of labor's rights under fascism. What had originally been conceived as an exposé in depth of the Jewish plight in central Europe became an extended analysis of the crisis all minorities confronted whether they were minorities of race, religion, nationality, class, or opinion.

The morals to be drawn, in case the careless reader missed them, were spelled out by Raymond Gram Swing in his introductory essay. The world was rapidly becoming polarized between the United States, "the central democracy of all democracies confronting Germany, the central dictatorship of all dictatorships." At stake was nothing less than the freedom of the human mind and spirit. "Over here," at home, the New Deal had won new gains for democracy—social security, welfare, the rights of labor; but there were failures as well—the denial of equal rights and opportunities to Negroes, Jews, and women, the persistence of mass unemployment, a static economy, and the growing concentration of economic power in the hands of the few. Time was running out, the crisis in the world must, therefore, act as a spur to accelerate reform in America, for if democracy were to survive it must practice tolerance and find effective ways to make the individual citizen secure in his person and in the enjoyment of his rights. The special number provided no blueprint, for democracy was "a process, not an achievement; an attitude, not a solution." The time when the United States could feel safe behind its salt-water moats was gone; with geography the nation could buy time, but that time had to be used "fully and fruitfully" or it would avail nothing.

Three times the size of the usual number of the *Graphic,* this special number went to more than 60,000 readers in addition to the usual subscription list of 25,000. Only one other special number—"The Americas: North and South"—published in March 1941 did better. Kellogg's inspiration, which he had stuck to when others on the staff tried to discourage him, had paid off, and the editor concluded that obviously here there was a mandate for the *Survey* to move out boldly and wrestle with the central crises of the times.[19]

"Calling America" set a line of argument which the *Survey* was to follow for the next two years: strengthen American democracy by overcoming social injustice, care for the refugee victims of war, begin to organize for peace and reconstruction when the day of liberation from tyranny should come, and (this last slowly and reluctantly) build the nation's military power should its employment become essential to the winning of the other goals. All through these months of gathering peril, the *Survey* never called for American military intervention; indeed right down to Pearl Harbor, Kellogg continued to seek a middle path between what he had called in March 1939 the "deadly choice of going to war [and] the deadening choice of doing nothing about it."[20] But the middle way was an elusive one, and Kellogg was never quite able to draw it clearly on a policy map. It involved a scrapping of neutrality legislation that did not discriminate between aggressors and the victims of aggression; it required the rescue and resettlement of refugees; at other times, it seemed to call also for the limitation of arms. Raymond Gram Swing saw the necessity in October 1940, of having the nation prepare for war even though he recognized that the use of force was always "a cruel and brutalizing procedure." The testing time had come, he declared, "and the supreme crisis of two thousand years of social growth is committed for solution, to a great degree, to Americans and America. If we fail, civilization is lost."[21]

More typical of the *Survey*'s position in these months than Swing's interventionist views was an article by Vera Micheles Dean published in June 1941, "Can Democracy Win the Peace?" Whether the United States joined the war or not (and it was that "whether" or "not" that set apart most *Survey* authors from Swing's position) there was no denying American responsibility in helping to create conditions for a just peace once the war was over. She for one had faith that "human intelligence" working through democratic means would be able to find paths to "a new order." It was the American responsibility and opportunity to set forth the premises upon which a just and lasting peace might rest; she had in mind no blueprint (*Survey* editors and authors never did), but the ingredients of a just peace would have to be made specific enough to persuade the German people that they need not continue the war out of a fear of a vengeful peace settlement.[22] In this hope, that a middle way could be found and that the United States might become the great neutral democracy whose power would be wielded for international justice and welfare without regard for national self-interest, Paul Kellogg and the friends whose articles he published harkened back to President Wilson's 22 January 1917 "peace without victory" declaration. It was that brand of Wilsonianism for which they were nostalgic.

In the meantime, the February 1939 special "Calling America" issue having been such a smashing success, Kellogg and Weybright decided to turn the number into a series. In October of that year the *Graphic* published a special number, edited by Beulah Amidon, on education in which schooling was viewed as "growth," as "process," as a way by which boys and girls, men and women, could gain the "capacity to live"; through democratic education democracy itself was broadened and made more vital, strengthened for the crisis which was facing civilization.[23] Number three in the series, February 1940, was devoted to "Homes: Front Line of Defense in American Life" in which the call went out for community and regional planning in order that people could live in a decent and liberating environment, free of congestion and decay.[24] The most successful of the series— measured by the number of copies sold (over 90,000 in all)— "The Americas: North and South," edited by Victor Weybright and published in March 1941; it was a plea for hemispheric solidarity and an exploration of the foundation upon which true democratic cooperation might be built. Although the number proved to be the most popular publishing venture in which the *Survey* ever engaged, its effectiveness was undermined to some substantial degree by its neglect of many of the unpleasant truths of Latin-American politics and society. To a critic who wrote to complain of these omissions, Weybright replied: "From one point of view, I could have made a devastating attack on the social institutions of nine-tenths, or more, of the twenty-one New

World Republics. My own choice, however, was to strike an affirmative note, and give mankind some hope in days like this."[25] It was not often that the *Survey* had ever so hedged and so deliberately accentuated the positive.

"Manning the Arsenal for Democracy," number five in the series, appeared on the eve of Pearl Harbor, November 1941. Its key concern the editors stated in letters that went out to contributors: "How can we speed defense production and at the same time preserve free labor and free enterprise?" The answers were implied in the question: union recognition provided a solid basis for orderly bargaining between labor and management; team spirit and mutual confidence were American customs that assured fair play and a rough sort of equity. Sidney Hillman's vigorous piece set a tone which other articles approached but did not exceed—America was involved in a great world struggle, not by choice but by the necessity of history; if Nazi Germany won the war there would be no freedom or security for any people anywhere; labor's cause was democracy's cause; the war would be won on the assembly lines of American factories; reconstruction at war's end would be secure if management, labor, and government continued their newly established practice of cooperation and collaboration; free labor could "shape a new world where men can walk again in security, in dignity, and in peace." It remained only for Beulah Amidon to ring the changes on "the passionate American faith in a better day, a better world," and on the American capacity to produce for plenty, for security, for freedom, if only men would, by foresight and planning, mobilize science and technology for the creation of "new levels of human life."[26]

A settlement worker who had been attending a conference at Christodora House in New York on 7 December 1941 later recalled the way she heard the news of Pearl Harbor. Paul Kellogg had left the conference room on some errand, and when he returned his manner commanded the delegates' attention—he "very quietly announced this incredible fact. The way he did it electrified us all." The delegates sent off a telegram of support to the president, and then they all went their separate ways. The war was on.[27]

If the American people were not fully prepared for the eventuality of war, the *Survey* was, for it had been thinking through the implications of belligerency for many months. In 1917, Kellogg had opposed America's entry into the war until April 6. This time he had fewer qualms, fewer anxieties. German, Italian, and Japanese tyrannies had to be ended and would be ended. They could be destroyed by the efforts of a free people in a democratic world in such ways that a just and lasting peace could be secured. The *Survey*'s wartime policy was of bedrock simplicity: fight the war by democratic means, prepare *now* for peace and reconstruction.

The policy line was clear but implementation proved difficult, for, just as in 1917-18, wartime conditions cut into revenue, cut down on newsprint, depleted the staff. Paul Kellogg himself came into the war years with below-par health. In 1939-40 he had an intermittent illness which the doctors were an unconscionably long time diagnosing correctly. When finally, after more than a half year of surveillance the physicians hit upon a hyperthyroid condition as the source of his problem, he had an operation, in July of 1940, that proved a success; he was unable, however, to handle his editorial responsibilities at anything like full capacity during the six-month convalescence, and then in December he cut his foot while chopping a tree at his weekend retreat at Cornwall. It was several weeks more after that before he could manage a full day and a full week at the office, and he never fully recovered his earlier vigor.

Victor Weybright had gone gaily off to war in April 1942, and Gertrude Springer said goodbye the first of that month. ("Isn't it just like me to pick April Fool's Day to toss my hat over the windmill?" she exclaimed to a friend.)[28] These departures left both the *Graphic* and the *Midmonthly* without managing editors. With Florence Loeb Kellogg and Beulah Amidon to fall back upon, Kellogg became his own managing editor for the *Graphic,* but it was a year and a half before he could locate anyone to assume responsibility for the *Mid.* Finally, in September 1943, Bradley Buell happily was persuaded to join the staff as executive editor with responsibility for finance, budget, admin-

istration, circulation, and promotion and with special responsibilities as managing editor of the *Midmonthly.*

Bradley Buell, "Si" as he was known to his many friends, was
an anomaly on the staff—a trained social worker with no experience in journalism whatsoever. He had earned a master's degree
from the New York School of Social Work and had held positions, at various times, as organization secretary of the American
Association of Social Workers (during its first three years of
existence), with the YMCA, as director of the New Orleans Community Chest and Council, and as field director for the National
Association of Community Chests and Councils, from which
position he came to the *Survey* where he stayed for the next four
years. Few persons at that time knew more about the whole wide
range of social services than did Buell, for his years with the
community chest movement had forced him to be a generalist
and to focus upon ways to coordinate the many different services
that each of social work's divisions provided. The peculiar need
of social work at that juncture in its development, as Buell saw
it, was to assist the family and the individual not by piecemeal
services but with a recognition of the basic wholeness of the
client. Intense specialization in the serving professions had undoubtedly contributed more information and more profound insights on the nature of human behavior, but new-found understanding was of little use unless the practitioner could synthesize
this diverse knowledge and put it to work for the client's benefit.
"Coordination" and "synthesis" were the concepts Buell stressed
in his years as executive editor.

The back-up assistant for Buell was Kathryn Close, a free-
lance writer with some experience in the welfare field, who had
joined the *Midmonthly*'s staff in 1938. Her skill and dedication
helped hold affairs together during the very difficult war years
when many others drifted away to war-related jobs. Walter F.
Grueninger oversaw the purely business end of the operation, a
task that often drove him nearly to despair not only because the
Survey always had trouble making ends meet but also because of
the unconventional and unsystematic budgeting procedures that
Kellogg followed in his reports to the board, procedures which
only Arthur had ever really been able to divine or to tolerate.

Then there was the problem of locating newsprint, and troubles at the print shop where unskilled workers, bad ink, and worn-out type were a constant plague. Articles dealing with government policy, especially if they concerned the welfare of servicemen or labor-management relations, had to be cleared through government censorship and although the *Survey* was never forbidden to print an article and sentences or paragraphs were never deleted, many printing deadlines were missed because of the delay that the bureaucratic routine of censorship inevitably involved. To save on newsprint the journals went from a two-column to a three-column layout, an economy which made for more words per page but also for a crowded and unappealing appearance. All graphic work, in both journals, had to be reduced severely. Typographical errors, for the first time since the first war, abounded. By 1945 the journals appeared gray and drab, particularly when compared with the life and visual beauty which had characterized the *Graphic* during most of the interwar years.

The difficulties were legion, but the mission clear—fight a democratic war democratically, plan now for a democratic settlement when victory had been won.

The first mandate called forth articles, in both journals, dealing with such diverse subjects as the treatment of Americans of Japanese ancestry who had been evacuated from the West Coast to relocation (internment) camps in the hinterland; the creation of foster day-care centers for the children of mothers who took defense jobs; services to troops in transit and to their wives and families who so often traipsed along from camp to camp; the use of volunteers to replace professionals who had been called to war service; the crisis in housing especially in congested defense centers; the planting of victory gardens; the rehabilitation of injured servicemen; the mobilization of overseas relief resources; the integration of Negro workers into defense industries and into the community life of war-boom cities; the drawing of labor into community chest and war chest drives; the prevention of juvenile delinquency with coordinated programs of education and recreation; services to the children of migrant workers; the origins and work of the United Nations Relief and Rehabilitation Administration; and the psychological tensions within young marriages of separation and, with war's end, of reunion. The *Midmonthly* devoted much of its space to brief, often one-paragraph, items which detailed in succinct prose what social service agencies, both public and private, were doing across the country and overseas in the fields of public health, medical care, race relations, manpower training and placement, security, housing and city planning, community organization, recreation, relief and reconstruction.

Of the special numbers printed during the war—there was one on health and one on juvenile delinquency, for example— the most ambitious project was the November 1942 issue on "Color: Unfinished Business of Democracy." The stimulus for the project came from the recognition that the denial of equal rights and equal opportunities to American Negroes was, at once, the sharpest flaw in American democracy and the chief obstacle to the winning of a just peace. So it appeared to the *Survey* staff as they began to plan this special number. America would have to set its own house in order if it were to win the war and win the peace, for whites were a minority in a world of color and when the war was over peoples of color would demand the right to determine their own destinies; centuries of white imperialism were clearly near an end. The United States would have constructive influence in such a world only insofar as it resolved the problems of racial discrimination at home. Furthermore, the American Negro himself now that he had been mobilized for war along with all other citizens would no longer be content to play a secondary role. As Elmer Carter counseled Kellogg during the planning stages of the issue: "It no longer matters if the Negro can paint or dance or sing—he's going to war. . . . race prejudice and discrimination must be at an end."[29]

Although Paul Kellogg called upon his old associate Alain Locke, who had edited the Harlem number in 1925, to be guest editor of this special number, it was Kellogg himself who did the greater part in conceiving, planning, and executing the issue. There was about his efforts a mood of intense urgency. As always, Kellogg had intended to maintain a fine balance between an exposé of the problem in all its ramifications and a program for constructive action. We must avoid "just a budget of abuses and injustices," he wrote to the Julius Rosenwald Fund asking for financial support; we must "interpret progress as well as problems. . . . On the other hand, nothing would be more self-defeating than to make the number an apology, much less a whitewash, of a deep and moving situation, where the pendulum swings in the balance between bitterness and mutual team play." The question in Kellogg's mind was whether the *Survey* could "give a realistic shove to belated gains here at home and at the same time hold out 'the promise of American life' so that here and abroad all who run may read, regardless of race or color?"[30]

The advice he got, especially the advice from Negro leaders, counseled him to avoid intellectualizing, to put the issue frankly and dramatically and not to be afraid of the expression of emotion. Walter White of the NAACP warned him against taking an "academic" approach because the depth of colored despair was too great. The issue must be written "with brutal directness to jolt people and government out of smug, blind stupidity," he said. We will have to live in a world of "white, black, brown and yellow peoples" who will tolerate no longer the "hypocrisy of whites towards Negroes."[31] The advice of another critic ran along the same line: "The simplest, most direct, most pungent and vivid statement of facts is required to reach peoples' hearts. It is not the minds of a few but the emotions of many that at this point must be aroused. There is enough understanding at the top and not enough below. I should therefore like to see this number far more flamboyant than seems to be contemplated."[32]

Kellogg took the advice seriously, and the issue as finally published although soundly based in objective fact did project that sense of urgency to which he had been persuaded. Lester Granger of the Urban League, for example, contributed a piece in which he described the persistence of patterns of segregation and exclusion in all segments of the nation's economic life, and he declared that it was not enough merely to end discrimination in defense employment by decree, for the Negro worker rarely possessed the skills required by modern technology; the Negro worker, it followed, would first have to be trained if his potentials were to be used to full capacity. Walter White slapped at the army and the navy for keeping the Negro in servile roles; there was not a single mixed division in the armed services, and Negro troops were not even given combat training. Elmer A. Carter identified most clearly and forcefully the basic issue which was at the heart of all manifestations of prejudice and discrimination. White and black could work together, but everywhere they were kept apart—in housing, in schools, in jobs, in the armed services—and it was the very fact of separation that rendered one group inferior and the other superior. Take education, for example; there were good Negro schools, "but the very fact of separation creates a spiritual hiatus between the races, fostering in the one a feeling of inferiority, and in the other an equally insidious superiority complex. It breeds resentment, suspicion and humiliation, and undermines the Negro's faith in democratic government itself."[33]

Kellogg knew that these views were not, at that time, in the mainstream of American concern, but he hoped to stimulate interest and provoke constructive social action. Fifty-five thousand copies were sold, a figure low enough to suggest that it was still to the "minds of a few" rather than the "emotions of the many" that the *Survey* appealed. That an analysis of segregation similar to Carter's became the chief justification for a series of Supreme Court rulings, most notably the Brown decision of 1954, can be taken in no way as proof of influence, but an indication merely that in this issue, as in so many others, the *Survey* anticipated, by years and often by decades, ideas that were on their way toward realization.

"Color: Unfinished Business of Democracy" looked both toward the strengthening of democracy on the home front and toward the possibilities of achieving a peace that would recognize the equal rights of peoples of all colors. The special number "From War to Work," published in May 1943, focused on planning now for the time when war industries would have to reconvert to peacetime production. Stuart Chase, who was called in by Kellogg to edit the special number, outlined the project to a panel of expert advisers: "A postwar program of full employment is an essential part of winning the war. Neither the boys in the Army nor the men and women in the war industries can do their part effectively if they are worrying about what is going to happen to them and their jobs when the war ends."[34] Men and resources had been mobilized for war—war was proof that planning worked; if the nation's labor force could find full employment building howitzers, it could find productive work building houses when the war was over. Man had at his disposal the means to provide security for everyone—"adequate food, shelter, clothing, medical service and educational opportunity."[35] Less formally, Stuart Chase wrote to Kellogg that the basic psychology of the issue should be to make each of its readers hopeful: "His mood when he finishes reading, should be 'Jesus! Look at all the fine jobs the future holds for me!' "[36] Between them, Chase and Kellogg recruited a distinguished list of advisers and contributors: Arthur Altmeyer, Marriner Eccles, Herbert Feis, Luther Gulick, Fred K. Hoehler, James M. Landis, Lewis Lorwin, Isador Lubin, Robert Nathan, and Beardsley Ruml, among others.

The central themes set forth in this number contained little that was new to long-time readers of the *Survey,* for the journal had been harping on them ever since the First World War. The ideas were brought up to date, of course, and given the authority of fresh statement, but to pronounce the right of every man to steady employment at a decent wage was a clear echo from the 1920s. The *Survey* had insisted then that management had the responsibility to regularize employment, but if hard times came it was the obligation of society through government to provide a job, or, failing that, unemployment benefits through social insurance. It was this formula that Elmo Roper set down in this special number as the basic faith of the American people in 1942. There were some new twists given to that basic formula, however. Marriner Eccles, for example, one of the few New Dealers to embrace Keynesian economics consciously and wholeheartedly, described in simple terms the ways in which fiscal devices could be used by the federal government to guarantee full employment and full production. And Alvin H. Hansen declared that in the postwar world there would be new outlets for capital investment that had hitherto been little exploited: urban redevelopment and national transportation, housing, and regional resource and river valley development. Stuart Chase stressed the same opportunities for investment and work in overseas relief and rehabilitation, slum clearance and housing, conservation of soils and forests, and hydroelectric dams. The world's work was to be accomplished, the means were at hand, the war experience demonstrated beyond doubt its feasibility—all that remained, it seemed, was for men to will that it should happen.[37]

From 1941 to 1945 the *Survey* was packed with such stories. When the Beveridge Plan outlining postwar social and economic policies for Britain was released in the winter of 1943, Paul Kellogg could not contain his enthusiasm, for it offered proof that just as in 1918 when British labor led the way, so now again Americans could learn from their cousins across the Atlantic. That America *could* learn he saw evidenced in the 1943 report issued by the National Resources Planning Board which provided a guide to full employment and comprehensive social insurance (including health insurance) in the postwar world. Other articles in other issues of the *Graphic* (and occasionally in the *Midmonthly* as well) listed the investments the nation could make with the labor and the capital released at war's end in schools, hospitals, recreation facilities, and civic beautification— all in the public sector. After so many frustrating years—in the 1920s when social sag was the mood, in the 1930s when the best the New Deal could do was not nearly good enough—it must have been exciting to contemplate the wonders that the postwar world might hold, if men would apply the lessons of war to the pursuit of peace.[38]

Victory and peace depended upon how Americans went about the business of winning the war and preparing for the peace, but they depended as well on international understanding and good will. To serve these ends the *Graphic* published a special number on America's Russian ally (February 1944) and on her British ally (May 1945). As in the "Americas: North and South" number, one of Weybright's last major editorial contributions, in which unpleasant comments on the state of Latin-American politics were avoided, so too in the Russian number Kellogg sought to put the best light on America's relations with her new partner.

To give it a good American twist, Kellogg hit upon playing up the common frontier heritage the two nations presumably enjoyed—frontiers not alone in the sense that both the American and the Russian people had expanded into open lands and carved out great nations where once there had been wilderness, but frontiers as well, as Kellogg put it, of "new horizons in technology, race relations, religious revival and the thrust of youth."[39] If the two peoples could "but understand each other and strike hands," then, by whatever divergent ways they had come, they could work together to realize "the promise for common men in the decades ahead."[40] There were articles on all phases of life in the Soviet Union at that time—economic, political, educational, cultural, social—but most of the contributors lacked the distinction of those who had written for earlier special numbers. In part because Kellogg tried so scrupulously to avoid authors whose reputations would identify them as being either anti- or pro-Soviet, he ended up with a rather bland group of articles.[41]

"The British and Ourselves" was no more distinguished, and its production may have been more notable for the trials and sorrows it caused the staff than for any contribution to understanding within the family of the English-speaking world. The idea had been, as with the Russian number, to emphasize those principles and traditions and opportunities the Allies had in common, and the original "scenario" (as Kellogg called the working outline drafts) had called for "an adventure in common understanding in what may be the last great chance open to our people and theirs to help shape the Future of the World."[42] Victor Weybright did some of the work at the British end, Lewis Gannett and Ferdinand Kuhn offered occasional advice, but of course (Kellogg wrote to Weybright in London) "they could give only fragments of their time." To Kellogg it seemed that there was always "a next bend of the river and more rapids ahead. . . . our shrunken staff overworked and tired, paper troubles, printers troubles, sickness troubles, issues late. . . . And me a rebellious and exasperating bottleneck!" And the manuscripts that came in were mostly abstract and impersonal, he complained, some were so bad that not even with skilled editing could they be salvaged. Some of the Americans, he continued, got carried away and wrote as though they were going to be published in the British quarterlies rather than in the *Survey*: " 'Apperceptions of behavior patterns within the compass of international, economic and social categories in a period of adjustment between civilizations marked by kindred but distinguishable characteristics.' Of course I'm outrageously exaggerating."[43] Of course he was exaggerating only a little bit; the number as a whole lacked coherence and the separate articles were, for the most part, flabby and unoriginal. Then, just as the issue was ready to go to press, everything changed: Franklin Roosevelt died, Germany surrendered, the United Nations met in San Francisco, the British government fell, and the breakup of the great wartime coalition began!

Kellogg had the resources of heart to see the funny side of the fiasco, although given his long admiration for British democracy it must have been a deep personal disappointment to him. It took a toll of energy and health which, by the 1940s, Kellogg could not afford to squander. At the time of Pearl Harbor he was sixty-two years old, on V-J Day nearly sixty-six, an age at which many men retire. He had been through two world wars, and he must have remembered how his hopes in 1918 for a reconstructed world had been utterly shattered by events in the decade that followed. He had enlisted his hopes again in Franklin Roosevelt and the New Deal and had finally to settle for less than he himself had thought possible. There had proved to be no middle way between going in and staying out of the war. It was war, which he abhorred, not reform, that had restored full employment to the nation. The war came; Victor Weybright and Gertrude Springer left; Beulah Amidon was sick for many months in the war years and even Ann Brenner had begun to fail. Kathryn Close and Bradley Buell somehow pieced together copy for the *Midmonthly*, so at least he didn't have to worry about that, but responsibility for the *Graphic*, for the special numbers (which taxed his energies far beyond what his reserves could stand), and for raising the money to keep the whole enterprise afloat was ultimately his alone. He had been overextending the limits of his energy for many years and by 1940 he had to begin to pay the toll—in numbing fatigue, in occasional but recurring incapacity to focus his attention on the business at hand, in momentary lapses of memory so fleeting that only his closest friends detected them.

At the old farm in Cornwall up the Hudson he could find temporary surcease from responsibility and the demands the *Survey* and the world made upon him. There, with Helen, he could find a haven, a respite, a place to restore his flagging spirits; to Victor Weybright he could still joke about matters very dear to his heart, but he was tired, often sick and tired, and not fully fortified for the challenges that came sweeping in with the war's end.

{XII}

The *Survey*'s Last Days, 1945–52

A DAILY newspaper or a weekly news journal prints news of events as they happen—politics, war, business, sports, the arts; they may have their eyes out for a scoop or they may hope to tell a story that all reporters are covering from some original angle, but their stories come to them. The world moves, events occur, presidents and senators are elected (and assassinated), bombs are dropped, corporations merge, a tournament is won (or lost), a new show is a sellout, men fly to the moon. But what if your beat is the welfare scene? What then are the big stories? What do you write about when public policy is deadlocked or stalemated and social workers are just going about their daily rounds? You can hash over old developments, you can try to stimulate new issues and provoke controversies on pressing social problems in which no one else seems much interested. Or you can "prophesy," write about what might be if only . . . But in journalism, as in life, a little prophecy goes a long way.

It was some such dilemma the *Survey* faced at the close of the Second World War. There were some natural stories to be followed, of course—overseas relief and rehabilitation, for example, the readjustment of the veteran to civilian life, and the reconversion of industry to peacetime production; but these were events that general newspapers and journals felt obliged to cover as well. And whereas most of them could keep staff in the field, the *Survey* journals had to depend largely on stories that came to them, for the tight budget under which they operated did not permit staff members to leave the office and run down stories as they had been able to do through most of the twenties and thirties. What Kellogg and Weybright and others had always feared might happen did happen—the staff, in the war and postwar years, became deskbound. A case in point is a poignant letter Kellogg wrote to Emily Greene Balch in the summer of 1946 as she was leaving for a meeting in Europe of the Women's International League for Peace and Freedom; he enclosed $350 to cover some of her expenses in return for which she would try her hand at a couple of stories on the convention itself, or perhaps something comparing reconstruction in the two postwar eras, after 1918 and after 1945. The press covers everything today far better than it did twenty-five years ago, he wrote, and there was at least a two-month lag, with the *Survey*, between the writing of an article and its publication. His advice, then, was for her not to write the news but to "get the tang of the meeting," to search out human interest, to illuminate a few strands, to relate her observations to a "friendly audience."[1]

It was not only that the daily press covered events more thoroughly than before the war; so, too, did the weekly and monthly journals with which the *Survey* had to compete for readers. In the interwar years the readership of the *Nation* and the *New Republic* ran in the same order of magnitude as subscriptions to the *Survey* journals, while the monthly quality magazines—*Harper's* and the *Atlantic,* for example—did very substantially better; but in the postwar years the latter journals came increasingly to publish articles in fields in which the *Survey Graphic* could earlier claim almost exclusive coverage. The quality monthlies, moreover, once they moved into welfare-related subjects, could pay their contributors far more handsomely than the one hundred dollars or so that went to established authors in the *Survey Graphic.* The *Survey* was losing out, on the other side, to the professional social work journals which, in the years after 1945, turned out specialized articles of wide appeal in welfare circles.

Paul U. Kellogg and the *Survey*

These were living realities to those whose responsibility it was to publish the *Survey*. Bruno Lasker, who had been a member of the staff when a very young man back in the years following the First World War and who had been a contributor and friend (and critic) of the journal for all the years that followed, wrote to Paul Kellogg in 1948 to counsel him on the matter of competition: "The critical situation which the Board now faces is not a falling off in public interest but a competition that can command the highest paid literary talents, the most lavish expenditure on illustration and make-up, the most far-flung publicity and promotion." He went on to urge that the new *Survey* should be written for "the sort of people who support social movements and social efforts," that it should publish articles that "a suburban board member of some local agency can successfully use to interest her scatter-brained neighbors."[2] Another long-time associate, Edith Pope, confessed to the editor that after a lifetime of reading the *Survey* she found that lately she had been glancing at it and setting it aside. Why? "Because of the number of specialized publications like *Mental Hygiene* and the *Journal of Social Case Work* and others and also the increased number of very good articles which appear in the better magazines about social work."[3] These were hard facts that the *Survey* had to confront.

So the *Survey* drifted, not knowing really what its mandate was in the changed conditions of the postwar world. It covered overseas relief, and the Full Employment Act (a partial but welcome fulfillment of its domestic reconstruction program), race relations, group treatment of the mentally ill, new ways of working with the aged, social hygiene, extension of social security benefits, and health insurance. There were articles on the Nuremberg trials and on the atom bomb, but these did not fall easily within the *Survey*'s traditional area of concern. More and more the *Midmonthly* became a social workers' exchange, more and more the *Graphic* became just another magazine concerned with domestic and world problems. The biting edge which had been their distinguishing mark was blunted.

Except for a special *Graphic* number on segregation, the later numbers in the "Calling America" series lacked the distinction of most of the earlier efforts. The survey of modern communications—radio, press, books, movies—published in December 1946 under the title "The Right of All People to Know," had much to say about free speech, the threats of monopoly and of government censorship and control, but the articles were repetitious and the prose often sodden, and after the point had been made that the free flow of information was vital both to reform at home and to peace in the world there wasn't much else to be said.[4] Beulah Amidon came back to the theme of education in a democracy, but except for a concerted attack on race prejudice and discrimination in the schools the special number contented itself with restating old propositions—education as problem solving, education as the means by which people learned to live together, education as the way to recognition of a world community and to the creation of a common order in society, and all the rest.[5] "Food for a Hungry World," number fourteen in the series (and the last), had been stimulated by a trip that Paul and Helen took to attend the second annual conference of the Food and Agricultural Organization of the United Nations meeting in Geneva in the summer of 1947. It afforded a dramatic picture of world hunger, outlined what was being done, and proclaimed America's special responsibility, but the number was not carefully planned; the home office could barely scrape up the money to pay the contributors, and many of the checks went out months late. Clearly the *Survey* didn't have the cash in hand or the other resources that money commands to try again.[6]

It is all the more remarkable, given these circumstances, that the special number on segregation, January 1947, was as hard-hitting and brilliant as it was. Although the number had a special guest editor, Thomas Sancton, a free-lancing young southern writer, it was Paul Kellogg again who did most of the planning and the final editorial work, although he was ably supported by Florence Kellogg who supervised the visual and graphic work and Kathleen Sproul who saw it through the press. The idea for the number had come from Dr. Will W. Alexander, vice-president of the Julius Rosenwald Fund, and one of the most influential white leaders in the field of Negro education during the interwar generation. Alexander wrote to Kellogg in the spring of 1946 describing at great length the persistence of segregation in schools, churches, housing, and the armed services, and it was he who cautioned against "over-emphasis on the achievements which are fragmentary and on the whole relatively insignificant." Good liberals had erred, he said, in placing their faith in attacks on discrimination and prejudice; it was the whole pattern of segregation, of the separation of the races both North and South, that had to go before prejudice and discrimination would begin to fade. Too many Americans of good will had accepted the pattern of segregation "as an inevitable and permanent characteristic of our society," and until that pattern was broken, the story would continue to be one of partial progress, futility and frustration. When Kellogg responded affirmatively and enthusiastically to Alexander's proposal the Rosenwald Fund made an initial contribution of $12,000 toward getting the project under way, and another $5000 from other foundations helped to see it through.[7]

As editor, Kellogg insisted that the contributing authors, whatever special area of segregation they explored, focus on the one central theme: that the fact of segregation lay at the heart of discrimination and prejudice, that the old principle of "separate but equal" had become a legal fiction, and that segregation was a national, not a regional or a sectional problem. Thomas Sancton's opening piece laid it on the line: segregation meant "a relentless system of frustration and rejection" for American Negroes, and for the nation "wasted resources"; among the wastes, most significant was the "psychological corrosion at work in the American character as the cost of imposing this thing upon a part of our people." It brought to all "subterfuge and self-deception . . . and cynicism." Then came the evidence of widespread (indeed, all but universal) segregation in every area and every institution of American life. No one and nothing was exempt. The roster of authors was a who's who of experts, black and white: Louis Wirth, Carey McWilliams, Ira Reid, Robert C. Weaver, Joseph Curran, Robert E. Cushman, Liston Pope, Charles Dollard, Donald Young, E. Franklin Frazier, Henry Lee Moon, Alain Locke, and Will Alexander among others. There were pieces illustrating how the pattern of segregation had been broken in the National Maritime Union and in the YWCA, but Kellogg held firm to Alexander's original warning not to overemphasize the positive steps, which were "fragmentary and on the whole relatively insignificant." The stress was rather on Robert Weaver's cry that the ghetto and ghetto psychology had first to be broken before anything else could be achieved: "there can be no equality of opportunity, equal protection before the law, or general feeling of belonging on the part of colored minorities, as long as America accepts segregation of ethnic groups."[8]

The special number reached double the usual subscription list of 30,000, with special bulk orders being distributed through the Federal Council of Churches, the YWCA and YMCA, the United Council of Church Women, the NAACP, the Urban League, the Committee on Church and Race, and the ACLU. Clipping service reports of news articles and editorials indicated that this number elicited a larger response throughout the nation than any other special issue of the *Graphic,* although several such numbers had sold more copies.[9] There is no way to measure the impact it had, but its significance can be tested by the clarity and the force with which the special number attacked, not discrimination which was still the prevailing white liberal strategy at that time, but the very heart of the problem—segregation in all its manifestations.

The number on segregation, moreover, provided a break from the drifting tendencies of the *Survey* in these postwar months and years; it gave something to focus on, something to bite down upon hard and clean in the clutter of other issues and subjects. But the nagging question remained: where was the *Survey* to go next, what policy lines could it lay down that would carry it into a new era? The Employment Act of 1946 and the G.I. Bill of Rights represented culminations of crusades the *Survey* had carried on in the years of depression and war. What next? It endorsed the creation of a new federal Department of Community Services which would encompass the fields of health, education, recreation, and welfare, and that notion was some ten years ahead of its time, but there was not much mileage in it at that moment.[10] It launched a series which took stock of new ideas and practices in the basic fields of welfare service and that proved to be a useful project, but it was more a summing up than an advance into unexplored territory, and it was that latter function in which the *Survey* had excelled. In preparing the series Kellogg wrote to his old associate and friend Adolf A. Berle, Jr., to solicit his advice on what lines the *Survey* might take in politics. A short time ago, he wrote, the answer "would have been almost exclusively the New Deal, plus what the LaGuardia Administration in its highest moments was doing in New York." The *Survey* was interested in identifying "what had permanently silted down from the New Deal," but weren't there new ideas since FDR? The preferred slogan was not "Back to the New Deal!" but "Forward to What?"[11]

The question of finding new guidelines of editorial policy was posed in the context of a myriad of other problems that the *Survey* faced, for there were other administrative and financial troubles in the postwar years (it was really a chronic condition by then). The monthly grind of getting out two journals with a skeleton staff during the war and postwar years left the editor and most of his associates physically and emotionally exhausted. Interoffice memoranda, and little notes from one staff member to another, bear evidence of recurring breakdowns in health and spirits. Ann Reed Brenner, who had helped keep the *Survey* solvent for so many years and who had always been a pillar of assurance and optimism, sensed that she could no longer keep up her old front. She was utterly fatigued and never free from pain; the loss of Roosevelt, she reported to a friend in May 1945, was "to be completely insurmountable. . . . One must somehow have faith that we will work something out and I am determined to be optimistic, though I don't quite know why."[12]

When Bradley Buell resigned as general executive editor for the *Survey* and as managing editor of the *Midmonthly* in the fall of 1947 (he had given notice many months earlier so that Kellogg would have plenty of time to find a successor) to head a special research project for Community Surveys, Inc., Kellogg had to face the prospect of finding and training still another chief associate. Several influential board members, perhaps a majority of those who were active in *Survey* affairs, recognized the need at this juncture to employ a man who, with several years' apprenticeship, could take over as editor in chief when the time came for Kellogg's retirement. For them it was a delicate negotiation because Paul Kellogg *was,* after all, the *Survey* and he had come, understandably, to be sensitive about his editorial prerogatives. Thus Alvin Johnson, a member of the board, wrote to assure Kellogg that the board had no intent of replacing him: "To me you are the heart of the Survey. You will remain its chief until the end of your days. . . . I am not a party to supplanting you, in whole or in part." But, he went on, new board members would be reluctant to accept nomination until they were assured that there was a good chief of staff, second in command, for that was the test of a sound organization.[13] Kellogg made offers to Irving Dilliard of the *St. Louis Post-Dispatch* and to Richard Neuberger of Oregon who had been an occasional (and brilliant) contributor to the pages of the *Survey.* Neither of them would consider it.

The position (it paid but $8000) went to George Britt, a reporter and free-lance writer who (like so many journalists) had worked for many different newspapers over his years as a newspaperman, and whose most recent assignment had been as representative of the Office of War Information in the Near East. An outspoken person, Britt, in making application for the job, expressed his affection and respect for the *Survey* but announced that he was "a great deal more interested in what the *Survey Graphic* might become than in either what it is or what it has been."[14] He was bound for frustration, and within fourteen months had feelers out for another job, saying that although he had been able to bring "some life to these pages within the rather narrow limits of the possible" the future of the *Survey* was uncertain and for him it was but a "temporary stopping place."[15]

Anxiety about the future of the *Survey* together with a very real present shortage of funds kept members of the *Survey* staff worried in these years and inhibited the hiring of new staff. Always in the past Paul Kellogg had been able to tap some new source of funds, and the special numbers in the "Calling America" series had all been financed by special grants from foundations and other patrons. Ever since 1930 the journal had been the beneficiary of an annual contract with the *Reader's Digest* that began at $900 and increased to $12,000 a year by 1945. The retainer granted exclusive right to the *Reader's Digest* to condense articles appearing originally in the *Midmonthly* and the *Graphic,* with additional honoraria to journal and author when an article was so selected. In some cases the *Reader's Digest* provided funds for the research and writing of an article to be placed in the *Survey,* then to be condensed and republished, and sometimes it merely "planted" one without a special grant of money, but always with the knowledge and permission of the editors of the *Survey,* of course. In a typical year, 1937 for example, the *Reader's Digest* condensed eight articles it selected from the run of *Graphic* and *Midmonthly* numbers; five more were written on the initiation of the *Digest,* printed in the *Survey,* and then condensed in the *Digest*; that year the *Graphic* rejected four manuscripts which the *Digest* sought to place in its pages.[16] But even that sum, on which the *Survey* counted year after year, was lost at the end of 1947 when the *Digest* went on a pay-as-you-go arrangement, and although DeWitt Wallace personally continued to contribute an annual gift directly to the *Survey,* it never matched the $10,000 or so a year that the previous contracts had provided.

In the interwar years, and into the war, publishing receipts had usually covered 55 to 70 percent of the *Survey*'s costs, the other one-third or more had been raised from cooperating members of Survey Associates, from large gifts by a few donors, and from occasional foundation grants. Members of the Associates willing to pay $10 a year, and sometimes $25 or $50 annually, held rather steady in their commitment; the *Survey* could count on $25,000 to $35,000 a year from these small donations. But by 1945 many of the patrons who had invested tens of thousands of dollars over the years in the *Survey*'s fortunes had died or withdrawn. Samuel Fels of Philadelphia, for example, had given over $100,000 from 1919 to 1950, and although he guaranteed about $2000 a year during the budget crisis in 1947 and 1948, the days of his support were numbered. Mr. and Mrs. Thomas W. Lamont had contributed $500 to $3500 a year from 1918 to 1945 for a total of approximately $40,000 over those years, but in the postwar era they cut back to a token $100 contribution. Agnes Brown Leach, wife of Henry Goddard Leach, editor of the *Forum,* was a wealthy woman in her own right; she served on the board from 1919 to 1949, and during those thirty years invested nearly $65,000, some years in amounts as high as $5000; but her donation in 1947 was cut to exactly $10. Robert W. de Forest had been a heavy subscriber to the *Survey* cause, $1000 to $2500 a year from 1910 to 1931, but the family had not carried his pledge after his death in 1931. And so the story ran: Harold Swift, William Rosenwald, Mrs. Willard Straight, the John T. Pratts and the George D. Pratts, the Herbert Lehmans, Felix and Paul Warburg, V. Everit Macy, Judge Julian Mack, Adolph and Sam Lewisohn, Thomas Chadbourne— by 1945 they were all gone, or were making small gifts as a sentimental gesture toward better years in another age.[17]

As for foundations, the Russell Sage Foundation had poured enormous sums into the enterprise in its formative years, and again in the depression it helped to cover the annual operating deficit and keep the journal going, but since the mid-thirties it had turned its attention to other matters. The 20th Century Fund, the Milbank Memorial Fund, and the Julius Rosenwald Fund had also made significant contributions, but by the postwar era they were interested only in making grants for specific projects (such as the special number on segregation) and not in helping to meet regular operating expenses.

One thing alone kept the *Survey* solvent from the mid-years of the Second World War through 1948—the special funds that had come to the *Survey* by bequest. Two of them were small, the Charles Cabot Fund whose capital value ran around $10,000, and the Julian Mack Fund which varied, these years, from $5000 to $10,000 in worth. Far more significant was the $80,000 fund which came from the estate of Justice Louis Brandeis after his death in 1941. Brandeis had specified that the income from the capital sum be used by the *Survey* in the fields of civil liberties and workers' education, but his interpretation of these fields was very broad, and there were really no binding restrictions on the ways the *Survey* could use the moneys. The terms of the bequest were purposefully ambiguous and left to the *Survey* broad discretion in drawing upon the principal as well as on the income from the investments. At least that was the liberal reading of the terms of the bequest made by legal counsel on the board, and it was an interpretation concurred in by members of the Brandeis family who were not about to dispute Paul Kellogg's judgment given his long years of friendship with the justice. Hard-pressed in 1947, the *Survey* borrowed $50,000 using the Brandeis stocks as security, and in the summer of the following year Richard B. Scandrett, Jr., at that time chairman of the board, was forced to sell more than $60,000 of the Brandeis Fund stocks in order to keep the *Survey* from bankruptcy—an act which left the *Survey* with fewer capital reserves to draw upon in future emergency. Some members of the board were understandably upset by these developments and raised the question of legality; Scandrett, who was a lawyer and an investor, had his reading of the terms of the bequest accepted by the board, but not before doubts and hard feelings had been aroused. For the moment the *Survey* was solvent, barely so, but looking ahead to the latter months of 1948 and to 1949, with the operating deficit mounting with every month, there seemed little hope that the journal could be rescued.[18]

Wealthy patrons on the board had often given generously to the *Survey,* but had never taken an active role in raising money beyond their own individual gifts and an occasional letter to a friend. When a fund-raising expert was added, temporarily, to the staff in 1946 to assist Kellogg and Ann Brenner in raising money she was shocked to learn that the board had no finance committee and "seemed to feel no responsibility for raising funds to support the organization" and that she "was expected to act as personal solicitor." When she sought out Mrs. J. Borden Harriman in Washington she was told, brusquely: "Go back and tell Paul Kellogg that this is not the way to raise money in 1946."[19] Time along with the money was running out on the *Survey.* By the spring of 1948 the cash balance was precariously low and the outstanding bank loans precariously high.

The editor by then was running largely on nerve and a half century's momentum, and what appeared to most of his colleagues as courage struck many others as sheer obtuseness. For many years (certainly since Arthur's death) he had recurringly explained to the board that too much was expected of him. A memorandum to the board at the close of 1936 had summarized the difficulty with deep poignance: "I have pinch-hitted first in one line and then in another; with the result that I am spreading out not too wide, but too thin in many places and too caught by detail in others," he wrote. "I am essentially charged with final editorial and financial responsibility. In administration, I am handling budgets . . . in finance and membership I am writing form letters, drafting major appeals, and doing a share of soliciting. In one or another capacity, I am attempting to coordinate staff activities; cultivate our board, authors, contributors; get out around the country; keep abreast of the simmering fields of social work . . . edit, rewrite and write. Such an exhausting, piecemeal use of my time is not only wasteful in itself, but chronically handicaps staff work."[20]

The board agreed (who would not?), but funds were always short, and Kellogg's talents never ran along administrative lines. Bradley Buell was able to bring some order into the *Midmonthly*'s affairs, but the *Graphic* and the office generally suffered from the lack of strong executive control in the years beginning in the mid-thirties. The troubles were compounded by Kellogg's recurring illnesses which kept him out of the office for long periods of time, sapped his strength, and blurred his editorial judgment. Correspondence went unanswered, manuscripts lay unread, staff meetings became perfunctory and were sometimes turned into occasions at which the senior associates could vent their bitterness with the way affairs were drifting. Kellogg could gather his strength and see through a brilliant issue—the 1947 number on segregation in which his was the chief inspiration and direction is a case in point—but such sustained efforts invariably depleted further the narrow margin of energy and judgment from which he could draw. The whole staff had aged and younger persons had not been brought on. What had once been a happy and lively family began to fall apart in petty bickering and squabbles. That intimacy which had been an essential ingredient of staff morale in the interwar years began to turn sour.

Paul U. Kellogg and the *Survey*

Members of the editorial staff sensed much of this, of course, and knew that all was not financially well with the journal, but they probably had little idea how very close it was to bankruptcy in 1947 and 1948. There was nothing they could do to find new funds and balance the budget, but they could, by self-analysis and self-criticism, hope to make the *Survey* a more exciting journal that would appeal to a larger audience. At least that was the hope that George Britt held out to the staff in the spring of 1948 when he asked for their candid appraisal of what the journal should do to meet the crisis. The memoranda of reply provide a unique insight into the strengths and weaknesses of the *Survey* as experienced insiders viewed them at that critical juncture. Obviously the makeup needed improvement, for the *Survey* was as drab and "dowdy" in appearance as it had become, through no fault of its own, during the war. Several suggested that Michael Davis's column on the economics of health care should be discontinued. The prose style was generally too much in monotone, most agreed, and there should be more and shorter articles.

But centrally what ailed the *Survey* was that it had become middle-aged—so replied the staff members oldest in seniority and themselves well into middle age (if one grants that "middle age" runs from thirty-five to fifty-five or thereabouts). We need to handle all our subjects "in a less middle-aged way," Beulah Amidon put it bluntly. The *Graphic*'s themes were youth's concerns—peace, housing, child care and education, emotional adjustment (including sex), and health—but in fact little was being done to give these themes the treatment youth would wish. "I think we are in a habit of turning to people who have written for us for a long time, and few of them are now young; I am very much in favor of some younger, newer writers, even if they don't write according to our traditional patterns—especially if they don't." Kathleen Sproul's advice ran to the same points. The *Graphic* had become static and too often defensive; it used to take up issues considered "raffish" but no more was that the case. "I think we should let our readers in on the secret that labor relations by now are more than young Sidney Hillman eating dinner with Mrs. Raymond Robins and the Chicago social workers," she added in a dig that was not entirely justified. And why not stir up a bit of controversy. "I think SG is essentially a magazine for middle-age. Youth wants to take sides—remember?" With these comments Britt agreed: "Why not aim at the idealistic young who are going to find themselves let down by [Henry] Wallace and not uplifted by [Harold] Stassen? . . . Why abandon them to cynicism?" The *Graphic* too often took for granted that "the values and personalities which came into full bloom under the New Deal have the same relative appeal today." To youth they did not. From retirement, Leon Whipple, still a loyal reader and sometime contributor, wrote that the *Graphic* had middle-aged "sag in the guts." To young readers it must appear that the *Survey* was "old hat, charity do-gooders, pryers and peepers into other folks business, red tape bureaucrats, humanitarian visionaries, damned social workers." And how to get youth to realize what the *Graphic* really was? Get young people to write, and lure a young (thirty-year-old) editor with newspaper training and set him loose.

There was both nostalgia and a realistic awareness of present shortcomings in the repeated self-criticism that the staff had lost touch with the outside world. "It is months (maybe years)," said Beulah Amidon, "since an outsider sat down at the library table with us, or came to staff meetings, to share experience or argue for a feature. This used to be our constant practice." Janet Sabloff, too, recalled the days when the staff got leads and contacts from visitors who would drop in for lunch or tea, and when the staff itself got out of the office and into the field. From those contacts everyone—friends, members of Survey Associates, authors, critics, staff—derived "a vital sense of belonging and backing a creative force for the betterment of civilization." That spirit was gone. Kathryn Close concurred: "No national magazine can expect to remain 'fresh' with its staff cooped up in New York."

For the staff Britt summarized the findings that had come to him in memoranda. The chief assets were a name and a tradition that carried respect and authority; the wisdom and experience of its senior staff; its tradition of special numbers; and the built-in loyal market it enjoyed with social workers. It suffered most from "middle age and penury." "In style, make-up, dress, subject matter and general appeal to eye and emotion, we are too much of an oak plank to be sawed through." But the opportunity was still present for the *Graphic* to be what at its best it had been. "The American people feel economically insecure and mentally uneasy, are divided into petty blocs and jealousies as never before." The times called for new programs, and "a new set of national *mores*." These had been the concerns of the *Graphic* historically; they could become so again. But "if the *Survey Graphic* is to survive, it must change into something different and with an initial fresh capital investment, and although this offers an inviting chance, the only sensible alternative if the board refuses is to stop the losses by killing it at once."[21]

That left it up to the board where, of course, the decisions would have to be made, for every constructive suggestion the staff had elaborated would involve the infusion of fresh capital into the enterprise. If the money was not there and could not be raised, nothing could be done to improve the *Survey* so that it could attract a wider audience. There was sharp irony in the dilemma, for the board had never initiated crucial decisions, or any decisions at all for that matter, and had rarely even participated in any meaningful sense in their making. That had been the editor's prerogative and power and the board had been content, by and large, to ratify and approve. Now, finally, in 1948 it was the board that had to make the decision to quit or go ahead.

At a surprise testimonial dinner given in 1928 by friends of the *Survey* honoring Robert W. de Forest, the board's first president, the honored guest responded to toasts and short speeches of praise with informal remarks, half in jest, about his relationship to the journal and its editor: Paul Kellogg *says* that he wants my advice on some matters, and he comes to see me or he writes a long letter, but what he really wants is approval, not counsel. "I am quite overwhelmed usually by his eloquence and also by his logic." If ever the paper should change its name again (and he'd been there for every change) it would have to be "Kelloggs Unlimited."[22] Pleasant banter set the tone for the affair that night, but de Forest's description was fully accurate, whether given in jest or in earnest, for the board and the Executive Committee of the board throughout most of the *Survey*'s life usually went along with whatever the Kelloggs proposed.

This is not to say it served as a rubber stamp; men of means and authority such as de Forest and Lucius Eastman, who succeeded him as president of the board, don't meekly do another's bidding. Nor do any men and women of the distinction that Kellogg was able to attract to board service. Board members were coopted, not really elected, and in their designation Kellogg always played the most prominent role. He built the board so that it would represent the profession of social work, the wealthy families whose financial support he needed, and the great foundations from which he hoped to win grants. In the first category, in way of illustration, were Jane Addams, Jacob Billikopf, Edward T. Devine, Fred K. Hoehler, Simon N. Patten, and Lillian Wald. From the foundations came John M. Glenn (of the Russell Sage Foundation), John A. Kingsbury (of the Milbank Memorial Fund), and William Rosenwald (with his family connection to the Julius P. Rosenwald Fund) among others. And the persons of wealth, many of whom also sat on the boards of many philanthropic foundations, included Alexander Bing, Blanche Ittleson, Agnes Brown Leach, Julian Mack, J. Noel Macy, V. Everit Macy, Rita Wallach Morgenthau, Mrs. George D. Pratt, Jr., Edward L. Ryerson, and Harold Swift. There was also a scattering of good names from the professions: Joseph Chamberlain (who happily was also a man of independent and substantial means), Lowell Shumway, Ordway Tead, Justine Wise Polier, James M. Landis, John Hanrahan, Adolf A. Berle, Jr., and Felix Frankfurter. Of the twenty-five board members who served at any given time, a simple board majority rarely turned out for the quarterly meetings, although the annual meetings were generally better attended. Kellogg set the agenda, in fact if not by constitutional fiat, and board discussions were frequently lively and helpful, but except for several crisis situations the board itself did not initiate discussion or action.

One test of editorial independence came in the winter of 1917 following Paul Kellogg's personal statement against America's entrance into the war in the pages of the *Survey,* and although the editor accepted a truce against the printing of any more such statements from whatever point of view the resolution of the conflict between Kellogg and some members of the board was, in the long run, interpreted as an affirmation of editorial independence and responsibility, both by the editor and by a majority of the board. In reaction to John Fitch's pro-union articles during the great steel strike of 1919, Robert de Forest contemplated resigning from the board so that his name would not be associated with a position so partisan, but Kellogg persuaded him of the accuracy and fairness of Fitch's reporting and of the *Survey*'s continued need for de Forest's support, and he stayed. John M. Glenn did withdraw as vice-president of the board in 1921 on the ground that the *Survey* was abandoning social work for industrial and social problems, but his resignation did not at that time affect adversely the relationships of the Russell Sage Foundation to the *Survey*. Kellogg's personal endorsement of LaFollette in 1924 created another minor stir, but once again the editor's prerogative was sustained.

So it was for the first time on a matter of surpassing importance that the board began in 1947-48 to wrestle with the *Survey*'s desperate financial plight. Costs were up, revenues were down, internal economies had already been instituted, gifts had fallen off badly—the deficits mounted. Everyone knew that new and large sums of money were needed at once if, in Kellogg's words, the *Survey* was to be turned "from a scrapbook of goodwill into a living force."[23] Outstanding bank loans which stood at $38,750 in January 1947 were up to $74,750 in January 1948. Early in June 1948, the board authorized Joseph Chamberlain and Richard B. Scandrett, Jr., to sell the stocks in the Brandeis and related funds to reduce the current indebtedness, but even with that drastic measure (the liquidation of assets came to around $62,000, leaving some $30,000 still in reserve) the *Survey* was left with an indebtedness of over $10,000, and the board estimated that the deficit would grow to $30,000 by the end of September, with the prospect of an additional $50,-000 deficit for 1949 if things continued as they were tending.

At the meeting of June 5 board members were polled on the question of whether money could be raised to cover the deficit and thereby to permit the *Survey* to continue publication. One by one they said "No." So Chamberlain recommended an immediate end to the journal and "orderly liquidation." If publication continued, he argued, more debts would be incurred and the process of liquidation at some time in the future made that much more difficult. But Kellogg pleaded for time; *he* at least was confident that the money could be raised, and so, out of personal loyalty and against their better judgment, the board deferred to the editor's wishes and appointed a special committee, chaired by Chamberlain, whose other members were Victor Weybright, Shelby Harrison, Lowell Shumway, and Richard B. Scandrett, Jr., with Kellogg serving as consultant. This special committee was authorized to make the decision to continue or to liquidate; if it was the latter course (and the clear presumption was that it would be) then the process of liquidation should be begun at once.[24]

Kellogg's strategy at this point was to suggest a consolidation of the *Graphic* and the *Midmonthly* into a single monthly publication, a move that the staff itself endorsed by secret ballot— 23 voting yes, 5 for immediate liquidation, and 4 abstaining. With a projected new budget based on this consolidation the special committee of the board accepted the proposal; they would watch the budget carefully and wait and see. In December Scandrett, who was aghast at the prospect of trying to keep the venture solvent, especially now that all the moneys in the Brandeis fund, the Cabot fund, and the Mack fund had been liquidated to cover the journal's indebtedness, resigned from the board, but a majority, led by Chamberlain, William Rosenwald, Mrs. Ittleson, and Judge Polier, voted to continue. The *Survey* was accorded a new (if precarious) lease on life.

Unexpectedly, the budget for 1949—which Adolf Berle had characterized as "poetry" when Kellogg submitted it to the board in December 1948—proved sound, not alone because of the economies that the merger of the two journals permitted, although that helped, but because a special new source of income opened in February of that year. The *Survey* learned that a Chicago manufacturer of a diet-supplement product, sold under the tradename Kyron, wished to establish a charitable foundation to receive the income from the business. The Continental Pharmaceutical Corporation, but eighteen months old at that time, had enjoyed spectacular success in 1948, earning profits of over a million dollars on a very small initial capital investment. The intent of the corporation was to shift from the 77½ percent individual tax rate on profits to the 25 percent tax rate on capital gains. As legal counsel put it in a memorandum to the *Survey* board: "The seller's objective is to obtain capital gains rather than current income out of the profits of his business up to the amount of the purchase price."[25]

A Kyron Foundation was established under the laws of Delaware, all of whose stock was owned by Survey Associates, Incorporated, and whose sole purpose for existence was to receive profits from the operation of the Continental Pharmaceutical Corporation. Morris Ernst, one of the lawyers advising Kellogg and the *Survey* on the transaction, estimated that the *Survey* could reasonably expect to receive, through its ownership of the Kyron Foundation, at least $75,000 in 1949 and more than $100,000 a year thereafter. The lawyers reported that the Kyron product was a reducing prophylactic which met the standards of the Pure Food and Drug Administration and to which the medical profession had raised no objections, and that the manipulation of its stock constituted "tax avoidance," not "tax evasion." There could be no doubt of the full legality of the transaction or of its morality, Ernst continued; there were no special foundation restrictions except the usual one that income of the foundation should be spent for "charitable, scientific and/or educational purposes," under which clause the *Survey*'s activities clearly fell.[26]

That Kellogg was uneasy about the implications of this arrangement is evidenced in a memorandum to all the staff, dated 29 March 1949, in which he reminded them that the *Survey*'s long-run function had been "chronicle, inquiry, interpretation, forum for discussion, *etc.* . . . With so much at stake this time, I am leaning backwards not to invite trouble by leading off with unsigned articles. . . . Notably in March issue, where clearly the writer put the *Survey* in position of supporting the President's Congressional program and urging readers to press Congress to enact it! Gist, blurbs, Common Welfare and all unsigned matter should be guarded likewise on this score."[27]

From March through July the *Survey* received $6250 a month, for a total of $31,250, through the Kyron Foundation. Profits were good for the Chicago firm in March and April, in May it broke even, in June and July it suffered losses. Business picked up a bit in the autumn and a double payment of $12,500 was channeled to the *Survey* in November, but by the winter of 1949-50 it was clear that the competition of several well-established drug firms, together with a business recession, meant the end of the marketing of that firm's product, and in February 1950, by act of the board of directors (only five of whom were present) the *Survey* sold its ownership to another charitable trust for a fee of $5000. Counting this fee, and subtracting from it the $1000 Survey Associates had originally paid for the stock, the total income realized from February 1949 to February 1950 was $47,750—a sum substantial enough to permit the *Survey* to operate without a deficit for the first time since 1944. Now, after a year's breather, the journal faced hard times again.

Kellogg had made good use of that time. It was not easy, because the traditional functions of both the *Graphic* and *Midmonthly* had now to be combined in an organic rather than a mechanical way so that the newly merged journal would have an authentic coherence of its own. Some old friends wrote in to suggest that the *Survey*'s primary audience was composed of welfare workers "who earnestly need help in understanding the minutiae of their day to day chores in relation to the general functioning of our society. . . . Most of the day's events have their impact in some way upon social services. My suggestion is that you constantly take current issues . . . and write of them for the case worker in Henrico County, Virginia."[28] To such advice, Beulah Amidon responded, setting forth the guiding philosophy of the new journal: "we here do not see the *Survey* franchise as limited to the working details of the social work profession. A score of specialized magazines provide that sort of material. . . . Our task, we feel, is to report and interpret trends and events in the broad field of social welfare. . . . Our job is to provide a forum for the discussion of these issues in relation not to the professional techniques of the social worker, but to the wellspring of the profession: its dedication to human welfare."[29]

In fact, the new *Survey* throughout 1949 was closer to the old *Graphic* at its best than to the *Midmonthly,* however dubious the source of funds which made its publication possible. (And whatever justifications the lawyers made, many staff members were dismayed at the Kyron arrangements which involved accepting cash subsidies from a commercial operation which, if legal, seemed on the margin of what the *Survey* had always considered legitimate.) It had never been a journal of opinion and it did not become one now, but it did regain a great deal of the dynamic, fighting spirit which had characterized it throughout so much of its lifetime. It focused on a backlog of unsolved problems which, in its view, cried for attention: housing (*more* than one-third of the nation were now scandalously ill-housed), health, inflation, city planning and conservation (soil, minerals, trees, and especially people). The American people, it seemed, were willing to let industrial progress and economic advance care for the problems of poverty; but the fact was, said a lead editorial in March, that millions of Americans had not shared in the general advance of prosperity, that millions lived in "low-income, bad-luck sections," and that millions endured "grievous lacks."[30]

The *Survey* seized upon the issue of health insurance, which it identified as one of the most crucial aspects of President Truman's Fair Deal. The United States had the highest standard of living in the world but not, by far, the highest standard of medical care, which was "not distributed even roughly in proportion to need." A comprehensive system of government health insurance seemed to be the "only way of providing widespread medical care at low cost," and to use an insurance system would "simply redistribute the financial burden" without adding to the nation's total medical bill. Health insurance, furthermore, was consistent with the investment the federal government had made in conservation for generations: if only 20 percent of the loss of worktime from sickness could be prevented, the nation would enjoy annual savings of $5 billion. Health insurance was designed, it followed, "to conserve our most precious resource, the lives and vigor of our people."[31] Also in the field of health, the new *Survey* hit hard at public lethargy in regard to care of the mentally ill. In the nation 650,000 persons were hospitalized (inadequately, in crowded institutions where services were substandard), and at least another 300,000 were equally in need, yet the nation had underway no program even to begin to meet this urgent condition.[32] Another article analyzed rotten-borough state legislatures in which legislators from rural districts, proportionally far overrepresented when contrasted with urban areas where the bulk of the people now lived, blocked programs to meet problems of housing, congestion, racial bigotry, and destitution in old age; the urgent need was for reapportionment to make state governments more responsive and more responsible.[33] Another came at the old problem of aging (financial dependency, lack of privacy, loneliness) with fresh insights and vigor.[34]

In 1949 and on into 1950, the new *Survey* restored its editorial column, went back to larger type and a two-column format (in place of the compact and unattractive three-column layout), and printed in each issue fewer and shorter articles. Segregation, new systems of parole, research on cancer and alcoholism, Canada's family allowance system, regional planning in the Missouri Valley, Point 4 assistance overseas, cooperative housing—these were the lively issues that the *Survey* handled with its own liveliness. The *Survey* leaped above the gray mediocrity into which it had lapsed in the hard-pressed postwar years. However inexpedient Kellogg's dealings with the Kyron Foundation may have been, however skeptical the staff had been of the implications of these dealings, there is no evidence that the *Survey* felt inhibited in driving hard on controversial issues, despite his cautious memorandum to the staff of 29 March 1949, and the evidence of the new *Survey* itself in these months demonstrates the effective use to which the moneys were put.

But the Kyron bonus lasted only a year, and at winter's end, 1950, the *Survey* had to begin to scrimp again. Publishing revenues just could not cover publishing and editorial costs; they never had, but now there was no extra income upon which the *Survey* could draw.

The board, under these conditions, began to fall apart. So did the staff. The constitution of Survey Associates called for a board of twenty-five members. There were no elections in 1947 or 1948, and by 1949 only thirteen persons were nominally on the board, and not all of them were active. During 1949 Lowell Shumway and Victor Weybright both resigned; it was a loss, for both of them knew the publishing business as other members of the board did not. In September Agnes Brown Leach, Kellogg's longest and closest associate, the person who had given more money to the cause than any other except Samuel B. Fels, felt compelled to withdraw, in sadness at good days gone and a true friendship broken. By the spring of 1950 even Professor Joseph Chamberlain, who had held firm when others despaired, could see no hope. Adolf Berle, who had approved the Kyron adventure, suggested three courses of action: immediate liquidation, the sale of *Survey* to McGraw-Hill publishers, or resignation of the entire board and the granting of authority to Kellogg to create a new board—options which simmered slowly for a couple of months. Fred Hoehler of the American Public Welfare Association, a man recognized throughout social work circles for his enormous integrity, was the next to drop away.

At the 2 June 1950 meeting of the board, Kellogg sat silent at the table while one by one the board resigned: Adolf Berle, Jacob Billikopf, Mrs. Henry Ittleson—old friends and loyal, all of them—William W. Lancaster, William Rosenwald. Only Chamberlain, in the chair, was left. Did Mr. Kellogg see any prospect of continuing? If so, "he was free as the new chairman to go ahead with a new Board," so the minutes read. "If, however, he found he could not swing this, then some of the old Board members would help him to liquidate." Board members would try, now, to raise funds to provide severance pay for members of the staff, but if the *Survey* went on that probably would not be possible. Chamberlain waited as Kellogg sat silent, and then continued. Mr. Lancaster and Mr. Berle had volunteered to help with all the legal processes of liquidation . . . And then the minutes record that Kellogg broke his silence: "Survey Associates can and should be conserved."[35]

With no board, dwindling resources, a disintegrating staff,

and certain of but one thing—that the *Survey*'s deficit would grow—Kellogg, age seventy-one, set out to recruit a new board. William Kirk, a settlement friend of Helen Hall's and director of the Union Settlement in East Harlem, agreed to come on. So did Alice Keliher, a professor of education at New York University; Elizabeth Ann Bacon, the wife of a senior partner of Ford, Bacon, and Davis; Louis Englander, an auditor (and there was no denying the need for a person of his professional training); and Katharine Lenroot, long-time chief of the Children's Bureau. Some others stuck with the sinking ship: DeWitt Wallace continued to send in his personal check ($4000 one year, $8000 another) even if the *Digest* no longer selected articles from the *Survey*. (In January 1950, with a check for $4000 Wallace sent encouraging words: "the country needs more of your indomitable fighting spirit.")[36] But it was to no avail. Running down the list of Survey Associate members in 1951, Janet Sabloff was able to stir up but $605 from thirty-nine individuals.

And the staff: Kathleen Sproul felt obliged to leave in the fall of 1948: "To contemplate producing a 'new' magazine for January in the face of all uncertainties and in the face of the limited budget proposed for the year seems to me ridiculous and impossible." George Britt, who had been thinking of resigning his post for some time but whose direction had helped to give the new *Survey* its lift in 1949, finally quit in June of 1950. In the fall of 1951, Kathryn Close wrote to an author to apologize for the delay in handling her manuscript, but the skeleton staff had to work in spurts; when deadlines came, all else was put aside and then there was a "frenzy of activity to get caught up on what gets lost in the shuffle and things that take a good deal of thought are apt to be put aside until there is a calmer period for reflection."[37] There were fewer such periods.

Paul Kellogg himself was less available. He was aging, bad colds slipped into pneumonia, his attention wandered, manuscripts gravitated, as one colleague put it, "to the bottom of the haystack on his desk."[38] He retreated to Cornwall, but even there the world intruded. A new super highway was going through; proposed plans made it cut the corner of the meadow not many rods from the front of the old farmhouse on the hill. One winter's day in January 1952 he walked the farmland with an engineer from the highway department, arguing with him, suggesting alternative routes. But the state's survey of the land and the route had to stick, sorry. Heartsick with the knowledge that the roar of trucks and cars would soon rise from the meadow, that the prospect down the hill and across the meadow would be broken by headlights and the blur of speeding vehicles, he prepared to be driven back to the city and his other home at Henry Street. He had suffered arteriosclerosis for some years; that night he had his first major stroke. The doctor was called.

And so was Joseph Anderson, then executive director of the National Association of Social Workers, to oversee the liquidation of the *Survey*. Anderson moved quickly. The last issue of the *Survey* appeared in May containing no notice that it was the end. Elizabeth Ann Bacon picked up the tab for April's deficit.

Hannah Gallagher, whose memory of *Survey* days went back to 1913, stayed on with an editorial assistant, Cora Emme, to close the office. On the last day, save one, in the dust and the darkness of the empty office, everything in shambles, Paul Kellogg appeared, pale and frail, and unsteady on his feet. Where was the rest of the staff? What was going on? Miss Gallagher, who had mothered him before, explained softly and gently that the office was being closed. "Oh, no," Paul said, "we can't close the office, not for good; we'll be open again in September."

They saw him back to Henry Street that afternoon. Some six years later, on All Saints' Day, 1958, he died.

These last years he spent with Helen in the settlement he had known as home, surrounded by the friendliness of neighbors and the settlement family, entering into the life around him as his health permitted. Weekends and summers he rested at Cornwall where, sitting on the side patio beneath the shade of a great Chinese chestnut tree he had planted many years before, he could contemplate the vista that stretched before him down the rolling valley of the Hudson. Although he came to talk about it less and less, he never surrendered the hope that someday the *Survey* might be revived.

{XIII}

A Summing Up

THE life and career of Paul U. Kellogg provide the historian an intensive case study of a sensitive reformer whose political proclivities and social attitudes can be traced from Roosevelt (Theodore) to Roosevelt (Franklin), from Square Deal through New Deal to Harry Truman's Fair Deal. To propose that a "case study" can be made is not to suggest that Kellogg can be treated as a "typical" reformer of the twentieth century, or that he somehow provides a "norm" against which other progressives can be measured: the development of his views, the loyalties to which he adhered, the friendships and alliances he made were peculiarly his own although they were shared by a goodly company of other concerned citizens. He does not fit comfortably or easily into any of the categories of old progressives who lived on into the New Deal years that Professor Otis Graham, Jr., has so brilliantly delineated in his *Encore for Reform,* although Kellogg is included, in that study, among those who "generally applauded" the New Deal, even though "they may have objected to certain laws or policies."[1]

Not a philosopher—not in any formal sense at least—not an ideologue, Kellogg was guided by certain first principles in the conduct of his life and in his role as editor, and although these axioms changed as events moved they demonstrated a remarkable consistency over the span of a half century. From the beginning of his career until its end, for example, he dedicated himself to making real the promise of opportunity for all human beings—the right of each individual to develop his own latent powers and talents in accord with his own desires and will. What he had set forth in a theme for a freshman course in composition at Columbia University in 1901 remained central: he sought ways to break the "rut" system of society that assigned roles and functions to particular individuals which they were powerless, by themselves, to escape or to transcend. "We are all of us working in a web of circumstance not of our contriving—trying to make it possible for life to come up through its meshes with greater freedom and joy," he wrote to a friend in 1925. "We don't make a great fist of it ourselves; the very toughness and cutting edges of the fibre take their toll upon us. But after all, I believe we are loosening things up a bit for those who come after, helping give a better chance for those who are here."[2] Self-determination of persons, social groups, neighborhoods, economic classes, communities, and nations—from this premise he never deviated.

Kellogg, although he made his living (and his life) with words, was not a dogmatist or a rhetorician but an activist. Deeds, not words, were the substance of what ultimately counted, although words themselves could become deeds, as he saw it. Because he abhorred the abstract and the nebulous and was devoted to the concrete, the evolution of his ideas can best be elaborated in the context of the real issues in which he was involved.

Take the developing profession of social work as a central example, for it was social service and social welfare that absorbed his attention (and the *Survey*'s). Although Kellogg himself was most at home with settlement workers, essentially because they appealed to his sense of fraternalism and participatory democracy and because they brought firsthand evidence to their work and were, therefore, more often than caseworkers aligned with reform groups and causes, he understood how central casework services were to the whole profession of social work. Too often, he felt, caseworkers saw their function only in relation to their clients without sufficient appreciation of their connection with and responsibility to the larger community. The relationship of the social worker and the client, he wrote in the mid-twenties to Richard C. Cabot, who has been called the father of medical social work, was "not that of an intruder—not that of a friend—not that of a doctor to his patient—but that, frankly and openly, of the agent of the community dealing with one of its members—on the ground that a person can not be as deep in distress as he pleases any more than he can be as sick as he pleases; the welfare of one being the concern of all."[3] It followed that these relationships were not to be cut and dried, but organically interrelated; the caseworker had an obligation not only to provide the best services he could with the resources at his command but also, as an "observer and explorer of human needs," to educate the community and help lead it to recognize the need for wholesale measures of prevention and constructive action to balance the retail provision of services. This "organic process" which combined "individual treatment with social action" was, it seemed to Kellogg, "the real alternative to an ingrowing, shortsighted retailing on the one hand, or a highfalutin' wholesaling on the other."[4]

Guided by the same insights, Kellogg sought to bring the many different divisions of social work together, to break down the barriers of specialized training and functions that tended to divide them. Professional social work education should begin, he believed, with what the different branches had in common, and the task of community betterment should not be left to those few workers who were formally engaged in what social work identified as "community organization."[5] By the same token Kellogg constantly urged upon program committees of the National Conference of Social Work the inclusion of plenary sessions that would deal with broad social problems, and the participation of persons not necessarily from the ranks of social work—if they represented insurgent points of view not often heard at professional conventions, all the better. It was important, he felt, for a conference not only to survey "what's doing" but to cover, as well, "what we should strike out for in the next year," and to include outside observers who saw "the seams as well as the shine of the programs."[6]

Familiar with all divisions of the serving professions, Kellogg was, as indicated above, most at ease with the settlement movement. A welcome visitor at annual conventions of the National Federation of Settlements, a member of its board and chief author and stylist of its Resolutions Committee for many years, he found the settlement spirit most congenial to his own style of life. Settlement workers were the general practitioners of social work, as he saw it; theirs was a synthetic function, drawing together all the resources of the community to advance the general welfare. Like the *Survey* itself the settlements were "listening posts" of society for they were in and of the neighborhoods they served. No branch of social service was closer to the community, he wrote; settlements avoided "superimposed institutions"; they were involved in the vital "process of give and take"; they were voluntaristic, plastic, decentralized, self-critical, and democratic; they were "centers of contact, understanding and impulse"; nothing human was alien to their programs, which touched health, education, recreation, the arts, research and social reform; they were engaged in "mutual adventures in community growth."[7] Whether or not the settlement spirit was in objective fact exactly as he described it, there can be no doubt that Kellogg ascribed those qualities to the settlements which he himself held most dear.

In regard to industrial conditions and the lot of labor, Paul Kellogg held advanced positions consistent with the views of the more progressive leaders of the settlement movement—Jane Addams, Mary McDowell, and Charles Cooper, for example. Like them, and many others, Kellogg had encountered the problems that working people faced in their daily existence in the early years of the twentieth century. The months he spent in Pittsburgh, 1907-8, especially, opened his eyes (and his heart) to the human suffering that accompanied unjust industrial conditions. Like many other reformers in that era Kellogg saw that government intervention was required, and so he joined with those who were fighting for legislative regulation or prohibition of child labor, maximum hour and minimum wage legislation (particularly to protect women workers), and the passage of workmen's compensation laws. Typically "progressive" also was his espousal in 1912 of the proposal to establish a Federal Commission on Industrial Relations which would have the authority to investigate the procedures by which wages, hours, and conditions of labor were determined and to recommend ways by which orderly processes could be established and a larger measure of "justice and order" brought into the "dislocated structure of . . . industrial life." Stressing the insecurity of the wage earner's life and the inequality of bargaining power between the workers and the corporations, Kellogg hoped that the processes of unionization might help make real the impulse toward self-governance, and that government concern and action might also protect the interests of what he termed the "third party to the industrial struggle," that is the general public.[8] Consistent with this essentially middle-class progressive position was the recurring role of the *Survey* in providing analyses in depth of industrial crises in order that informed public leaders might bring their influence to bear for order and human rights. "The *Survey* has no axes to grind on either side of the industrial cleavage," Kellogg wrote to a number of friends in 1922 on the occasion of the publication of the special number on the coal industry. "We have a very real concern that the public shall understand what it faces in the present crisis, and what indications there are of enduring solutions for the future."[9]

There persisted in Kellogg's thinking, then, the progressive notion that there was a "public" interest involved in every industrial dispute, separate and different from the special interests of labor and management. But Kellogg also believed in self-determination, and that meant in this context the right of labor to organize. That was the lesson the British labor movement held for Kellogg—the lesson of industrial democracy from shop council right on up to Parliament, for if labor were to be an effective force in its own right it had to organize for political action just as for direct economic action in shop and industry. He possessed the progressive desire for "order," but he knew that there was no social order without social justice.

Thus, when many others found conspiracy at the heart of the great steel strike of 1919, Kellogg visited Pittsburgh, talked with workers and with field investigators of the Interchurch World Movement, and quickly discerned that the strike was "a clean and law-abiding old line labor struggle." It was not a political strike foisted upon unwitting workers by clever radical leaders seeking their own nefarious ends, as the newspapers tended to report and the public to believe. Rather he found a profound gulf between "thousands of obscure workers who have been holding out against the pressure of empty pay envelopes and public obloquy—and the well-to-do dominant class in the community."[10] The *Survey*'s articles on the strike, written by John Fitch, made clear that union recognition was vital to an orderly and humane settlement of the dispute. So, again, during the coal strike in the same year, Kellogg felt that the public concern for the supply of coal should be matched by an equal "concern for the pinch of an inadequate work schedule upon the household incomes in the coal industry."[11]

Several years later, during the strike of the textile workers in Passaic, New Jersey, in which the employers refused to deal with the striking union ostensibly because it was led by men the employers chose to identify as Communists, Kellogg joined with Rabbi Stephen Wise, John Lovejoy Elliott of the Hudson Guild Settlement, and the Reverend John Howard Melish in an offer to represent the union directly with the employers. In a letter to the striking workers the four spoke of their grief at the ruthlessness of the city's police and at the stubborn and misguided refusal of the employers to bargain with the union, even though the radical union leaders had "scrupulously avoided" injecting their own political views into the conflict. They proposed "to serve as a body of your representatives who shall negotiate on your behalf," and assured the workers that they were prepared "to urge the acceptance of the demands made by you, and to submit the results of our negotiations to you and your General Strike Committee before the final acceptance thereof." The workers accepted the proposal, the employers did not, but before any further steps could be taken the secretary of labor had intervened. To some this may have seemed a quixotic gesture, and there was a touch of the romantic in much that Kellogg did, but in a larger sense the offer reflected his concern for workers as human beings and for the essential justice of labor's demand to be recognized.[12]

As for the unionization of social workers, this too he endorsed in a letter to the publication *Social Work Today*: "I'm in favor of 'protective organizations of social workers along trade union lines,' " he wrote in response to a request for his views. "You can write me down as for (a) demonstrations, (b) picketing, (c) stoppages, (d) strikes (which you didn't mention). Also

I am for extraction, amputation and the Cesarian operation, but I should not be for resorting to them in ordinary cases of toothache, broken legs or child birth." Unionization, after all, was not an end in itself, and the tactics that any union chose to use in a given situation depended upon the objectives to be won. The question, he concluded, was not so much whether social workers had the right to organize—of course they did; the question rather should be how labor tactics were going to be employed and for what ends.[13] His reply ran true to form: on the labor issue as on others he clung to a few absolute dogmas, he was a pragmatist and a relativist in most practical matters and always concerned that means and ends, ends and means, be considered as interrelated parts of a single organic process. His faith rested in method, not in set plans or fixed goals.

In other ways, also, he remained an old-line progressive—in his cultivation of liberal business leaders, for example. His hope that enlightened business leadership might seize the initiative and move toward more democratic structures in industry ran particularly strong during the decade of the "new era" economics in the 1920s, and although his enthusiasm was subsequently dampened he never quite gave up the notion that management could be converted to fair procedures (including recognition of independent unions). Business leaders were reasonable men and the logic of events and the weight of self-interest lay on the side of industrial democracy. Thus the *Survey* never tired of seeking out examples of corporation executives who were attempting to regularize production and employment, to involve workers' councils in the evolution of shop policies, and to include workers in the distribution of rewards through profit-sharing or stock-option devices. If Sidney Hillman and David Dubinsky were the kind of labor leaders he admired, Morris Leeds, Edward A. Filene, Henry S. Dennison, Samuel B. Fels, and Lucius Eastman represented the best of industrial statesmen. His bitterness against the Hoover administration reflected dashed hopes, for he had expected that one who was known both as the Great Engineer and the Great Humanitarian would have engineered society toward humane ends. The book he had edited in the early 1930s for Samuel Fels, which was serialized in the *Survey,* set forth a program for partnership between liberal capitalism and liberal government, and Fels remained one of the most generous financial contributors to Survey Associates. With such men Kellogg felt at ease, just as so many New Nationalist progressives had felt comfortable in the presence of enlightened business leaders in the years before the First World War.

Kellogg had faith in enlightened men of capital and enlightened men of labor because he believed in man's essential rationality; and if reason were to hold sway man had to be free to pursue the truth wherever it carried him and free to proclaim the truth as he found it. Even in times of crisis—*particularly* in times of crisis—free speech and free press were essential if democracy were to survive. For a time during the First World War he wondered if Western civilization possessed the intelligence and the courage to hold true to the principle of liberty when dissent appeared to threaten the security of the state. Spending Christmas alone in Rome in 1917, he began to muse whether dissent were any more respected now than in the days of the Roman Empire. "Have we more faith in the triumph of light over darkness by the ways of light—by free discussion, education, toleration, the interplay of ideas," he wrote home to his wife; "or do we cling after all to suppression and vested might?"[14] The test lay in what a people did in times of stress. And he had cause to worry: censorship was the rule everywhere, and at home those who opposed the war and those who could not in conscience submit to the draft were being hounded and harassed. He had urged, unsuccessfully, that the American conscription act make individual conscience rather than membership in particular religious societies the test of conscientious objection.[15]

Like other civil libertarians, Kellogg was appalled by the wave of hysteria that followed the First World War. He protested against the deportation of alien radicals and against the Palmer raids; he assailed those who attempted to discredit labor unions by proclaiming their leaders to be "reds"; in the *Survey* he ran articles exposing the Ku Klux Klan; he leaped to the defense of social workers dismissed from public positions without a hearing for unspecified beliefs or acts; and during the second red scare that followed the Second World War he insisted that a political test for holding a job was inappropriate in a democracy.

No cause was more significant than the celebrated Sacco and Vanzetti case. The Kellogg brothers and their families together with Leon and Katherine Whipple were vacationing at the Kelloggs' summer place at Lake Memphremagog in August 1927 when news reports made it clear that the two immigrant anarchists, after years of judicial maneuvering, were truly going to be executed for a crime that millions of concerned persons around the world thought they had not committed. Earlier that summer, Paul Kellogg later wrote to an associate, he and his family had toured New England. "You see some of our ancestors came from the early coast settlements; and we in Michigan have a special loyalty to New England," he explained. "Then came the dog days with justice and liberty dragged pretty low; the very juxtaposition of things burning in upon me."[16]

The crisis had not come unannounced, of course, although in late September of that year, after the two Italian-Americans had been executed, Kellogg blamed himself and others for not having exerted themselves many months sooner.[17] The fact was that Kellogg, like so many others, had followed the case carefully ever since 1921 at the time of the trial, and in the spring and summer of 1927 the *Survey* had carried unsigned editorials (undoubtedly written by the editor in chief) decrying the denial of a fair trial, charging prejudice on the part of the trial judge, and asking for executive clemency so that the governor would have the time to reexamine the whole case. The trial, he wrote, had "left the judicial area" and had become "a political issue," and surely Governor Fuller must know that to carry out the execution in the face of a "tremendous body of opinion believing them innocent, will shatter the prestige of the courts."[18]

It was that line that the vacationers at the lake retreat took in an open letter to Governor Fuller which was also telegraphed to the *New York Times*. The letter, whose strategy was originally Leon Whipple's inspiration, did not claim that Sacco and Vanzetti were innocent of the Braintree murders; it asserted rather that there was widespread skepticism about their guilt and a firm sentiment that they had been denied a fair trial, and asked for a stay or commutation of the execution order. "We did not think it would count with Fuller," Kellogg wrote to Mary Ross in the *Survey*'s home office, "but might help in stretching the imagination of some newspaper readers as part of the re-education of people right and left if America isn't to lose its heritage. . . . The best we could think to do was to stand up and be counted; in the hope that it would help even if only a little to show that others besides the various 'ists had a stake here."[19] In response to the open letter came a blunt telegram from Felix Frankfurter, one of the chief leaders of the Sacco and Vanzetti Defense Committee in Boston, which urged that Kellogg come at once to Boston to mobilize sentiment for this strategy. Kellogg could not deny his old friend—or his own conscience—and he was off to Boston where for ten days (and another two days in New York) he labored to stir up broad public support on the part of responsible Americans for a stay of execution.

During the week of August 15-21, Kellogg and those who gathered around him in Boston sent out over nine thousand form letters and telegrams and made countless long-distance telephone calls to persons around the country whom they assumed to be sympathetic to this point of view. By Sunday the 21st the ad hoc committee had received over five hundred favorable replies. Through the good offices of John F. Moors, senior partner of the Moors and Cabot stock brokerage firm in Boston and a conservative financier close politically to Governor Fuller, Kellogg was able to arrange an interview with the governor for Monday the 22nd. The afternoon of that day Kellogg and Moors, together with Dr. Alice Hamilton (an early Hull House resident and professor of medicine at Harvard University), John Lovejoy Elliott (assistant leader of the New York Ethical Cultural Society as well as director of the Hudson Guild Settlement in New York), the Reverend Edward Staples Drown (of the Episcopal Theological Seminary in Cambridge, Massachusetts), and Waldo L. Cook (editor of the *Springfield Republican* in western Massachusetts) were able to claim an hour of the governor's schedule.

From the memoranda written by Kellogg's five associates (memoranda composed independently in the early autumn following the event and mailed to Kellogg at his request) and from

Paul Kellogg, vacationing at Lake Memphremagog.

the memoranda set down by Kellogg himself (a long one dated 4 September 1927 and afterthoughts composed November 30 and December 1-2) it is possible to piece together the general tenor of the audience as it appeared to these participants. The governor was clearly on the defensive, as they saw it: he tried to force an argument with them charging that they had come to plead for the lives of guilty men and that they came at the manipulation of Felix Frankfurter, one of the "chief conspirators" in "breaking down the enforcement of law and order in Massachusetts." To Elliott it seemed that the small committee of six was dealing with "a man whose mind was not only made up but closed." Kellogg, the chief spokesman for the group, replied that the petition they carried, signed by over five hundred responsible citizens from Massachusetts and throughout the nation, was in no way related to the activities of the official Defense Committee, and that their mission was not to discuss the guilt or innocence of Sacco and Vanzetti but merely to win a stay of sentence in order that the governor would have the time to review the entire case again until all doubts could be resolved. Others joined in the discussion to support this position, but to no avail. "As the hearing went on," Kellogg reported in his first memorandum, "it seemed more and more like pressing in on a rubbery surface; as soon as the pressure relaxed, a plea made, the surface sprang back to its old contour."

Paul Kellogg's confidential memorandum, set down a fortnight after the events and preserved by him apparently just for the enlightenment of posterity, is worth quoting at some length, for not only does it describe the interview with the governor as he viewed it but it also reveals his own persisting confidence in the essential and ultimate reasonability of man and the efficacy of open and candid discussion. "Whether it was due to our own ineptness, to our personal limitations or our burdened sense that our only hope lay in the respectability and reasonableness of our appeal, none of us rose to any heights of eloquence or feeling," he confessed; "there was nothing of the Hebrew prophets in our assault on the Governor's will. We might have been playing hide the slipper with him as the argument passed from hand to hand. No doubt we exercised restraint too long and the opportunity passed. . . . As it was, sticking to our lower key, we came away both with the feeling that we had overrun, one after another, his lines of defense but that it made no dent on his determination." Most frustrating of all were the guarded hints they had from the governor that he had secret assurances of the certain guilt of Sacco and Vanzetti which he could not divulge— assertions which Kellogg and the others felt the defense had no means of knowing or of challenging. And so "the Governor, hugging these beliefs and secret assurances of the guilt of Sacco and Vanzetti, resented doubts on the part of others."

Their mission failed, of course. All their efforts and the efforts of thousands of others proved to no avail. Sacco and Vanzetti were legally killed, and so embraced martyrdom. The "eleventh hour" efforts of professional men and women to stay the hand of injustice were "too few, too futile, too feeble," Kellogg wrote Mary Ross after the terrible day.[20]

The long and futile days, the shock of the execution, "the last wrenching days of that episode pretty well used up everybody in it," Arthur Kellogg observed. "Everybody who worked on the job went to pieces afterward. Paul had to take an extra two weeks' vacation because of a 'hole in the back of my head.' "[21] Paul never did shake the memory of those awful August days; the impact of the events lived on as a nagging doubt at the back of his head that affairs in life did not always come out all right, that injustice was not easily overcome, that some men were not easily persuaded—or not persuaded at all—by the force of reason. The outcome did not make him cynical, he was too much of an affirmer and a believer for that; the events did not make him a skeptic, for he had always been a questioner. But more than the frustration of the long crusade for the twelve-hour day, more than the disappointment that accompanied a quarter century's battle to secure national prohibition of child labor, more than the disillusionment that came with the collapse of Wilsonianism in the early postwar years, the death of Sacco and Vanzetti stuck in his heart as a central failure of American democracy, a crucial failure of reason and good will in human affairs. None of these failures ever embittered him, but they did give him pause. "I think we all try to look for scapegoats on the one hand, and heroes with shining swords on the other," he wrote to an intimate friend soon after the execution. "The point as I see it is that we are all to blame on this thing—all elements in American democracy."[22] Here expressed at this moment of despair was a new sense of complexity, a new awareness that even men of reason and good will could fall short.

There were two further consequences of the Sacco and Vanzetti affair for Kellogg. It cemented his friendship with Felix Frankfurter, to whom he had been close since the day the Harvard law professor took over as chief legal adviser to the National Consumers' League when Louis Brandeis went to the Supreme Court in 1916, and for the next decade, until Frankfurter himself joined the Court in 1939, Kellogg drew upon his advice and sympathy in many matters pertaining to *Survey* policy. Secondly, it deepened Kellogg's opposition to capital punishment. As editor of the *Survey*, Kellogg tried to keep himself aloof from causes that might embarrass the journal and dissipate his own energies; he could not afford to be a professional "joiner." To some causes he lent his name and prestige: on special occasions he permitted his name to be used by the NAACP, the National Urban League, and the ACLU, for example, for civil rights and civil liberties placed high in his priorities. He was for a time a very active member of the board of the Foreign Policy Association, and came to be caught up in the movement to relieve the refugees of the Spanish Civil War. But these were the exception to his general rule of not compromising the authority of his editorship by an indiscriminate joining of reform societies. The other major exception was his long-term active membership on the board of the American League to Abolish Capital Punishment. "It's not merely the killing that is bad," he confided to Lillian Wald in 1930, "but the man hunt that is staged in the popular imagination every time that a big murder trial is put on. . . . Of course, I think the thing that gets me hardest, is that it sets man up in judgment, with life and death in the scale. No modern man can play at God that way . . . without doing violence to my sense of democracy as well as humanity. . . . We see that in executing an innocent man, society makes a heart-breaking mistake. Socially speaking, it's as big a mistake to execute a guilty man. It makes us all murderers behind the law."[23]

Kellogg's commitment to civil rights is more difficult to evaluate. He conferred professionally with leaders in the Negro community and enjoyed good relations particularly with directors and staff of the Urban League, in part because of their social work orientation and program, but he could probably count only Alain Locke, editor of the special Harlem number of the *Graphic* in 1925, as a friend, and no Negro ever served on the *Survey* board or staff. Yet far more than other progressives he was sensitive to the issue of color and race and the *Survey* pioneered in covering the Negro welfare news front; the three special numbers on the black community—1925, 1942, and 1947— were far in advance of their time. With the printed word and in graphic illustrations the *Survey* broke away from set stereotypes, and by pointing up the special needs and problems of Negro workers, women, and children it moved beyond consideration of the black elite alone. As in his expectation that immigrants would come in time to be incorporated into the mainstream of American life, so did he hope that Negroes could be made integral and fully participating members of the American community.

Still there were anomalies in the record. Following publication of the pace-setting Harlem number in 1925, Kellogg considered having Survey Associates play host to a special dinner, such as there had been to mark the publication of the special numbers on coal and on electric power. A dinner for blacks and whites might be an affair that would further understanding, he believed, "by the simple process of bringing people together." But, to a white friend in the South, Rossa B. Cooley, head of the Penn School in South Carolina, he wrote to ask if such a dinner would be "misconstrued in the South; so much so as to hinder rather than to help the educational purpose of the number; and to prove a boomerang to the *Survey*'s work in other fields." Miss Cooley replied that it was better that prejudice should "be left to slumber," for then "the sooner it is likely to die out . . . and we feel that is, in the end, the larger service to the Negroes themselves too." Whatever the reasoning the *Survey* decided not to go ahead with the dinner.[24] But that spring Kellogg visited the Hampton Institute and on his return wrote a letter to George F. Peabody, a wealthy patron of the institute, setting forth reforms that he felt should be instituted at once. Hampton was dedicated to interracial cooperation, Kellogg observed, yet there was but one Negro member on the Board of Trustees. "In the day of inter-racial councils, is that proportion one which will carry conviction with the rising generation?" he asked. "You have one head of a department at Hampton who is a Negro. Is that, after 50 years, the highest way-mark which can be reached by the talent and industry of the Hampton trained man or woman—or is the proportion rather a heritage of an earlier day when white teachers were your chief resource?" He urged that the entire faculty should be brought in to help shape the school's policies, and that a special national advisory council to the board, with broad representation, be created.[25] Later, in the 1930s, and especially when he served as president of the National Conference of Social Work, Kellogg worked consistently, quietly and behind the scenes, to include more Negro social workers on NCSW programs, and to use the commercial weight of the organization in persuading southern cities to provide equal hotel and eating facilities for Negro delegates to the annual convention and in demonstrating within the South itself the contributions that Negroes had to make to the common welfare.

Paul Kellogg's sensitivity to the issues of color, which ran ahead of the views of most of his contemporaries, may be ascribed in some substantial part to his closeness to the settlement movement which was in a strategic position to recognize and interpret the felt needs of rural southern Negroes as they moved rapidly into the cities of both the North and the South. Although Kellogg was in touch with the Negro in the rural South through his visits to the Penn School, it was primarily the urban Negro whose condition he knew best. Not only in the three special numbers devoted to the race issue, but in number after number of both the *Graphic* and the *Midmonthly,* the special problems and opportunities of American blacks were set forth in matter-of-fact articles that rarely showed the slightest tinge of condescension or patronage of white toward black.

It was in action, in practice, that Kellogg evolved a working philosophy of life. But from time to time throughout his long career, as was appropriate for a journalist, he put his precepts into words. Metaphors often reveal better than formal prose the concepts by which a man is moved. During a half century of writing—letters, editorials, articles, memoranda, pleas for money—he employed a number of words and phrases all of which conjured up the frontier experience of the American people. On state occasions (as in his presidential address to the National Conference of Social Work), or when sending fatherly advice to his son, he began with the West, with the pioneers, with the "self-dependent, self-employing men" of Lincoln's frontier land of the Middle West. The pioneers were both rebels and builders; they were self-reliant individuals but they joined together in team play; alone they mastered their environment but they created self-governing communities; they moved ahead both by "private adventure and voluntary effort" and those things they could not accomplish as single individuals or families or by voluntary cooperative enterprise they did "collectively through government."[26]

Late in the autumn of 1920, Paul Kellogg wrote his nine-year-old son a long letter from the rough camp at Lake Memphremagog where he had stayed on to assist the local handyman in building the great stone chimney in the cabin which they had constructed that summer. The long descriptive letter detailed the work they did—the search for just the right field stones, the track of small logs they laid along which the great stones could be rolled to the site of the cabin, the primitive tools with which they worked, the process of lifting the stones and cementing them firmly in place. But the letter was no more about engineering than *Moby Dick* was a handbook for whaling—it was, of course, a little morality story. There was a model for self-sufficiency and pride in craft in Mr. Wilcox, the chief architect and carpenter and straw boss of the operation, whom Kellogg describes as "master of the wilderness." He was a jack-of-all-trades, a rugged man who knew how to win "comfort and food and shelter and beauty from nature," a man with a profound intuitive understanding of "earth and stone and wind and frost and fire and metals, and the laws of three dimensions and human nature and whatnot." Together, under his direction, they built a chimney which would *last*, and he imagined the warmth the fire would bring on a chilly day, and the friendship and comradeship which would be kindled around the hearth. To bring the heavy stones in from the field they had had to clear a path by cutting down a number of beautiful trees (and Pat must have known even then his father's love for all growing things, especially trees), but the lesson was clear—"you must tear down in order to build." Some people went through life, he added, just tearing down; the virtue lay in clearing the way for constructive ends.[27]

The frontier-pioneer experience had meant struggle, too, and sacrifice and a long, hard fight for liberty and brotherhood and elbowroom. In the midst of the second great war for democracy,

Paul U. Kellogg and the *Survey*

Paul Kellogg reminisced about the boyhood days with Arthur back in Kalamazoo when they had been awakened and stirred by stories of Columbus, Valley Forge, the Civil War, and the epic story of the covered wagon. "These things stood for discovery, adventure, struggles against tyranny and slavery. They stood for all manner of men who struck out for independence and the wilderness." As young boys they heard firsthand accounts of the underground railroad that had operated through their hometown, and from the mixture of immigrant folk in that frontier state—Irish, Hollanders, Germans, and Scandinavians—they learned stories "of breaking away from yokes of state, or church, or landlordism or militarism." From all these traditions they had been made aware of "the essential brotherhood of all sorts and conditions, races and religions of men whose traditions blended in the new adventure of America."[28]

Adventure . . . discovery . . . struggle—these were the "keys to the human quest everywhere," and why America was "kin" to those who risked "everything for freedom and the world round." In times of peril when it seemed that the human quest for freedom might be quenched, America offered an example of "freedom, security, opportunity," and the nation had an obligation, therefore, to assist all those who stood against tyranny. "We have had the chance to experiment with fresh relationships that the world never had room for before. A new continent for our laboratory."[29]

There was nothing novel in Paul Kellogg's vision of America, of course, but he proclaimed a people's mission with peculiar intensity and sought to apply the lessons to an industrial and urban era in which the pioneer virtues might seem outmoded and irrelevant. That was what progressive movements for reform were all about, as he saw it—the application of established traditions, deeply rooted in the American experience, to new social and economic conditions. The *Survey* itself, symbolized by the jaunty and daring caravel of Columbus's fleet, represented a joint enterprise of adventure and discovery—new pioneering on new frontiers of knowledge and society. In Kellogg's view, pioneering in the new and highly complex society of twentieth-century America demanded cooperation and team play. "Team Play," in fact, was the title he gave to his essay celebrating the silver anniversary of Survey Associates: "Team play no less than individualism was inherent in American life from the outset," he wrote. "The settler who had cleared his own land joined in barn raising, in laying a corduroy road over the swamp, in setting up a school."[30]

Evidence of the pioneering function is scattered throughout this book: *Charities and the Commons* broke into the open the problems Negroes from the rural South faced when they moved to northern cities; its exposé of housing and health conditions in the nation's capital provoked the great Pittsburgh Survey; the Pittsburgh study, in turn, strengthened the movements for workmen's compensation and for the elimination of the long day in the steel industry; the journal dared broach the social and health implications of venereal disease at a time when the subject generally was taboo. The *Survey* opened up discussion in welfare circles of vocational guidance and child guidance clinics during the teens, a decade before these two welfare movements really took hold. The special number on the Harlem renaissance, and the later numbers on segregation, 1942 and 1947, broke new ground for analysis and understanding in the field of race relations. In the 1920s the *Survey*'s central themes dealt with economic and social planning, the rights of labor, preventives and cures for unemployment, and comprehensive social insurance— thus forecasting central ingredients of the New Deal. Its special numbers on heart disease and on syphilis stimulated public action in the health fields. The journal hammered at the need for health insurance and public housing a generation before it became feasible even to engage in public debate about their prospect. The *Survey* sought to "win hearings for subjects which, as the general run of periodicals look at things, the public is not ready for," Kellogg declared to readers in 1928. "We must forecast or even provoke what in due course people will be pricking up their ears about."[31] A decade or so later, in 1942, he confided to Samuel Fels the hazards involved in playing this role: "There have been times in our *Survey* work that we have been so far in advance of the procession that while we later gained a reputation as prophets, we altogether failed to spur public opinion and action." He was proud to have been ahead of the times, but he preferred to be of practical service.[32]

But what does it really mean to "pioneer" or to be "ahead" of the times? It cannot be claimed that the *Survey* entertained a unique vision of the future, that it stood apart from central themes that characterized America in the first two generations of the twentieth century, that it always swam against the current. Its politics, it is true, stood over against the majority programs and styles of Harding, Coolidge, and Hoover in that decade of the 1920s which was generally inhospitable to reform, but by no means did it reflect, even in these years, the positions of a small minority. Paul Kellogg and the journal he edited were never "alienated" from their times. The *Survey* was part of a goodly company of liberal, humane, enlightened, pragmatic progressives (at least that is how they perceived themselves), who believed in intelligence, in democracy, in reform, in variety, in an open and malleable universe. The *Survey* may often have provoked public discussion of unpopular issues but it rarely if ever played the prophet crying in the wilderness. It was too professional, too bourgeois, too reasonable, too respectable a journal for that. It was, in the words of Katharine Lenroot, "unangry." It went about in white (if unstarched) collar, not hair shirt.

Paul Kellogg often espoused causes "ahead" of his times, but in a more significant sense he lived at the vital center of his times, and he never felt "alone." He was a man very much of and in his own times. He was at home in the universe and in each new era as it came. He was numbered among the pioneering few to travel occasionally by air when commercial flights were experimental and not without risk. Disappointments he knew, heartache, frustration, and fatigue, for they are part of the human condition from which he was not immune. He was no stranger to loneliness, although he was always surrounded by love; in the death of Arthur, just at the moment he was beginning a new life of his own, he suffered an irreparable loss. All these— but never alienation.

Even when he was striving the hardest to adapt the pioneer tradition to modern urban conditions, Kellogg could not shake off that nostalgia for what he called, time and again, "Lincoln's plain people." The point of departure was always Michigan and the great valley of democracy through which the Mississippi River flowed. To William Allen White, who shared so many of these ideals, Kellogg wrote in the early months of the Second World War: we must gain a sense again of "a great, loose-hung democracy," for if "democracy means anything, it means that its wellsprings should be in the hills and plains."[33] And in the concluding paragraph of his essay on the need to establish the pioneer tradition of "team play" he appealed to the men and women who lived in crowded urban and industrial centers, who looked "down streets where the wind rattles sooty leaves, who must get out to the woods to breathe the remembrance of the wilderness they sprang from."[34]

To Kellogg, the notion of returning to the wilderness was not merely a rhetorical flourish, but a pressing need. He had watched slum children go off for a week or two in the summer camps that the settlements provided beyond the sooty rim of the sprawling, congested cities of modern America, and had seen them come back tanned and gay. He had sat with adult clubs of men and women who were alumni of the settlement camping experience and listened as they laid plans for their own children to enjoy the great out-of-doors. He joined the crusade to save the Palisades of the Hudson from industrial and commercial despoliation; he solicited myriad articles for the *Survey* on the movement for national parks, not alone for the conservation of resources but especially for the preservation of unspoiled, wilderness areas where men might repair to be restored. At the lake place in Quebec he found refreshment of spirit, and escape from the noisome cities; cleansed in soul by fresh air and clear water and the breeze through the trees, his mind cleared of the city's clatter, he would hike through the woods to the rough field above the cabin and there, on great yellow pads of notepaper he would begin to outline the *Survey*'s plan of action for the next year and begin to set down in rough draft editorials and appeals for the autumn's work. Later in life, when he and Helen Hall bought the farm at Cornwall, an hour's drive up the Hudson from Henry Street, he found the same kind of respite, weekends and summers, from the week's and the year's routine. There, in his fifties and sixties, as at Memphremagog when he was a younger man, he cut down brush and saplings to open up vistas down which he could see far distant the winding valleys and gentle rolling hills. It is difficult for all of us not to read our own sentiments and needs into other men, for mankind (it is easy to believe) is one; and although Paul Kellogg believed in variety and had experienced variety in the men and women he met and with whom he lived, he could not but believe that they shared with him this hunger of body and soul for the quiet and peace of wilderness and woods.

Yet he knew that not many men, in fact, could escape to the countryside. Economic dependence and social interdependence were the facts of life, not individualism which presumably had characterized America's first three centuries of history. Exploitation, not self-reliance, was the mark of an industrial civilization. In the modern era men were insecure, they could not provide by themselves against the risks of accident, sickness, and unemployment, and against the certain hazards that came with old age. What then could be salvaged from the past? What adaptations could men make to their new environment, so drastically transformed by the factory, the mine, and the city?

Kellogg gave many answers, none perhaps more comprehensive than the explanation he made in a letter to Robert W. de Forest, president of his board, concerning his personal endorsement of the presidential candidacy of Robert M. LaFollette in 1924. In private conversation he had replied to de Forest's query about why he was for the Wisconsin senator by saying "that I was from Michigan." This answer must have been mystifying, his letter began, but it was the place to start. His grandfather had gone to Michigan when it was still a wilderness and in his lifetime it had been turned to "farms and communities." But then came the industrial revolution and economic troubles for the average man in the Middle West who found himself "at a disadvantage—as producer and consumer, employe, and shipper and householder, when set off against the corporate machinery . . . that ran the mills and railroads and the other great instruments of common service." He had known firsthand these disadvantages, for the family lumber business had failed in the

1890s and as a boy he had come "to know life as the average experience it." It didn't seem fair or just that the gains of "science and progress" took such "a long time getting spread around." That is how he came to join forces with Edward Devine and Graham Taylor and de Forest and all those who from "various angles were interested in getting at the causes of poverty and distress; and in laying the foundations for a new social statesmanship."

In those years, at the beginning of the new century, Kellogg continued, it was LaFollette who worked for the people, bringing the power of the state to the assistance of the common citizen, "turning the state university and state services to new and constructive uses," and harnessing "this genius for team play" to the needs of the "new corporate epoch." It was at that time that he had gone to Pittsburgh to direct the Survey and there he saw "developing rapidly a social composition strangely like that of Europe. Would we let this drift continue; classes develop and harden in layers; and create a serried social order, which would repress life for a few generations and lead, as overseas, to explosion from below? Or would we have the self-mastery to control these headlong industrial forces, and recapture opportunity for each oncoming generation?"

Here expressed was the progressive anxiety that America might be divided into conflicting classes, and lose the harmony and cohesion and common purpose which presumably had been the quality of the nation in its younger years. If industry destroyed the unique openness which had been America, Kellogg cried, "then what rhyme or reason in having a New World—if we were to be just a belated edition of the old countries?" In America the progressives, in Britain the labor movement, had promised a "new social statescraft" which could, with the "help of the social engineers," achieve organic progress. That is what LaFollette represented in 1924, Kellogg concluded: a broad party built not along class lines but under leadership "native to that mid-western pioneering spirit which I knew as a boy: 'headworkers,' farmers and townsfolk—stretching tent ropes to include workers with hand." Such a coalition of "Lincoln's plain people," who were "my kind" of people, could shape, as the English had, a "new balance between individual liberty and human welfare, self-government and state action."[35]

Kellogg had lived in New York most of his adult life and in eastern cities he had found his friends and allies, and still he did not shake loose the ancient prejudice, typified by Bryan and LaFollette, that somehow men of the West, men who lived close to nature and in the wide open spaces, and drew their sustenance directly from the soil, were truer to the American dream. When he cited LaFollette's coalition (as he perceived it) to include " 'head-workers,' farmers and townsfolk [and] . . . workers with hand" he was, unwittingly without doubt, paraphrasing that old romantic notion pronounced by the Knights of Labor when he was a boy that workers of "hand and brain" could join together and govern the nation. It was a glorious concept of what might be, and consistent with the visions of Jefferson and Whitman, but it flew in the face of much of what history in his own time demonstrated about class and self-interest and power. Charles Beard had challenged the *Survey*'s easy perception of city and regional planning back in the mid-1920s—because it ignored the wellsprings of human behavior in property, self-interest, and class.

It was Coolidge, not LaFollette, who won out in 1924; then Hoover, for whom so many social workers had entertained such high expectations; and then, of course, came the depression and drift. With the depression a year old and no sign of constructive leadership from Washington, Kellogg wrote to an old fellow Bull Mooser, Gifford Pinchot of Pennsylvania, to complain of Hoover's "fumbling leadership": "It seems to me that the Hon. H. H. with his persistent reiteration of sturdy individualism as the answer to all our industrial ills, quite misses the point. . . . After all he was in South Africa, Australia, China, in the very years in which Roosevelt and the rest of you Progressives were educating America on the possibility of the use of government as a friendly implement of democracy rather than a policeman's club."[36] Where Hoover had fallen short it seemed that Roosevelt might strike through to new levels of constructive government action, and he did in some substantial measure, but never to the degree that Kellogg thought both desirable and feasible. The New

Deal had established the principle that "what's wrong anywhere is everybody's concern," but it had not moved on to comprehensive social planning, save perhaps in the Tennessee Valley Authority.[37]

In the modern era of mass insecurity, Kellogg believed that nothing short of comprehensive social planning, from neighborhood to nation, would suffice. Procedures would have to be democratic—that is, the citizens would have to be involved at every stage of planning; planning by decree, by edicts issued from above, could not work without destroying initiative and liberty. Cities and regions were the units of planning out of which national planning, where appropriate, could rise. And in this matter, as in so many others, the nostalgia for an older and simpler America would not down. A sense of fellowship came when people worked together toward common goals, and that kind of natural neighborliness had its best chance to flower when intelligent planners, working in their own localities, could get away "from the big city idea with its houses piled on houses and the ugly crowding together of industrial buildings."[38]

The name with which Kellogg conjured in this instance was Sir Patrick Geddes, Scottish sociologist and city planner who, during a visit to New York in 1923, had spent a day with Kellogg and the *Survey* staff. It was one of those chance occasions that take on larger meaning with the passing of time, for until his last sickness Kellogg would tell again and again the excitement of those hours when Geddes sat on a "hard bench under the gnarled old tree in Gramercy Park," and gave the assembled group a "visualization of the things we dream about when we read of Socrates in Athens."[39] Geddes was such a man as Kellogg extravagantly admired—romantic yet practical, philosophical yet down-to-earth, visionary yet rooted in the experience of precise city planning—and he stood for democratic, decentralized planning, common citizens and the experts working together in a partnership for the common good.

Planning necessarily implied that men could in fact control their own destinies, and to Kellogg it seemed that (in America at least) mankind could consciously and deliberately and intelligently guide the course of human events along progressive lines.

Paul U. Kellogg and the *Survey*

Once again it was a "pioneer" characteristic that he extolled, for the American, as he conquered the wilderness and built communities, gained a "zest for fashioning life." That spirit of discovery and building led "men to welcome change as a natural experience and to share in it; that leads in turn to faith in human volition as something which can shape and direct change." In the modern era life had become so complex that simple common sense would no longer suffice in the provision of guidelines and blueprints: the inductive methods of the social sciences would have to be utilized as tools for social control. In a paper prepared in collaboration with Neva Deardorff and delivered at the International Conference of Social Work in Paris in 1928 the successful attack on tuberculosis was taken as a model for all phases of social engineering. Here there was a natural sequence beginning with investigation and research, moving on to public education, care, and preventive measures which culminated in control; from this sequence men were fortified in their belief "that the human spirit could assert itself over circumstances, that democracies by taking thought might cure themselves of some of their ills."[40]

If Geddes was the prophet of city and regional planning whose disciple Kellogg chose to be, his philosophical mentors were John Dewey (although there is no indication that he ever labored through Dewey's professional articles and books), James Harvey Robinson, Louis Brandeis, Roscoe Pound, Simon N. Patten, and Charles A. Beard. Pragmatic instrumentalism came as naturally to Kellogg as all other parts of his world view. As editor he mistrusted potential contributors who saw life in blacks and whites and who had pet (and pat) solutions to the world's problems. He saw one chief mission of the *Survey* to be that of provoking critical discussion of established methods of social service and of set patterns of welfare programs and policies. One had to begin with the facts, inductively established as valid, but "to stuff the public with masses of information," he declared, "is like trying to cram school boys with facts."[41] As long as citizens were involved, at every stage and at every level, in the processes of social engineering, one need have no fear of totalitarianism. The universe, including human society, was in process; the world was not closed and finished but open and in flux, and men could share in the processes of evolution.

Study, research, and contemplation found their justification in purposeful social action; in the *doing* one found meaning in life. Kellogg favored men with "living faiths," and he himself sought "to contribute something to the long struggle of man with his universe, his mastery of his environment, of himself, his genius for team play for common ends." He looked for men who were moved by "forward promptings," for men who had "the feel of social engineering—of wind, and stream and the joy of energising power, as against the lassitudes of dead calms, or the neutralization of crosscurrents and choppy seas—that's a beginning in getting an approach to a dynamic as against a static social order."[42]

Kellogg believed in man, in his intelligence and his good intentions, although in war he saw evil forces that could turn man "back to savagery," as he once wrote to his son.[43] His faith finally was in the sure expectation that "if you can give people a foot-hold for life . . . they will find out what to do with that opportunity."[44] Like the settlement workers, he hoped to find ways to reconcile classes, religions, and peoples, to resolve divisions and antagonisms so that social harmony, the fruit of reason, would prevail; he abhorred power (and undoubtedly did not really understand it). He knew that compromise was an essential ingredient of reaching an agreed consensus and that no man, no group, had a monopoly on the truth. He was impatient with exploitation and injustice but finally patient in the face of evil because he believed in the ultimate beneficence of history. Katharine Lenroot, chief of the Children's Bureau, summed it up accurately in a statement eulogizing the *Survey* soon after its demise. The *Survey* was "unangry," she observed, "even when its presentation of issues was most pressing and urgent. Paul Kellogg feels that, when people really understand, their actions will be right and just. He has never stopped trying to get them the facts on which understanding will be based."[45]

He believed in "Lincoln's plain people," yes, but he knew that the people had to be led, and so the *Survey* was aimed at the elite in each community—professional men and women, teachers, lawyers, doctors, social workers, responsible business and labor leaders, engineers, ministers, priests and rabbis, architects —"a leaven of people who are not content with the past, people who are exchanging ideas, people who are groping, inventing, experimenting, people who within the span of their own professions have a gleam of a better day."[46] It was to this audience that the *Survey* was addressed.

Kellogg never hoped for or worked toward a large mass circulation for his journal; he aimed rather at these expert professional groups of "socially-inclined folk" who could move the community ahead without waiting for popular opinion to support constructive social innovations.[47]

The man was one with the philosophy. Gentle in his relations with others, he expected like treatment in return. Assured and self-confident in professional and public matters, he often backed away from personal confrontations that threatened to be unpleasant. Although unwittingly he sometimes ruffled the feelings of others, he could never bring himself to face awkward or disagreeable situations. Sentiment and loyalty sometimes overrode his own best judgment. Reflective, balanced, and thoughtful, he seldom responded quickly to crises, but rather took his time in carefully exploring all facets of a new issue before declaring himself. Rarely doctrinaire in his responses, he consulted persons on all sides of all issues and kept his own counsel until, for him, the facts were in. He took his time because he wanted the stories the *Survey* printed to be right; he took his time so as not to do injustice to any living person or cause. As the *New York Times* editorialized when the *Survey* ceased publication: "It has had a deep humanity as well as a sound instinct for accuracy. . . . It has been a heart as well as a brain."[48]

In appearance Kellogg was an unprepossessing person. He dressed casually—even carelessly—and there persisted in him a boyish charm which often provoked possessive concern on the part of his female staff. One of his secretaries, Sadie Stark, who had worked in the office for several years just following the First World War, recalled that she found the editor at first a "shabby, slumped-over blonde man with thin rumpled hair and a completely unassuming manner."[49] And there was good-humored self-deprecation in Kellogg's reply to a request for a photograph to be used by the National Conference of Social Work when he was president: "Most of my pictures don't adorn, they smudge— because except for my nose, I seem to be lacking in eyebrows, hair, whiskers or other features that stand out." His desk was as untidy as his personal appearance was careless and rumpled. "My desk looks like a threshing floor," he confessed to a friend on one occasion; and on another wistfully admitted, "my desk is my weakest point."[50] Victor Weybright, who became very close to Paul Kellogg in the years he managed the *Graphic,* commented, years later, that the poet's claim that "disorder can be heaven's highest law" applied perfectly to his chief; the disorder came naturally, not by design, but that quality did also represent the unaffected openness of Kellogg to new ideas (and manuscripts) and that habit of gathering evidence from many different sources until it sifted down into some true order and sense.

Perhaps his finest virtue as an editor was his intuition for the significant new issue. He was curious about everything that touched people, and quick to sense when new troubles were brewing. To say as much is not to suggest that he was an innovator or a "prophet"; he had a creative but not an original or even an analytical mind: its prescience and creativity were exercised in divining new lines of investigation and reporting and in getting to the root of things that mattered to common people. Closely related to this instinct for fresh insights was Kellogg's knack for uncovering fresh talent. He obtained photographic and graphic work from Lewis Hine, Joseph Stella, and Hendrik Willem Van Loon when they were still relatively unknown. He solicited articles from David Lilienthal, Lewis Mumford, and Richard Neuberger, for example, before their reputations had been fully established. A gentle teacher, he could lead others to recognize ideas and insights they didn't know they had, and he helped countless persons to find themselves and to develop their potential. It was a knack that Paul Kellogg himself ascribed to his mother, to whom he was passionately devoted. "She was a wonder at getting the drama and meaning out of people she was thrown with," he wrote to his son en route to Europe in the early summer of 1928. " 'Mommy'—your grandmother Kellogg—was gifted at that. She could get more drama and personality out of chance encounters than any one I've ever known."[51]

After Arthur's death only Victor Weybright could be counted as a person who had the talent, the ambition, and the strength ever to challenge Kellogg's authority or to be thought of as a fit successor should he ever retire; but the *Survey* was too confining a place for a man of Weybright's vaulting talents and drive. Kellogg knew how to delegate authority and responsibility; once new staff members were trained and had proven themselves, they were given their head and encouraged to become fully participating members of the editorial staff. It was all the more surprising, then, that Kellogg proved constitutionally unable to take on an associate to whom, in time, he might have turned over his position as editor in chief. Perhaps he was a victim of bad luck and bad timing. It is equally likely that after a half century of being chief, Kellogg could not psychologically contemplate stepping down or aside. Unlike Edward Devine, for whom editing the *Survey* was only one of many commitments so that he could relinquish that responsibility to Paul Kellogg in 1912 without personal trauma, the *Survey* was for Kellogg both vocation and avocation. It became so much an extension of himself that to withdraw was psychologically to die; his friends and his wife, who knew this was so, encouraged him to stay on. If the *Survey* had any remote chance of surviving, the failure to find a successor proved the fatal flaw.

Although he learned to move at ease in sophisticated and wealthy social circles there was always about Paul Kellogg an aura of natural innocence. He never mistrusted the motives of others. For all his years in the big city, for all his experience reporting social problems, for all his travels and contacts with exploitation and callousness and social calculation, he remained unpretentious, unaffected, whimsical, puckish, romantic, unconcerned with rank or authority, and (some said) naive. Or it may have been that what appeared as naiveté was an expression of that central openness to other persons and other ideas: at his desk, around the evening dinner table at Henry Street, in a railroad car, or on the terrace at Cornwall, he would suck on his pipe (which would never stay lit), his clear Dutch blue eyes intent on the person speaking, listening and waiting, quietly shaping a story in his mind.

Kellogg played the role of reporter with great skill, but his larger contributions came from intellectual courage and integrity, open-mindedness, and responsiveness to new social needs. Unlike so many other of the reformers who had been converted to progressivism back at the turn of the century, he moved easily with changing times. He managed to keep his balance because he had the capacity for sustained intellectual effort interlaced with a love of gaiety. Because of his openness and interest in people, he was surrounded by loving and loyal souls his life long.

He was at home. In Kalamazoo, in New York City, in Mexico City and in London, at Memphremagog and at Cornwall he was at home. If he never cared for stylish clothes and paid more attention to dinner conversation than to what he was eating, he knew about the earth and was at home in it. He was quickly at home in the settlements where he lived or visited—Greenwich House, Hull House, Kingsley House (which had been his home base during the Pittsburgh Survey), and best of all, of course, the House on Henry Street. He was quickly at ease with all sorts and conditions of humankind, perhaps because he had very early in life learned how to be open to others without exposing his own most private thoughts and moods. He moved with equal facility among Scottish miners and the elite of the rich Jewish community in Manhattan. He counted friends among poor Mexicans, and the Gypsies he met at Hull House. He understood the language of Sidney Hillman and Samuel Fels, Florence Kelley and Edward Ryerson. He joked with Felix Frankfurter and with backwoods farmers in Kentucky. His was an insatiable curiosity about humankind.

He shared the enthusiasms of progressive reform-minded America in the wonderfully exuberant years before the First World War. He caught the vision of a new world with Wilson. The New Deal, at its best, was his America. With so many of his associates and friends he shared an expectation, during the second great war, that surely *this* time society could be reconstructed according to heart's desire. The twenties he had found inhospitable, but even then he took comfort and found excitement in the visual and performing arts and in the exploration of the psyche which was then the rage. Things hadn't always worked out as he had hoped. Reaction, not reconstruction, was the hard fact of two postwar eras. Roosevelt (Franklin that is) never went far enough or fast enough to keep pace with his own program and his own calendar. But still he was at home in time and space —his time, his place, his times, his places. He was unable finally to admit to himself that the time might be out of joint or that life might involve tragedies and defeats which lay beyond redemption. In the midst of some of the most awe-full events of the twentieth century, he remained a believer and an affirmer. He was constitutionally unable to say "no."

Testimonials and eulogies rarely constitute reliable evidence for the biographer; yet occasionally on state occasions and at death the essential truth is spoken. Homer Folks, a towering figure in the health and welfare movements of the first third of the twentieth century testified in 1940, when Paul Kellogg was being honored at a banquet, that the *Survey*'s editor had kept him from self-satisfaction, that he had always prodded him forward and had never let him rest: "He has been the great stirrer-up, the tireless reproacher, the super you-can't-possibly-stop-there man. He has agitated my conclusions, my self-respect, my desire to be in some slight degree consistent with myself, and my desire to really know something . . . and to have accomplished something." That rang true. So did the remarks of William Hodson, commissioner of welfare in New York City, on the same occasion: "Paul has understood the sorrow and misery of humble people but he has never lost faith in them nor in the ultimate ability of America to give them a better break." An unsolicited compliment came from Ella C. Parmenter, of Oberlin College's publicity bureau, in 1944, that contained another fragment of the truth: "I turn with joy to the *Survey,* which can criticize without using a bludgeon, and which always builds, or at least points the way to building, after razing any tottering structure or condition." When Kellogg died, Adolf Berle observed that Paul's life had been "all of one piece from the beginning to the end. Essentially, he wanted to liberate other human beings." Another evaluation was attributed to Walter Rauschenbusch, chief prophet of the social gospel movement: "If a fellow has the New Testament and the *Survey,* he ought to be able to be a good Christian."⁵²

What difference did it all make—what contributions did the *Survey* really make? It takes a bold man to draw lines of influence and consequences. Can it ever be "proved" that the *Survey*'s was an effective voice in moving the nation toward those goals which were its declared intent? Can the writing of biography ever establish what a man's impact on his times truly was? It is a risky and uncertain business to attempt answers, and yet certain deductions can be made, certain inferences essayed.

The *Survey*'s role for the developing professions of social service cannot be gainsaid—it served a synthesizing function in an age of specialization. For two generations of social workers the *Survey* was their "bible" (as so many of them put it). For all branches of social work—casework, group work, community organization, research and education, and administration—the *Midmonthly* was the one indispensable reference. It reflected, it informed, and it helped to mold the serving professions in their formative years. Its concern for rural health and welfare was casual and sporadic, but that was a neglect that characterized urban social work generally. It helped to educate untold thousands of lay citizens, who came as amateurs and volunteers to the social service fields, to the intricacies of welfare programs and policies. If, all by itself, it did not bring about the eight-hour day, or the abolition of child labor, or social security, it was an effective ally in the movements that sought these ends and it served to provoke discussion of these issues among community leaders who counted. It was certainly one vital force, among others, in keeping alive the social action component of social work when many factors operated with contrary tendencies and in opposite directions.

And if the writing of history has any special justification, the *Survey* can be justified, in turn, as a great journal of record, a reservoir of historical evidence because it was written from such a strategic position so deeply within its times.

But questions of influence and impact and consequence are not the only ones the historian may attempt to answer. Perhaps they are not even the most appropriate questions to raise. If one recognizes that lives and acts do have consequences and count, then the existential questions of what a man was and what he did justify not only his life but the telling of it.

The *Survey* itself, in one of its last (unsigned) elaborate and philosophical editorials, took a position just short of that. It opened with a long quotation from William James's *Will to Believe*: "If this life be not a real fight, in which something is eternally gained for the universe by success, it is no better than a game of private theatricals from which one may withdraw at will. But it feels like a real fight—as if there were something really wild in the universe which we, with all our idealities and faithfulnesses, are needed to redeem; and first of all to redeem our own hearts from theisms and fears. For such a half-wild, half-starved universe our nature is adapted." Such was the text for the day. The editorial then went on to assert the *Survey*'s pride in "many stoutly-won successes—no assumption that they were eternal or universal, but successes which proved to be substantial human gains." So, in December 1948, on the eve of a new year, the fight had meaning still. "The burdens left by war or carried over from prewar days can be unloaded from humanity's back only by action, through agitation for disinterested help and in the light of understanding. It is in these functions that *Survey Graphic* has done its work in the past." The editorial asserted that "civilization and human dignity" faced another time of acute peril, and for such a crisis the *Survey* had no "readymade patterns" of response, no formulas to apply; but it had a method, and a dedication to a "world of peace and good will, of less violated decencies and more equal chances."[53]

Such was the justification that the *Survey* made in its own behalf—not only on this late occasion, but so often in other words, in other ways, at other times throughout the half century it was the nation's leading journal in social work and social welfare. The *Survey* claimed no ultimate, no "eternal or universal" justification. Perhaps for the *Survey* and for Paul Kellogg it is unnecessary to claim any more than that. Perhaps it is enough merely to say that the justification lay in the being and the doing.

NOTES AND BIBLIOGRAPHIC NOTE

Notes

CHAPTER I. THE ORIGINS OF SOCIAL WORK JOURNALISM

1. Edward T. Devine, *When Social Work Was Young* (New York: Macmillan, 1939), pp. 103-104.
2. *Charities*, 1 (December 1897), pp. 4-5.
3. *Charities*, 1 (August 1898), 1. I have also drawn here on my essay from *America Discovers Poverty—Again* (New Orleans: Tulane University, School of Social Work, November 15, 1967).
4. *Charities*, 1 (17 December 1898), p. 1.
5. Report of Homer Folks, in *Charities*, 3 (17 June 1899), p. 7.
6. *Charities*, 6 (5 January 1901), p. 1.
7. *Charities*, 9 (6 December 1902), p. 541.

CHAPTER II. THE MAKING OF AN EDITOR

1. I shall return to this theme later, but for the moment, just by way of illustration, see Paul U. Kellogg (hereafter cited as PUK), "Touchstone of American Temper," comments on the 25th Anniversary of the Foreign Policy Association, 1943, in Survey Associates (hereafter cited as SA) Papers, Folder 662; "Buffalo and Points West: The Span of a Century in Our Struggle for Footholds for Democracy," presidential address, National Conference of Social Work, *Proceedings, 1939*, pp. 3-29. PUK to Judge Mack, 27 September 1933, SA Papers, Folder 722; PUK to Judge Florence Allen, 29 December 1938, SA Papers, Folder 343.
2. From "Daddy" to "Dear Pat," n.d., c. 1919, in PUK Papers, Folder 5.
3. PUK to William Hard, 27 July 1934, SA Papers, Folder 594.
4. PUK to Pat, 23 June 1934, PUK Papers, Folder 11.
5. This and other documents I draw upon here are located in the chronological folders of personal papers in the PUK Papers, Folders 3-19. Some of the stories come from a series of interviews with various surviving members of PUK's family.
6. The quotations above and some of the other information are taken from PUK to Pat, 18 February 1929, PUK Papers, Folder 10.

7. PUK Papers, Supplement.

8. Themes for English I, November 1901, PUK Papers, Folder 23.

9. These paragraphs are based on the New York COS folder in the PUK Papers, Folder 27, on columns in the *Charities* detailing the Summer School work, on clippings in the Arthur P. Kellogg (hereafter cited as APK) Scrapbook, 1893-1903, which is located in the PUK Papers, Folder 50. See also PUK to Edward T. Devine, 1 October 1937, SA Papers, Folder 492. PUK's account, "The Summer School in Philanthropic Work," was published in *Charities*, 9 (26 July 1902), pp. 90-92. See also Edward T. Devine's account, *When Social Work Was Young*, pp. 108-109.

10. Memorandum PUK to Edward T. Devine, January 1903, COS files in papers of Community Services Society Archives, New York City. It is an unsigned statement, but the context and the language indicate clearly that Kellogg was the author.

11. PUK to Jane Addams, 7 March 1932, on the occasion of Florence Kelley's death, SA Papers, Folder 335.

12. *Charities*, 14 (24 June 1905), pp. 857-860. Memorandum on response, dated 24 February 1906, in COS Charities Publications, 1904-11, CSS Archives.

13. *Charities*, 12 (2 July 1904), pp. 687-688.

14. CSS Archives, folders in COS files, folder on Charities Publications, 1904-11: 23rd Annual Report, the COS, 1904-5, in CSS Archives; see especially PUK's memorandum dated 18 May 1905.

15. Quoted by Devine in *When Social Work Was Young*, p. 110.

16. Model letter in COS Charities Publications, 1904-11, CSS Archives.

17. *The Commons*, 10 (October 1905), p. 530.

18. "Philanthropy and Justice," *The Commons*, 32 (31 December 1898), pp. 8-9.

19. *The Commons*, 1 (February 1897), pp. 5-6.

20. Editorial excerpted and used on the letterhead of the merged publications.

21. Edward T. Devine, presidential address, in *Charities and the Commons*, 16 (2 June 1906), pp. 340-345. See also PUK's summary of the whole conference, ibid., pp. 291-293.

22. Ibid., p. 293.

23. Edward T. Devine, year's end report to readers, *Charities and the Commons*, 19 (7 December 1907), pp. 1147-48.

24. Edward T. Devine, lead editorial, *Charities and the Commons*, 19 (4 January 1908), p. 1305a.

25. Edward T. Devine, lead editorial on opening of new volume, *Charities and the Commons*, 17 (October 1906), pp. 1-3.

26. Edward T. Devine, "What We Believe," *Charities and the Commons*, 20 (5 September 1908), p. 635.

27. Edward T. Devine in *Charities and the Commons*, 19 (2 November 1907), pp. 947-948; Cabot's article appeared in the same number, pp. 1001-10. These points of view could be documented, of course, by reference to any number published during these years, 1905-9.

28. Edward T. Devine, lead editorial, *Charities and the Commons*, 21 (3 October 1908), p. 2.

29. Henry R. Seager, "Outline of a Program of Social Reform," *Charities and the Commons,* 17 (April 1907), pp. 828-832.

CHAPTER III. THE PITTSBURGH SURVEY AND THE *SURVEY* JOURNAL

1. Alice B. Montgomery to PUK, 11 June 1906, PUK Papers, Folder 330.

2. The story of the origins of the Pittsburgh Survey has been pieced together from the published volumes themselves and from Devine, *When Social Work Was Young,* p. 112; Shelby Harrison, typescript biography of John M. Glenn of the Russell Sage Foundation, Chapter 9 (lent to me by the author); typed memorandum in 1920 folder (no. 489) of SA Papers which relates the background of the study and includes quotations from an April 1910 statement of the editors of the *Survey* journal on the subject; and PUK to Charles C. Cooper, 25 February 1925, on the death of Robert A. Woods, in SA Papers, Folder 454. The articles on social conditions in Washington, D.C., were published in *Charities and the Commons,* 15 (3 March 1906).

3. PUK to Edward T. Devine, 13 February 1907, in COS Publications folder, CSS Archives.

4. PUK, *The Pittsburgh District; Civic Frontage* (New York: Survey Associates, 1914), p. 492.

5. Ibid., p. 515.

6. The quotations in this paragraph are all drawn from Edward T. Devine's summary preface to ibid., pp. 3-5.

7. PUK in ibid., pp. 510-512. See also his evaluation of the significance of the Pittsburgh Survey in PUK and Neva R. Deardorff, *Social Research as Applied to Community Progress* (N.p.: International Conference of Social Work, 1929), pp. 7-12.

8. The story was often told on ceremonial occasions later in PUK's life, and members of his family recalled, more than fifty years after the event, the pride that he had taken in this sequence of events. It is also told in Shelby Harrison's typescript biography of John M. Glenn; in Devine, *When Social Work Was Young,* p. 113; and by PUK in a letter to Jane Addams, 31 October 1925, SA Papers, Folder 332.

9. PUK to Francis Tyson, 4 December 1919, SA Papers, Folder 854.

10. Copies of these memoranda, dated January through April 1907, can be found in SA Papers, Folder 652.

11. COS, Charities Publications, 1904-11, CSS Archives.

12. PUK to Robert W. de Forest, 25 July 1908, ibid.

13. Typescript memorandum, c. 1906, in PUK Papers.

14. Letters and minutes in COS, Charities Publications, 1904-11, CSS Archives.

15. The original board included Jane Addams, Robert S. Brewster, Robert W. de Forest, Edward T. Devine, John M. Glenn, V. Everit Macy, Julian W. Mack, Charles D. Norton, Simon N. Patten, Frank Tucker, Paul M. Warburg, and Alfred T. White. Articles of Incorporation, SA Papers, Folder 1.

16. *Survey,* 31 (4 October 1913), cover and pp. 31-32.

CHAPTER IV. AN ERA OF REFORM AND
THE COMING OF WAR

1. PUK to Lillian Wald, 19 November 1937, Wald Papers, File 3, Drawer 3. This in reply to an 18 November 1937 letter from Miss Wald: "I have not forgotten that I felt young and hopeful. Despite the confinement to a house and a room and a bed . . . I still feel young and hopeful and love, as I always have loved, 'my white haired boy.' "

2. Edward T. Devine, "Politics and Social Work," *Survey*, 29 (5 October 1912), pp. 8-10. Allen F. Davis, *Spearheads for Reform: the Social Settlements and the Progressive Movement, 1890-1914* (New York: Oxford University Press, 1967), pp. 194-207.

3. PUK, news story on the election campaign, *Survey*, 28 (24 August 1912), pp. 668-670.

4. PUK to Waldo Cook, editor of the *Springfield Republican*, 23 April 1946, SA Papers, Supplementary Folder Coo-.

5. PUK to Josephine Goldmark, 18 March 1946, SA Papers, Supplementary Folder Glu-Gon. See also PUK to Jane Addams, 9 February 1929, and her reply, 6 March 1929, SA Papers, Folder 333; PUK to Edward T. Devine, 30 December 1910, SA Papers, Folder 652; PUK Papers, Folder 331, which includes among several other documents a copy of a letter from Theodore Roosevelt to George W. Perkins, 23 August 1912, acknowledging that "our best plank, the plank which has really given our party its distinctive character," came from the social workers. "They are doing literally invaluable work."

6. For PUK's role in these affairs see PUK Papers, Folder 313; PUK to Mary Van Kleeck, 25 November 1919, SA Papers, Folder 857; PUK to John A. Fitch, 8 May 1940, SA Papers, Folder 536. On the commission itself see Graham Adams, Jr., *Age of Industrial Violence, 1910-15: The Activities and Findings of the United States Commission on Industrial Relations* (New York: Columbia University Press, 1966); and Allen F. Davis, "The Campaign for the Industrial Relations Commission, 1911-1913," *Mid-America*, 45 (October 1963), pp. 211-228.

7. Typescript of PUK annual report, October 1914, in SA Papers, Folder 3; PUK to Samuel Z. Batten, 30 April 1912, SA Papers, Folder 370.

8. Edward T. Devine, "A Profession in the Making," *Survey*, 35 (1 January 1916), pp. 408-410.

9. Edward T. Devine, "Preparedness," *Survey*, 35 (18 March 1916), pp. 732-734.

10. *Survey*, 31 (3 January 1914), pp. 383-402.

11. John M. Glenn to PUK, 8 July 1916, PUK Papers, Folder 131.

12. PUK, typescript memorandum, 20 February 1915, probably for the information of the Industrial Relations Commission, in PUK Papers, Folder 204.

13. *Survey*, 30 (5 April 1913), pp. 3-4; PUK Papers, Folder 131.

14. PUK Papers, Folder 332.

15. PUK, signed editorial, *Survey*, 36 (17 June 1916), p. 304.

16. PUK, "Three Platforms," *Survey*, 36 (24 June 1916), pp. 336-340.

17. Typescript copy of statement, October 1916, in SA Papers, Folder 329.

18. Jane Addams, 25 October 1916, and APK to Jane Addams, 28 October 1916, in SA Papers, Folder 329.
19. Frederic Almy to PUK, 16 December 1916, SA Papers, Folder 344.
20. PUK, typescript of remarks before the U.S. Commission on Industrial Relations, 1915, PUK Papers, Folder 204. He was comparing the autocracy which ruled the Krupp works in Essen with the industrial autocracy which still prevailed in Pittsburgh, eight years after the Pittsburgh Survey. Here, as in many other places, I am also indebted to Robert Wiebe's analysis of progressivism in his *The Search for Order, 1877-1920* (New York: Hill and Wang, 1967).
21. PUK Papers, Folders 308-310; see also PUK's correspondence with Jane Addams during the years 1914-17 in SA Papers, Folder 329.
22. PUK, editorial, *Survey*, 33 (3 October 1914), p. 29.
23. PUK to Jane Addams, 9 February 1917, SA Papers, Folder 329.
24. PUK to Jane Addams, 14 February 1917, SA Papers, Folder 329.
25. PUK, undated memorandum, c. late February 1917, in PUK Papers, Folder 242.
26. PUK, "The Fighting Issue," *Survey*, 37 (17 February 1917), pp. 572-577.
27. PUK Papers, Folder 242; PUK to Richard C. Cabot, 21 March 1917, SA Papers, Folder 417.
28. Copy of letter of John M. Glenn to Richard C. Cabot, 7 April 1917, SA Papers, Folder 417, explaining the board's action ordering a moratorium on the printing of any more articles of whatever persuasion.
29. PUK to Cabot, 2 April 1917; Richard C. Cabot to PUK, 3 April 1917; and PUK to Cabot, 4 April 1917, SA Papers, Folder 417.
30. PUK to APK, 11 October 1917, SA Papers, Folder 654.
31. PUK to Richard C. Cabot, 16 April 1917, SA Papers, Folder 417.

CHAPTER V. WAR AND RECONSTRUCTION

1. PUK, Personal Papers, Folder 4.
2. PUK to Marion Kellogg, from Paris, 16 November 1917, PUK Papers, Supplement.
3. PUK to Jane Addams, 21 June 1917, SA Papers, Folder 329.
4. PUK to editors of *Social Work Today*, Fall 1934, SA Papers, Folder 661.
5. PUK to Newton D. Baker, 26 March and 18 April 1917, SA Papers, Folder 363.
6. PUK, memorandum to staff, undated, c. summer 1917, SA Papers, Folder 654.
7. Flyer describing the new department, c. 1917, SA Papers, Folder 654; and *Survey*, 1917, *passim*.
8. PUK, Annual Report, *Survey*, 39 (24 November 1917), pp. 191-196.
9. APK, memorandum to staff, 10 May 1917, SA Papers, Folder 654.
10. PUK, memorandum to APK, 5 September 1918, SA Papers, Folder 655.
11. The story of these months has been pieced together essentially from letters home to his wife which were lent to me by her; there are also some

letters detailing his Red Cross experience scattered in Folders 6, 54, 329, 363, 466, and 654 of SA Papers.

12. PUK to APK, 24 January 1918, SA Papers, Folder 655.

13. PUK, typescript of address to Women's International League for Peace and Freedom, 20 February 1940, PUK Papers, Folder 35.

14. PUK to Jane Addams, 26 February 1918, SA Papers, Folder 329.

15. The quotation is from a letter to Felix Frankfurter, 20 June 1918, in SA Papers, Folder 558. See also, in SA Papers, PUK to Charles W. Eliot, 13 and 23 April 1918, Folder 501; PUK to John A. Fitch, 17 June 1918, and John A. Fitch to PUK, 19 June 1918, Folder 530. With Arthur Gleason, PUK wrote a book, *British Labor and the War: Reconstructors for a New World* (New York: Boni and Liveright, 1919), which reported on their combined experience observing the British labor movement; it includes appendixes of various statements and programs of British labor during the war.

16. PUK, report to annual meeting of SA, October 1914, SA Papers, Folder 3.

17. *Survey*, 33 (6 March 1915), pp. 603-624.

18. PUK, memorandum to APK, 5 September 1918, SA Papers, Folder 655. See also Shelby Harrison's memorandum for the Russell Sage Foundation, 24 October 1918, SA Papers, Folder 600.

19. Edward T. Devine, lead editorial, *Survey*, 41 (16 November 1918), p. 179.

20. Edward T. Devine, "Between War and Peace," *Survey*, 41 (16 November 1918), pp. 181-185.

21. Summary of the conference, 29-30 November 1918, *Survey*, 41 (7 December 1918), pp. 287-317.

22. Report of special committee of the Conference on Social Agencies and Reconstruction, *Survey*, 42 (7 June 1919), pp. 402-409.

23. PUK to Jane Addams recounting again the crisis on the board which followed his 17 February 1917 article, 7 December 1918, SA Papers, Folder 329.

24. PUK, editor's statement to the board, 25 May 1917, SA Papers, Folder 5. See also Bruno Lasker's memorandum on the *Survey*'s role once war came, 27 March 1917 in PUK Papers, Folder 248.

25. PUK, typescript memorandum, no date, but c. mid-April 1918, in PUK Papers, Folder 319; PUK to Joseph P. Chamberlain, 11 April 1918, SA Papers, Folder 423. The comment on the Socialist party is implied in earlier documents, but put sharply and explicitly by PUK in a letter to Edward T. Devine, 2 July 1918, SA Papers, Folder 488.

26. Minutes of 23 April 1918 meeting, SA Papers, Folder 542.

27. Minutes, summer and fall 1918, in SA Papers, Folders 497 and 542. PUK to Frederic Almy, 16 November 1918, SA Papers, Folder 344.

28. Minutes of board meetings in SA Papers, Folder 542; see also PUK to Charles Cooper, 13 March 1919, SA Papers, Folder 452.

29. *Survey*, 42 (21 June 1919), p. 451.

30. PUK, "To the Unfinished Work," *Survey*, 42 (5 July 1919), pp. 513-514.

31. Letter to PUK, March 1919, SA Papers, Folder 563.

32. Letter to PUK, 30 April 1919, SA Papers, Folder 563.

33. Arthur Gleason to PUK, 8 July 1919, SA Papers, Folder 575.
34. Arthur Gleason to PUK, 28 July 1919, SA Papers, Folder 575.

CHAPTER VI. *SURVEY GRAPHIC* AND THE
MIDMONTHLY IN THE 1920S

1. PUK to Richard C. Cabot, 21 May 1924, SA Papers, Folder 418.
2. PUK to Crystal Eastman, 20 January 1927, SA Papers, Folder 499.
3. PUK to Ramsey MacDonald, 18 February 1926, SA Papers, Folder 718.
4. PUK to Elwood Street, 15 December 1926, SA Papers, Folder 837.
5. PUK to Richard C. Cabot, 26 August 1919, SA Papers, Folder 417.
6. Board minutes and letters from the editor, 1919-23, contained constant reference to these points; for example, all in SA Papers, PUK to Jacob Billikopf, 7 April 1922, Folder 378; PUK, memorandum to board, 16 December 1920, Folder 8; Minutes of board meeting, 17 June 1922, Folder 9; PUK, undated memorandum, c. April 1922, Folder 378; PUK to S. Adele Shaw, 19 August 1920, Folder 820; PUK to Jacob Billikopf, 25 May 1923, Folder 378.
7. Letter to PUK, 4 April 1922, SA Papers, Folder 378.
8. APK to PUK, from Cincinnati, 18 March 1920, PUK Papers, Folder 132. Here, and elsewhere when I have written about personalities, I have had to depend on inferences one can draw from a great body of personal correspondence and also on a number of interviews I had with persons associated in one capacity or another with the *Survey*. These former staff members, secretaries, board members, lawyers, printers, family, and friends proved open and friendly to my project; they were eager to have me know the truth as they saw it. Their relationships with the *Survey* and PUK were deep enough in the past so that I detected very little that was self-serving in the stories they told. Almost without exception they wished me to draw freely from the interviews, but preferred that I not identify one observation and another, one story and another, as coming specifically from them.
9. Financial records are located in the SA folders holding board minutes; I have had to make my own summaries from these quarterly and annual reports.
10. PUK to Ethel S. Dummer, 28 January 1922, Dummer Papers, PUK folder, Radcliffe Archives.
11. PUK memorandum, undated, c. 1923, SA Papers, Folder 584.
12. The quotations are from PUK, lead editorial in the first *Graphic* number of the *Survey*, 47 (29 October 1921), p. 185.
13. PUK, lead editorial, *Graphic* number of the *Survey*, 47 (29 October 1921), pp. 184-185.
14. PUK to Edward T. Devine, 10 August 1922, SA Papers, Folder 490.
15. PUK to John Palmer Gavit, 30 September 1921, SA Papers, Folder 565.
16. The rationale appeared in almost every report and appeal Kellogg made during the years roughly 1923-39. The quotations, in order, may be found in request for funds to Rockefeller Foundation, 22 October 1924, SA Papers, Folder 1567; PUK to Robert W. de Forest, 23 April

1930, SA Papers, Folder 168; model letter of solicitation, April 1929, SA Papers, Folder 722; PUK, annual report to SA, 1924, PUK Papers, Folder 108.

17. PUK, remarks at testimonial dinner to Robert W. de Forest, 9 February 1928, SA Papers, Folder 484.

18. PUK to S. Adele Shaw, 29 September 1919, SA Papers, Folder 819.

19. PUK to Newton D. Baker, 21 November 1918, SA Papers, Folder 363. There are hundreds of such letters as over the years the *Survey* faithfully followed these procedures.

20. Letter to PUK, 26 July 1949, SA Papers, Folder 50.

21. I have selected these from literally thousands of letters. Since they are intended to be representative, the recipients will not be identified here.

22. PUK to Geddes Smith, 9 July 1925, SA Papers, Folder 827.

23. John Palmer Gavit to PUK, 10 February 1927, SA Papers, Folder 566.

24. Patrick Geddes to PUK, 3 September 1924, PUK Papers, Folder 185.

25. Alain Locke to PUK, 10 December 1946, SA Papers, Folder 1517.

26. Cora Emme to Kathryn Close, 20 December 1946, SA Papers, Folder 1590.

27. PUK to Sydney Teller, 9 June 1938, SA Papers, S. Teller Folder.

28. APK to PUK, 20 July 1922, SA Papers, Folder 656; "B.L." is a reference to Bruno Lasker, another staff member at that time.

29. APK, description of office, 18 March 1932, in SA Papers, Folder 548; PUK, editorial note, *Survey*, 41 (8 March 1919), p. 819.

30. PUK to Newton D. Baker, 25 July 1932, SA Papers, Folder 363.

CHAPTER VII. THE *SURVEY* JOURNALS: SERVICE AND REFORM

1. Abraham Flexner, "Is Social Work a Profession?" NCCC *Proceedings* (1915), pp. 576-590.

2. Mary Ross and PUK, "New Beacons in Boston," *Survey*, 64 (15 July 1930), p. 341.

3. In the paragraphs above I have borrowed liberally from Chapter 4, "The 'Cause' and 'Function' of Social Work in the 1920's," of my own book, *Seedtime of Reform: American Social Service and Social Action, 1918-1933* (Minneapolis: University of Minnesota Press, 1963). See also Roy Lubove, *The Professional Altruist: The Emergence of Social Work as a Career, 1880-1930* (Cambridge, Mass.: Harvard University Press, 1965).

4. Karl de Schweinitz to APK, 11 October 1918, SA Papers, Folder 486.

5. PUK and Neva Deardorff, *Social Research as Applied to Community Progress*, p. 47.

6. PUK to Jacob Billikopf, 4 May 1927, SA Papers, Folder 379.

7. Homer Folks to. PUK, 20 April 1928, and PUK to Homer Folks, 25 April 1928, SA Papers, Folder 540.

8. PUK to Philip Cabot, 9 September 1920, SA Papers, Folder 416; such explanations were legion, but other particularly clear statements appear in PUK to Alice Hamilton, 28 June 1918, SA Papers, Folder 590; and PUK to Francis Hackett, 24 April 1923, SA Papers, Folder 584.

9. APK to John Palmer Gavit, 26 July 1919, SA Papers, Folder 565.

10. Special number of the *Survey* on the long day in steel, 45 (5 March 1921); the quotation is taken from a news story on the annual meeting of SA in *Survey*, 46 (7 May 1921), p. 163. See also, in SA Papers, PUK to Charles Cooper, 3 September 1919, Folder 453; John M. Glenn to PUK, 10 November 1919, Folder 578; and William H. Matthews to PUK, 19 September 1923, Folder 730.

11. Karl de Schweinitz, "Are the Poor Really Poor?" *Survey Midmonthly*, 59 (15 January 1928), pp. 517-519.

12. See, for example, Robert W. Bruère, "Unconstitutional and Void," and Homer Folks, "Home Life for the Aged," in *Survey Midmonthly*, 53 (15 October 1924), pp. 69-72; Ordway Tead, "Unemployment and Old Age Destitution," *Survey Midmonthly*, 62 (15 August 1929), pp. 526-527.

13. The quoted words are from an editorial in *Survey Midmonthly*, 53 (15 October 1924), p. 76, but again, as in other matters, examples could be selected from almost any number during these years, 1923-29.

14. Bruno Lasker to PUK praising the *Graphic*'s early issues, 31 January 1923, SA Papers, Folder 657.

15. PUK, "Gangway," *Survey Graphic*, 51 (1 December 1923), pp. 245-247.

16. Maida Castelhun Darnton, "A Playhouse of Wide Interests," *Survey Graphic*, 53 (1 January 1925), pp. 395-398, 423-424.

17. *Survey Graphic*, 58 (1 June 1927).

18. Joseph Lee, "Play, the Architect of Man," *Survey Graphic*, 12 (1 November 1927), pp. 123-126.

19. *Survey Graphic*, 60 (1 April 1928).

20. Articles on social planning were scattered through many different issues of the *Graphic*, but see especially the special number edited by Lewis Mumford on regional planning, *Survey Graphic*, 54 (1 May 1925).

21. PUK, editorial note, *Survey Graphic*, 51 (1 October 1923), p. 2.

22. PUK to Hendrik Willem Van Loon, 17 November 1923, SA Papers, Folder 862.

23. Gifford Pinchot in *Survey Graphic*, 51 (1 March 1924), pp. 561-562.

24. Joseph K. Hart, "Power and Culture," ibid., pp. 625-628.

25. Charles A. Beard, "Some Regional Realities," *Survey Midmonthly*, 56 (15 April 1926), pp. 85-87. It is curious that Beard's rejoinder was published in the *Midmonthly* when the enthusiasm for social planning found outlet primarily in the *Graphic*.

26. PUK, "Gist of It," *Survey Graphic*, 59 (1 October 1927), p. 5. The Irish number appeared on 26 November 1921 and the special number "Mexico: A Promise" in *Survey Graphic* on 1 May 1924.

27. PUK to Rossa B. Cooley, 12 March 1925, SA Papers, Folder 447.

28. PUK in *Survey Graphic*, 53 (1 January 1925), p. 376. ̄

29. Correspondence between Locke and Kellogg in the planning of this issue is located in SA Papers, Folder 710. See also PUK to George Peabody, 13 March 1925, SA Papers, Folder 761.

30. Alain Locke in *Survey Graphic,* 53 (1 March 1925), pp. 629-634.

31. *Survey Graphic*, 59 (1 March 1928).

32. Louis Brandeis to PUK, 11 March 1928, SA Papers, Folder 396.
33. Louis Brandeis to PUK, 4 April 1928, and PUK to Brandeis, 12 March 1928, SA Papers, Folder 396. On exactly the same points of employment regularity see the correspondence between PUK and Senator James Couzens of Michigan in the spring of 1934, SA Papers, Folder 458. See also PUK to Judge Julian W. Mack, 28 March 1931, recalling Brandeis's influence, SA Papers, Folder 722.
34. Beulah Amidon, "Our Stake in Steady Jobs," *Survey Graphic*, 62 (1 April 1929), p. 5.

CHAPTER VIII. DEPRESSION AND THE COMING OF THE NEW DEAL

1. William M. Leiserson to Beulah Amidon, 4 February 1930, SA Papers, Folder 698.
2. PUK in *Survey Midmonthly*, 64 (15 May 1930), p. 177.
3. PUK to Shelby Harrison, 17 December 1930, SA Papers, Folder 601.
4. PUK to Jacob Billikopf, 23 April 1931, SA Papers, Folder 381.
5. See, for example, Gertrude Springer, "Ragged White Collars," *Survey Midmonthly*, 67 (15 November 1931), pp. 183-184.
6. PUK, *Survey Graphic*, 64 (1 April 1930), p. 3.
7. On this point see William Hodson, "An Open Letter to the President on Federal Relief Appropriations," dated 13 October 1931 and published in full in the *Survey Graphic*, 67 (1 November 1931), pp. 144-145.
8. PUK's testimony is filed in the Personal Papers, Folder 31, and his letter to APK, 29 December 1931, is in SA Papers, Folder 660.
9. William M. Leiserson, "Who Bears the Business Risk?" *Survey Graphic*, 65 (1 March 1931), pp. 596-600, 622.
10. Frances Perkins, "Unemployment Insurance: An American Plan to Protect Workers and Avoid the Dole," *Survey Graphic*, 67 (1 November 1931), pp. 117-119, 173.
11. PUK, "Security Next," *Survey Graphic*, 67 (1 December 1931), pp. 237-240.
12. Harry Lurie, "Case Work in a Changing Social Order," *Survey Midmonthly*, 69 (15 February 1933), pp. 61-64; William Hodson, ibid., 69 (15 April 1933), pp. 147-149.
13. PUK, introduction to special planning number, *Survey Graphic*, 67 (1 March 1932), p. 565.
14. The quotations from Lewis Lorwin's article are from ibid., p. 637.
15. Evans Clark to PUK, 27 May 1931, SA Papers, Folder 431.
16. PUK to Mrs. Morris L. Cooke, 15 September 1932, SA Papers, Folder 50.
17. Unsigned editorial, *Survey Graphic*, 53 (1 October 1924), p. 49, with added personal note.
18. PUK to Jane Addams, 25 October 1928, SA Papers, Folder 332.
19. SA Papers, Folder 627.
20. SA Papers, Folder 622.
21. PUK to Lillian Wald, 29 March 1930, SA Papers, Folder 871.

22. PUK to Harold Ickes, 11 April 1932, SA Papers, Folder 629.
23. PUK to J. F. Rettenmayer, 27 October 1932, SA Papers, Folder 634.
24. Frances Perkins to PUK, 23 November 1932, and PUK to Frances Perkins, 28 November 1932, SA Papers, Folder 763.
25. *Survey Midmonthly*, 68 (15 December 1932), p. 673.
26. PUK to Margaret Bondfield, 20 September 1933, SA Papers, Folder 389.
27. *Survey Graphic*, 22 (August 1933), p. 394.
28. Harry A. Overstreet, "The Eighth Adventure," *Survey Graphic*, 22 (August 1933), pp. 404-406, 436-437.
29. Harold Ickes, "The Social Implications of the Roosevelt Administration," *Survey Graphic*, 23 (March 1934), pp. 111-113, 144.
30. Mrs. Henry Goddard Leach to PUK, 9 November 1934, SA Papers, Folder 691.
31. Arthur E. Morgan, *Survey Graphic*, 23 (January 1934), p. 5.
32. All in SA Papers, except as noted: PUK to Frances Perkins, 8 May and 23 May 1933, Folder 763; PUK to John Palmer Gavit, 1 June 1933, Folder 569; PUK to William Hard, 16 June 1933, Folder 554; PUK memorandum to Felix Frankfurter, 11 July 1933, Folder 559; PUK to Richard Patrick Kellogg, 16 August 1933, in PUK Papers, Folder 10; Beulah Amidon to PUK, 18 August 1933, Folder 661; Bruno Lasker to APK, 18 December 1933, Folder 686.

CHAPTER IX. YEARS OF CRISIS

1. PUK to Janet Sabloff, 18 July 1928, Sabloff Papers.
2. PUK to Michael M. Davis, 27 July 1934, SA Papers, Folder 472.
3. PUK, memorandum to board, 15 December 1936, SA Papers, Folder 21.
4. Gertrude Springer to Helen Cody Baker, 3 October 1934, SA Papers, Folder 360.
5. PUK to Janet Sabloff, 4 May 1937, SA Papers, Folder 662.
6. APK to PUK, 17 August 1933, PUK Papers, Folder 10.
7. Leon Whipple, "AK—Managing Editor," *Survey Graphic*, 23 (September 1934), pp. 435-437.
8. Brief notice of death, "1878—Arthur Kellogg—1934," *Survey*, 70 (August 1934), p. 253.
9. APK, "To my Brother Paul and any others concerned," 30 July 1924, PUK Papers, Folder 48.
10. Beulah Amidon to PUK, 9 February 1937, SA Papers, Folder 662.
11. Beulah Amidon to PUK, 28 May 1935, SA Papers, Folder 661.
12. Beulah Amidon to Ned Dearborn, 23 June 1941, SA Papers, Folder Dea-; see also her reply to a group of Japanese editors, 17 July 1951, SA Papers, Folder 639.
13. Beulah Amidon to Eveline Burns, 11 March 1938, SA Papers, E. Burns Folder, 1937-51; see also her letter to John Carroll, 5 October 1944, SA Papers, Folder 50.
14. Gertrude Springer quoted in *Survey*, 88 (January 1952), pp. 38-39.
15. Gertrude Springer to David C. Adie, 10 February 1938, SA Papers, Folder 339.

16. Gertrude Springer to Grace Abbott, 7 April 1936, SA Papers, Folder 327.
17. Gertrude Springer to Harry Hopkins, 9 October 1936, SA Papers, Folder 623.
18. Gertrude Springer to Ann Reed Brenner, 1947, SA Papers, Folder 830.
19. Gertrude Springer, memorandum to APK, October 1933, SA Papers, Folder 487.
20. Gertrude Springer to APK, May 1934, in SA Papers, Folder 829.
21. Gertrude Springer to APK, April 1931, SA Papers, Folder 829.
22. Gertrude Springer to Beulah Amidon, 7 August 1931, SA Papers, Folder 347.
23. Gertrude Springer to Lawrence Blair, 27 October 1937, SA Papers, Folder 386.
24. Gertrude Springer to Edith Abbott, 5 January 1942, SA Papers, Folder Abb-Abi.
25. Gertrude Springer to Helen Cody Baker, 6 January 1942, SA Papers, Folder 362.
26. Gertrude Springer to Mrs. Lawrence Blair, 20 and 27 March 1942, SA Papers, Folder Bla-Blh.

CHAPTER X. THE *SURVEY* AND THE NEW DEAL, 1935-41

1. Hanrahan's reports, dated 1932 and 1933, may be found in SA Papers, Folders 592 and 15.
2. In order, in SA Papers, John D. Kenderdine to PUK, 23 November 1932, Folder 663; Richard C. Cabot to PUK, 23 June 1933, Folder 419; Hugo Van Arx to PUK, 16 June 1935, Folder Ar-; Eleanor R. Wembridge to Gertrude Springer, 28 September 1936, Folder 886; Noel Macy to PUK, 11 December 1936, Folder 724; minutes of board-staff meeting, 16 January 1937, Folder 560.
3. The paragraphs above are drawn from Leon Whipple's eight-page memorandum to PUK, dated 17 June 1935, SA Papers, Folder 889. PUK's memorandum to the staff, 19 June 1935, picked up many of Whipple's criticisms, SA Papers, Folder 570.
4. Leon Whipple to Ann Reed Brenner, 14 June 1936, SA Papers, Folder 889.
5. John Palmer Gavit to PUK, 2 August 1935, SA Papers, Folder 570.
6. Victor Weybright has told his own story in *The Making of a Publisher* (New York: Reynal and Company, 1966). Chapter IV, "A Bright Oasis in the Dismal Social Sciences," details his career on the *Survey*.
7. Victor Weybright to PUK, 21 April 1935, SA Papers, Folder 887.
8. Gertrude Springer to Joanna C. Colcord, 25 July 1935, SA Papers, Folder 435.
9. Victor Weybright to Richard Neuberger, 6 June 1939, SA Papers, Folder 750.
10. The four-page printed statement is located in SA Papers, Folder 661; see also PUK Papers, Folder 341; PUK exchange of correspondence with Newton D. Baker, May 1934, SA Papers, Folder 363; *Survey*

Graphic, 23 (June 1934), pp. 283-284, 302, 304. Others who signed the statement included Bruce Bliven, Paul Brissenden, Edward T. Devine, John Dewey, John Lovejoy Elliott, Morris Ernst, Helen Hall, Helen Harris, Arthur P. Kellogg, Freda Kirchwey, Agnes Brown Leach, Henry Goddard Leach, Lucy Mason, and Oswald Garrison Villard.

11. PUK to Frances Perkins, 9 May 1934, SA Papers, Folder 763.
12. PUK, remarks to annual meeting, 4 February 1935, SA Papers, Folder 16.
13. PUK, statement to *Christian Science Monitor*, 3 December 1935, PUK Papers, Folder 307.
14. PUK to Sam A. Lewisohn, 16 January 1935, PUK Papers, Folder 307. In addition to these extensive materials see, in SA Papers, PUK to Joseph P. Chamberlain, 22 November 1934 and 20 February 1935, Folder 424; PUK to Neva Deardorff, 8 February 1935, Folder 479; State of Social Policy Committee, New York, 20 February 1935, Folder 492; PUK to John A. Fitch, 15 January 1935, Folder 533; PUK to William M. Leiserson, 22 November 1934, Folder 699; Beulah Amidon to Frances Perkins, 22 August 1934, Folder 763; Mary Ross to Frances Perkins, 4 December 1934, Folder 763; PUK to Frances Perkins, 31 January 1935 and 4 May 1935, Folder 764; Isaac Rubinow to PUK, 24 January and 11 February 1935, and PUK to Rubinow, 28 January 1935, Folder 800; PUK to Frank Bane, 21 October 1935, Folder Bane-; PUK to Josephine Roche, 15 February 1935, Folder Moore-; Helen Hall, typescript of "Unfinished Business," pp. 70-73.
15. PUK to Bruce Bliven, 29 September 1936, SA Papers, Folder 388.
16. Mary Van Kleeck to PUK, 9 March 1934, and PUK's reply, 12 March 1934, SA Papers, Folder 860.
17. Victor Weybright, memorandum to PUK, 20 November 1936, which Kellogg later used, in December, with the board, SA Papers, Folder 21.
18. Appendix to PUK memorandum to board, 15 December 1936, SA Papers, Folder 21.
19. William T. Foster, "The Bill for Hard Times," *Survey Graphic*, 25 (April 1936), pp. 200-203, 264-266.
20. PUK, "Postscript," *Survey Midmonthly*, 75 (August 1939), p. 244.
21. J. F. Fishman and V. T. Perlman, "Let's Abolish the County Jail," *Survey Graphic*, 28 (January 1939), pp. 26-27.
22. Dr. Thomas Parran, "The Next Great Plague to Go," *Survey Graphic*, 25 (July 1936), pp. 405-411, 442-443. Also of interest are PUK-Parran correspondence in SA Papers, Folder 759; and follow-up articles: Thomas Parran, "No Defense for Any of Us," *Survey Graphic*, 27 (April 1938), pp. 197-202, 248-253; and "Are We Checking the Great Plague?" *Survey Graphic*, 29 (April 1940), pp. 217-221.

CHAPTER XI. REPRISE: WAR AND RECONSTRUCTION

1. PUK remarks in minutes of Foreign Policy Association Executive Committee, 18 March 1927, SA Papers, Folder 545.
2. John Palmer Gavit to PUK, 7 and 28 August 1927, SA Papers, Folder 566.

3. There is scattered correspondence on all these issues in SA Papers: Foreign Policy Association, Folder 547; John Palmer Gavit, Folders 569 and 570; Agnes Leach, Folder 692; Lillian Wald, Folder 872; editors of *Social Work Today*, Folder 661; Thomas Brennock, Folder 398.

4. PUK to Richard Patrick Kellogg, 25 August 1936, PUK Papers, Folder 12.

5. PUK to Samuel B. Fels, 14 September 1936, SA Papers, Folder 521.

6. Ibid.

7. PUK to John A. Fitch, 9 September 1936, SA Papers, Folder 535. Exactly the same phrase was repeated in letters to many other friends. PUK to Anita Eldridge, 5 April 1937, SA Papers, Folder Eld-. See also Tay Hohoff, *A Ministry to Man: The Life of John Lovejoy Elliott* (New York: Harper, 1959), pp. 169-170; Helen Hall to Lillian Wald, 21 August 1936, Wald Papers, File 3, Drawer 3.

8. See PUK correspondence, 1936-39, in SA Papers, with Jay Allen, Long Editorial File; Adolf A. Berle, Jr., Folder 375; Harold Ickes, Folder 629; and Attorney General Frank Murphy, Folder 747.

9. Roger Baldwin to author, 22 July 1965; on this episode also see memorandum of Herman F. Reissig, executive secretary of the Spanish Refugee Relief Campaign, to PUK, 3 March 1940, PUK Papers, Folder 339; PUK to Samuel Guy Inman, 6 March 1940, PUK Papers, Folder 339; "The Inside History of the SRRC: A Statement to Make Clear the Basis of the Present Controversy, 12 April 1940," memorandum signed by majority members of the Executive Board, including PUK, PUK Papers, Folder 340; PUK to Adolf A. Berle, Jr., 16 April 1940, SA Papers, Folder 375; National Federation of Settlements Papers, Folder 143, which contains publicity material relating to the 1 February 1940 testimonial dinner to PUK.

10. See, for example, Anna Louise Strong, "Children of the Spanish War," *Survey Graphic*, 26 (September 1937), pp. 459-462; statement of Clarence Pickett of the American Friends Service Committee, ibid., p. 463; and William Allen White, "Caring in a Nightmare: The Children of Spain Are Calling," *Survey Graphic*, 27 (August 1938), p. 405.

11. PUK to John Palmer Gavit, 26 February 1939, SA Papers, Folder 572.

12. The quoted phrase is in a letter to Clara Sturges Johnson, 31 October 1939, SA Papers, Folder Joh-.

13. PUK, address, 20 February 1940, PUK Papers, Folder 35.

14. PUK to Edward Ryerson, 18 March 1941, SA Papers, Folder 803; also PUK to Dorothy Dunbar Bromley, 14 March 1939, SA Papers, Folder Brock-; and PUK to Alexander Smith, 29 March 1939, SA Papers, Folder Smith-.

15. John Palmer Gavit to Victor Weybright, 4 September 1937, SA Papers, Folder 887. Another more bitter and biting letter followed 21 January 1938, ibid.

16. Victor Weybright to Jacob Billikopf, 17 April 1942, SA Papers, Folder 383.

17. Victor Weybright to Richard Neuberger, 20 August 1940, SA Papers, Folder 751.

18. PUK to Harry Emerson Fosdick, 29 November 1939, SA Papers, Folder 1387.

19. *Survey Graphic*, 28 (February 1939). SA Papers, Folders 1387 and 1388, contain the working papers, memoranda, manuscript drafts, and much of the correspondence concerned with the publication of this special number. Also PUK, memorandum to board, 31 January 1939, Folder 17; PUK to Shelby Harrison, 6 April 1939, Folder 51; correspondence of PUK and John Palmer Gavit, 1938-39, Folder 572; and Oscar Janowsky to PUK, 19 June 1938, Folder 662.

20. PUK in *Survey Graphic*, 28 (March 1939), pp. 226-228.

21. Raymond Gram Swing, "The Challenge of Crisis," *Survey Graphic*, 29 (October 1940), pp. 485-486; for other positions along the line see PUK in *Survey Graphic*, 28 (March 1939), pp. 226-228; and Frank Kingdon, "Toward a Dynamic Democracy," *Survey Graphic*, 29 (September 1940), pp. 453-456; "People without a Country: A Challenge to Civilization," *Survey Graphic*, 29 (November 1940), pp. 572-592.

22. Vera Micheles Dean, "Can Democracy Win the Peace?" *Survey Graphic*, 30 (June 1941), pp. 340-346.

23. *Survey Graphic*, 28 (October 1939); SA Papers, Folder 1395.

24. *Survey Graphic*, 29 (February 1940); SA Papers, Folders 1398 and 1399.

25. Victor Weybright to Mrs. Frankie G. Merson, 20 May 1941, SA Papers, Folder Mer-; also Folders 1401-2, and 18; and *Survey Graphic*, 30 (March 1941).

26. *Survey Graphic*, 30 (November 1941); the quotations from Hillman and Amidon are from pp. 573-575 and 637; see also SA Papers, Folders 1406-9.

27. Lois Smith to Helen Hall, 11 November 1958, PUK Papers, Folder 44.

28. Gertrude Springer to Helen Cody Baker, 6 January 1942, SA Papers, Folder 362.

29. Remarks of Elmer Carter in minutes of meeting of staff and visiting experts, 1 June 1942, SA Papers, Folder 1412.

30. PUK to Julius Rosenwald Fund, 4 June 1942, SA Papers, Folder 1414.

31. Walter White, remarks at planning session of staff and experts, 23 April 1942, SA Papers, Folder 1412.

32. Letter to PUK, 2 June 1942, SA Papers, Folder 1414.

33. Elmer A. Carter, "Shadows of the Slave Tradition," *Survey Graphic*, 31 (November 1942), p. 554.

34. Stuart Chase, remarks to panel of experts, 4 August 1942, SA Papers, Folder 1416.

35. Stuart Chase, preliminary outline of special issue, 15 September 1942, SA Papers, Folder 1416.

36. Stuart Chase to PUK, 7 May 1942, SA Papers, Folder 1417.

37. "From War to Work," *Survey Graphic*, 32 (May 1943).

38. It would be folly to attempt to cite all the articles illustrative of these points, but as examples see in *Survey Graphic* "Report on the Beveridge Plan." 32 (January 1943), pp. 5-7, 30; "Freedom from Want: The National Resources Planning Board Report," 79 (April 1943), pp. 106-

109; Eduard C. Lindeman, "Pursuit of Happiness in Wartime," 31 (March 1942), pp. 146-149; Herbert Lehman, "When Freedom Rings," 32 (August 1943), pp. 310-312; Raymond Massey, "Free Men Are Not 'Ersatz' People," 79 (September 1943), pp. 227-229; Eveline Burns, "New Perspectives in Social Welfare," 80 (January 1944), pp. 15-17; Beulah Amidon, "The Future Is Already Here," 34 (January 1945), pp. 6-7.

39. Scenario for special number, undated, c. fall of 1943, in SA Papers, Folder 1420.

40. PUK to Henry A. Wallace requesting a manuscript from him along these lines, 9 December 1943, SA Papers, Folder 1447.

41. *Survey Graphic,* 33 (February 1944).

42. PUK, scratch scenario, 31 October 1944, SA Papers, Folder 1450.

43. PUK to Victor Weybright detailing his troubles, 24 May 1945, SA Papers, Folder 1476.

CHAPTER XII. THE *SURVEY'S* LAST DAYS, 1945-52

1. PUK to Emily Greene Balch, 3 July 1946, SA Papers, Folder 364.

2. Bruno Lasker to PUK, 16 November 1948, SA Papers, Folder 687.

3. Edith Pope to PUK, 3 December 1948, SA Papers, Folder 51.

4. *Survey Graphic,* 35 (December 1946); SA Papers, Folders 1480-82.

5. *Survey Graphic,* "Education for Our Time," 36 (November 1947); SA Papers, Folders 1525-45.

6. "Food for a Hungry World," *Survey Graphic,* 37 (March 1948); SA Papers, Folder 1546.

7. Minutes of staff meetings with Alexander and others, 28 March, 16-17 April 1946, SA Papers, Folder 1499; PUK to Dr. Will Alexander, 8 January 1947, SA Papers, Folder 1500; PUK to Richard B. Scandrett, Jr., 5 February 1947, SA Papers, Folder 807.

8. "Segregation," *Survey Graphic,* 36 (January 1947), *passim.*

9. Report of PUK to Julius Rosenwald Fund, 21 August 1947, SA Papers, Folder 1500; memorandum of Walter F. Grueninger, 13 March 1947, SA Papers, Folder 31.

10. Leonard Mayo, "A Cabinet Post for the Home Front," *Survey Graphic,* 81 (August 1945), pp. 203-206; see also Bradley Buell to Senator George D. Aiken, 19 March 1947, SA Papers, Folder Add-Ald.

11. PUK to Adolf A. Berle, Jr., 7 July 1947, SA Papers, Folder 375; see also George Britt to Gardner Murphy, 24 October 1947, SA Papers, Folder Mur-.

12. Ann Reed Brenner to Robert Mayer, 21 May 1945, SA Papers, Folder May-.

13. Alvin Johnson to PUK, 19 March 1947, SA Papers, Folder Joh-.

14. George Britt to PUK, 24 November 1946, SA Papers, Folder 662.

15. George Britt to Walter Davenport of *Collier's Weekly,* 10 June 1948, SA Papers, Folder 401; there are also similar letters to *Fortune* magazine and to the *New York Times,* 2 July 1948, ibid.

16. Victor Weybright, memorandum to PUK, 28 January 1938, SA Papers, Folder 777.

17. Much of this material was summarized from the personal folders

on board members and other large contributors and from board minutes by my graduate research assistant, Clarence Griep.

18. Board members who complained of the confusion that PUK's quarterly and annual budget reports created have their anxieties and skepticisms confirmed by any reading the historian can make of these records, which are filed in various places, most of them together with board minutes, but also in personal correspondence with Joseph Chamberlain and Richard B. Scandrett, Jr., for example, in scattered folders of PUK's Personal Papers, and in the Agnes Brown Leach Papers. There can be no imputation of dishonesty or of mismanagement of funds by PUK or anyone connected with the *Survey* staff or board; but the accounting, particularly in the years of the forties and the fifties, was careless and while not designed to confuse, certainly had that consequence.

19. Mrs. Beulah W. Burhoe to PUK, 22 April 1947, SA Papers, Folder 662.

20. PUK, memorandum to board, 15 December 1936, SA Papers, Folder 21. For evidence that these were chronic problems going back before the time of APK's death see PUK to Richard C. Cabot, 12 December 1919, and 5 January 1922, SA Papers, Folders 417 and 418.

21. Britt's original memorandum of inquiry is dated 15 April 1948, his summary memorandum 7 May 1948. Replies were received from Beulah Amidon, Walter F. Grueninger, E. F. O'Halloran, Dorothy Putney, Rosamond Lee, Irene Headley Armes, Florence Loeb Kellogg, Loula Lasker, Janet Sabloff, Kathleen Sproul, Leon Whipple, E. Lansing Lancaster, and Kathryn Close. All are located in SA Papers, Folder 1600.

22. Stenographic account of de Forest's remarks, February 1928, in SA Papers, Folder 167.

23. PUK to J. Lionberger Davis, 13 February 1948, SA Papers, Folder 467.

24. References here and above are to the board minutes in SA Papers, Folder 19; but the personal papers of Agnes Brown Leach contain letters to and from board members at this time which provide other insights.

25. Memorandum, 3 February 1949, PUK Papers, Folder 126.

26. The papers on this episode of the *Survey*'s financial history are located in PUK Papers, Folder 126, and in Board of Directors Papers, and not in the official records of SA itself. The supposition is that PUK kept all board minutes, legal memoranda, and correspondence on these events in his own personal files rather than together with all the other official administrative files of the *Survey*. The above is drawn from PUK, memorandum to the board, 11 February 1949; minutes of board, February and March 1949; Morris Ernst to PUK, 18 and 22 March and 19 May 1949; PUK to Joseph Chamberlain, 12 May 1949.

27. PUK, memorandum to all staff, 29 March 1949, the only copy of which is in the George Britt Papers.

28. Letter to Beulah Amidon, 21 March 1949, SA Papers, Folder Cors-.

29. Reply from Beulah Amidon, 24 March 1949, SA Papers, Folder Cors-.

30. Editorial, *Survey,* 85 (March 1949), p. 131.

31. Alfred Baker Lewis, "Why Government Health Insurance?" *Survey,* 85 (June 1949), pp. 327-329.

32. Dr. George S. Stevenson, "Yardstick for Citizenship," *Survey,* 85 (July 1949), pp. 356-359.

33. Richard Neuberger, "Our Rotten-Borough Legislatures," *Survey,* 86 (February 1950), pp. 53-57.

34. Ollie A. Randall, "The Family in an Aging Population," *Survey,* 86 (February 1950), pp. 67-72.

35. Board minutes, 2 June 1950, PUK Papers, Folder 111.

36. DeWitt Wallace to PUK, 23 January 1950, SA Papers, Folder 878.

37. Kathryn Close to Maurine Neuberger, 16 October 1951, SA Papers, Folder 749.

38. George Britt to Bruno Lasker, 1949, SA Papers, Folder 687.

CHAPTER XIII. A SUMMING UP

1. Otis L. Graham, Jr., *An Encore for Reform: The Old Progressives and the New Deal* (New York: Oxford University Press, 1967), pp. 71, 77, 102-106, 109, 125, 145.

2. PUK to J. Prentice Murphy, 25 November 1925, SA Papers, Folder 748.

3. PUK to Richard C. Cabot, 3 May 1924, SA Papers, Folder 418.

4. PUK to Richard C. Cabot, 15 June 1926, SA Papers, Folder 418.

5. In SA Papers, see, by way of illustration: PUK to Porter Lee, 14 December 1932, Folder 694; PUK to Mary Anderson, 6 October 1933, Folder Anderson, 1932-34; memoranda of special National Conference of Social Work Committee on Social Action, 19 November 1943 and 14 December 1943, Folder 536.

6. In SA Papers, PUK to Mary Anderson, 19 January 1934, Folder Anderson, 1932-34; see also PUK to Howard R. Knight, 10 April 1929, Folder 668; PUK to Frank Bruno, 9 July 1935, Folder 409; PUK to Stuart A. Queen, 10 November 1935, Folder Pug-.

7. PUK, "Social Settlements," 1934 edition of the *Encyclopaedia of the Social Sciences,* pp. 157-162.

8. PUK, *Work-Relationships and Democracy,* pamphlet for the Industrial Relations Committee, 1912; and "The Field before the Commission on Industrial Relations," *Political Science Quarterly,* 28 (December 1913), pp. 593-609; for a particularly poignant account of the human dimension of a mine disaster see PUK, "Monongah," *Charities and the Commons,* 19 (4 January 1908), pp. 1313-28.

9. PUK to Jacob Billikopf, 1 April 1922, SA Papers, Folder 378; and to others inviting them to a special dinner meeting arising out of the publication of the special number on coal.

10. PUK to Rabbi Stephen S. Wise, 5 December 1919, SA Papers, Folder 894.

11. PUK to Henry R. Seager, 25 November 1919, SA Papers, Folder 814.

12. PUK and others to strikers in the textile industries of Passaic, March 1926, SA Papers, Folder 894; PUK to Robert W. de Forest, 21 and 26 April 1926, SA Papers, Folder 483.

13. PUK to editors of *Social Work Today,* 10 December 1935, SA

Papers, Folder 661. His remarks were printed in *Social Work Today*, 3 (January 1936), p. 5.

14. PUK to Marion Kellogg, 26 December 1917, PUK Papers.

15. PUK to Newton D. Baker, 2 May 1917, SA Papers, Folder 363; memorandum of Crystal Eastman, executive secretary of the American Union against Militarism, to the board, 14 June 1917, detailing the division within the board in regard to priorities, SA Papers, Folder 499.

16. PUK to John F. Moors, 30 August 1927, PUK Papers, Folder 334.

17. PUK to Jacob Billikopf, 26 September 1927, SA Papers, Folder 379.

18. The quotations are from an editorial in *Survey Graphic*, 58 (1 June 1927), pp. 284, 292; see also editorial in *Survey Midmonthly*, 58 (15 April 1927), p. 78.

19. PUK to Mary Ross, 11 August 1927, SA Papers, Folders 659 and 793.

20. PUK to Mary Ross, from Boston, just before returning to his vacation retreat, 24 August 1927, SA Papers, Folder 793. The account above is based on documents in the Sacco and Vanzetti files of the PUK Papers, Folders 334-336, including the several memoranda referred to in the body of the text and assorted letters from PUK and APK written in August and September of 1927. See also PUK's account, "One Show of Hands," in *Survey Midmonthly*, 58 (15 August-15 September 1927), pp. 533-535, 571; summary of the case by Adolf A. Berle, Jr., in *Survey Graphic*, 58 (1 September 1927), p. 489, and unsigned editorial (probably written by PUK), pp. 512-513; Louis Stark, "The Grounds of Doubt," *Survey Graphic*, 59 (1 October 1927), and PUK editorial, pp. 46-47.

21. APK to John Palmer Gavit, 7 September 1927, SA Papers, Folder 566, and to Francis Hackett, 13 September 1927, Folder 584.

22. PUK to Jacob Billikopf, 26 September 1927, SA Papers, Folder 379.

23. PUK to Lillian Wald, 14 October 1930, SA Papers, Folder 871.

24. PUK to Rossa B. Cooley, 26 January and 5 February 1925, Miss Cooley to PUK, 1 February 1925, SA Papers, Folder 447.

25. PUK to George F. Peabody, 28 April and 11 May 1925, SA Papers, Folder 761.

26. PUK, "Buffalo and Points West," *Proceedings* of the National Conference of Social Work, 1939, pp. 3-29.

27. PUK to Richard Patrick Kellogg, 23 October 1920, PUK Papers, Folder 5.

28. PUK, "Touchstone of American Temper," typescript essay, undated, c. 1943-44, in SA Papers, Folder 662.

29. Ibid.

30. PUK, "Team Play," *Survey Graphic*, 26 (1 December 1937), p. 621.

31. PUK in *Survey Midmonthly*, 61 (15 November 1928), pp. 261-264.

32. PUK to Samuel B. Fels, 17 December 1942, SA Papers, Folder 1418.

33. PUK to William Allen White, 16 March 1942, SA Papers, Folder 890.

34. PUK, "Team Play."

35. Rough draft of a letter from PUK to Robert W. de Forest, 29 September 1924, SA Papers, Folder 166. There exists in the folder no carbon copy of a finished and polished draft, so the letter as drafted may never have been sent; whether it was received by de Forest or not is, of course,

beside the point here, for it sets forth, in fourteen typed pages, Kellogg's heartfelt views at this time.

36. PUK to Gifford Pinchot, 18 August 1930, SA Papers, Folder 769.

37. The quotation is from a letter from PUK to Carl Sandburg, 16 July 1937, SA Papers, Folder San-; Kellogg's reference was not directly to the New Deal in this instance, but the principle was one he often ascribed to the Roosevelt administration.

38. PUK, address to Lincoln, Nebraska, Council of Social Agencies, clipping from Lincoln *State Journal,* 21 February 1929, in PUK Papers, Folder 38. Gertrude Springer, in a letter to Helen Cody Baker, 2 March 1938, SA Papers, Folder 361, discusses the penchant for neighborliness which was "very precious to certain desks in this office."

39. PUK to Sir Patrick Geddes, 20 June 1923, PUK Papers, Folder 184.

40. PUK and Neva Deardorff, *Social Research as Applied to Community Progress,* p. 47. The sections I have quoted from, the introduction and the conclusion, are clearly from Kellogg's pen; one cannot miss his characteristic rhetorical style of writing, or the examples he selects in way of illustration. Large parts of the paper were published under his authorship alone as "Our Hidden Cities: And the American Zest for Discovery," *Survey Graphic,* 60 (1 July 1928), pp. 391-392, 409-411, 416.

41. PUK and Deardorff, *Social Research as Applied to Community Progress,* p. 47.

42. PUK to Geddes Smith, 26 July 1926, SA Papers, Folder 827. The concepts paraphrased in this paragraph can be found scattered throughout fifty years of writing, but for a few explicit examples in SA Papers, see PUK to Bruno Lasker, 29 April 1947, Folder 687; recommendation of A. J. Kennedy for a Guggenheim Foundation grant, 1944, Folder Kel-Keo; memorandum to Robert W. de Forest, fall 1923, Folder 482. For a long article by one of the *Survey's* associate editors which summarized PUK's and the *Survey's* attitudes on these matters see Joseph K. Hart, "The World in the Teacher's Mind," *Survey Graphic,* 48 (1 August 1922), pp. 559-564, 585, for it is important constantly to remember that by the selection of articles to appear in the *Survey* and by their careful editing, PUK wrote himself into the views of others and infused the whole *Survey* with his spirit.

43. PUK to Richard Patrick Kellogg, 30 December 1922, PUK Papers, Folder 6.

44. PUK, "Out of the Depression," in *Quarterly Bulletin* of the New York State Conference on Social Work, April 1933.

45. Katharine Lenroot, statement at the National Conference of Social Work, 26 May 1952, in United Neighborhood Houses Papers, Folder 336.

46. PUK, speech to League of Women Voters, Greenwich, Conn., March 1929, PUK Papers, Folder 38.

47. The quoted phrase is from a letter to Mrs. Ethel S. Dummer, 28 January 1922, SA Papers, Folder 498.

48. *New York Times* editorial, 28 May 1952, p. 28.

49. Sadie Stark, remarks printed in Omaha *Bee-News,* 17 January 1924, PUK Papers, Folder 38.

50. PUK to Lillian Wald, 23 June 1936, PUK Papers, Folder 143; PUK

quoted in interview in *New York Daily Mirror,* 30 January 1939, PUK Papers, Folder 40.

51. PUK to Richard Patrick Kellogg, 14 June 1928, PUK Papers, Folder 9.

52. Homer Folks to Robert P. Lane, 1 February 1940, SA Papers, Folder 540; William Hodson to Robert P. Lane, 1 February 1940, SA Papers, Folder 616; Ella C. Parmenter to PUK, 4 January 1944, SA Papers, Folder Park-; Adolf A. Berle, Jr., to Helen Hall, November 1958, PUK Papers, Folder 41; Walter Rauschenbusch, quoted by Jacob Billikopf in a letter to PUK, 12 March 1929, SA Papers, Folder 380.

53. Editorial in *Survey Graphic,* 37 (December 1948), p. 491. The unsigned editorial could have been written by PUK almost any time in his long career, for it expressed views which he had embraced for many years; the style of the editorial and PUK's own failing powers by that time suggest, however, that the editorial was probably composed by George Britt. The exact authorship is not the crucial point to establish, in this instance, for it is sufficient to note that the substance of the editorial was entirely in keeping with the long pragmatic tradition of the *Survey* journal.

Bibliographic Note

To a larger extent than general histories, biographies must rest essentially upon primary documentation. The footnotes will indicate those secondary works from which I have borrowed directly at one point and another. It would be foolish, and probably gratuitous, to list all those general studies, special monographs, and articles to which I am indebted for evidence and insights throughout this study. With every year one's indebtedness to the work of other scholars grows. After nearly a quarter of a century of reading and writing history, I could not begin to note those historical works that have informed my understanding of events in the twentieth century or to note the literature of social work and social welfare from which I have learned the little I do know of the serving professions.

As the footnotes demonstrate, this book rests upon a great body of primary documentation contained in the Survey Associates Papers and in the Paul U. Kellogg Papers. Although both collections contain some records dating from the years before the First World War, the bulk of the evidence covers the years 1917-52. Detailed descriptive inventories of these two collections are included in *Descriptive Inventories of Collections in the Social Welfare History Archives Center, University of Minnesota* (Westport, Conn.: Greenwood Publishing Corporation, 1970), pp. 111-166 and 533-614. The finding aids, in each instance, were prepared by Andrea Hinding, curator of manuscripts.

There are also papers bearing on the history of the *Survey* deposited at the Minnesota Center by George Britt, Mary Katz Golden, Agnes Brown Leach, and Janet Sabloff. I had access to a good number of letters from Paul Kellogg now in the possession of Helen Hall, Marion Kellogg, Mercy Kellogg, and Richard Patrick Kellogg.

There are a few Paul Kellogg papers scattered in the Papers of the National Federation of Settlements and of the United Neighborhood Houses of New York, both on deposit in the Minnesota Center. I also found some material on Paul and Arthur Kellogg in the Graham Taylor Papers, Newberry Library, Chicago; the Edith and Grace Abbott Papers, the University of Chicago; the Ethel Sturges Dummer Papers, Radcliffe College; the Lillian Wald Papers, New York Public Library; and the

Bibliographic Note

New York Charity Organization Society Papers, in the Archives of the Community Services Society, New York.

I read in their entirety all the issues of the *Survey* (under whatever title published) and the journals that preceded it.

Most of Paul Kellogg's writings were published in the *Survey* or in the *Proceedings* of the National Conference of Charities and Correction (later the National Conference of Social Work). I consulted, in addition, the following items, listed here chronologically:

"The Civic Responsibilities of Democracy in an Industrial District," Address before the Joint Convention of the American Civic Association and the National Municipal League, Pittsburgh, 16 November 1908. 16 pp.

"The Field before the Commission on Industrial Relations," *Political Science Quarterly*, 28:4 (December 1913), pp. 593-609.

"Addresses by Paul U. Kellogg, Samuel Gompers, and William English Walling on the British Labour Party's Program of Reconstruction after the War and the Stockholm Conference," National Civic Federation, New York City, 16 March 1918.

The Fourth Year in Belgium: How Help Has Reached the Lowlands through the American Red Cross (Washington, D.C.: American Red Cross, 8 April 1918). 32 pp.

British Labor and the War: Reconstructors for a New World, with Arthur Gleason. New York: Boni and Liveright, 1919.

"Lillian D. Wald: Settler and Trail-Blazer," *New York Sunday Times,* 13 March 1927.

Ten Years of the F. P. A., 1918-1928. New York: Foreign Policy Association, 1929. 21 pp.

Social Research as Applied to Community Progress, with Neva R. Deardorff. International Conference of Social Work, 1929. 49 pp.

"Magic Lenses," review of Jane Addams's *The Second Twenty Years at Hull House* and of Lincoln Steffens's *Autobiography,* in *Yale Review,* 21:1 (September 1931), pp. 196-198.

"The World's Economic Dilemma, Want in the Midst of Plenty," Address before the Conference on the Cause and Cure of War, 18 January 1932.

"Out of the Depression," *Quarterly Bulletin: New York State Conference on Social Work,* 4:2 (April 1933), pp. 50-61.

I have enjoyed many interviews with Helen Hall and Richard Patrick Kellogg, and spoke also with Marion Kellogg and Mercy Kellogg. Others who shared with me their memories of the *Survey* and of Paul and Arthur Kellogg were Margaret Berry, George Britt, Bradley Buell, Kathryn Close, Alice Taylor Davis, Michael Davis, Abraham Friedman, Mary Katz Golden, Albert J. Kennedy, Mary Dublin Keyserling, Mary Kirk, William Kirk, Agnes Brown Leach, Harry Moak, Janet Sabloff, Richard B. Scandrett, Jr., Hyman Schroeder, Kathleen Sproul, Victor Weybright, Mrs. Leon Whipple, Gertrude Folks Zimand, and Savel Zimand.

INDEX

Index

Addams, Jane: settlement pioneer, 6; and National Publications Committee, *1905*, 23; political positions, *1912-16*, 48, 55; urges health insurance, *1913*, 54; views on World War I, 56, 59, 62, 68; on *Survey* board, 203; mentioned, 216

Adler, Felix, chairs Conference on Demobilization, 70

Advisory Council on Economic Security, 153, 155-157

Alcoholism, 51

Alexander, Dr. Will W., 191-192

Allen, Jay, 169

Almy, Frederic, 18, 55

Altmeyer, Arthur, 183

American Association for Labor Legislation, 63, 71

American Association of Social Workers, 93-94

American Civil Liberties Union, 63

American Friends of Spanish Democracy, 169-170

American Union against Militarism, 57-58, 63

Amidon, Beulah: concern for education, 107, 175, 191; *Survey Graphic* editor, 107, 141, 175, 177, 200-201, 207-208; on employment, 117, 119-120, 176; covers economic crisis for *Survey* journals, *1928-30*, 119-120; early career, 141;

political views, 141-142; personality, 143; views on American intervention in World War II, 171

Anderson, Joseph, 212

Andrews, John B., 47, 51

Atlantic, 189

Bacon, Elizabeth Ann, 211-212

Baker, Newton D., 55

Balch, Emily Greene, 58, 68, 189

Baldwin, Roger: drafts letter to Wilson in *1917*, 63; supports *Social Work Today*, 160; and Spanish Refugee Relief Campaign disputes, 169-170

Barrows, Samuel J., 20

Beard, Charles A., 111, 238

Berle, Adolf A., Jr., 203, 210, 244

Billikopf, Jacob, 203, 210

Bing, Alexander, 203

Birth control, 51

Booth, Charles, 23

Brackett, Jeffrey R., 11, 18, 26

Brandeis, Louis: relations with *Survey* and Paul Kellogg, 55, 105, 238; advocates employment regularity in *1928*, 116-117; bequest to *Survey*, 197-198

Brandt, Lilian, 20

Brenner, Ann Reed: member of Pittsburgh Survey staff, 36; *Survey* fund raiser, 81-82,